Jacob's Family Dynamics
Climbing the Rungs of the Ladder

by
Gad Dishi

DEVORA
PUBLISHING
NEW YORK◆JERUSALEM◆LONDON

Jacob's Family Dynamics
Climbing the Rungs of the Ladder
Published by Devora Publishing Company
Text Copyright © 2010 Gad Dishi

COVER DESIGN: Shani Schmell
COVER ILLUSTRATION: BINYAMIN LAUKSTEIN
TYPESETTING: Daniella Barak
EDITORIAL AND PRODUCTION DIRECTOR: Daniella Barak
EDITOR: Sorelle Weinstein

Maps created by Benjie Herskowitz
Photo of the Jordan River is reprinted with permission by Gal Forenberg.
Photo of the Jabbok Tributary is reprinted with permission by Stefan Meierhofer.

Excerpts from The Five Books of Moses: A Translation with Commentary, translated by Robert Alter; copyright © 2004 by Robert Alter; used by permission of W.W. Norton & Company, Inc.

Soft Cover ISBN: 978-1-936068-08-1

E-mail: publisher@devorapublishing.com
Web Site: www. devorapublishing.com

Distributed by:

Urim Publications
POB 52287
Jerusalem 91521, Israel
Tel: 02.679.7633
Fax: 02.679.7634
urim_pub@netvision.net.il

Lambda Publishers, Inc.
527 Empire Blvd.
Brooklyn, NY 11225, USA
Tel: 718.972.5449
Fax: 781.972.6307
mh@ejudaica.com

www.UrimPublications.com

First edition. Printed in Israel

❧ DEDICATION ❧

I recall a conversation I had prior to my Aliyah with my late father, *a"h*, discussing the prospects of employment in Israel. During the course of the discussion, the idea of teaching Jewish studies arose and was likened to "selling sand at the beach." I believe there are many people, in various aspects of their lives, who are attempting to become the best sand-salesperson to ever reach the beach.

This book is dedicated to all those sand-sellers who simply refuse to quit.

CONTENTS

ACKNOWLEDGMENTS

I acknowledge with great gratitude the Almighty God for constantly providing me with new insights, for synchronizing the myriad of life factors so that I could write this book, and for allowing me to do so in Alon Shevut, while overlooking "*derekh avot*" the physical path our forefathers tread upon, in His Holy Land.

I acknowledge with love my dear wife, Abby, whose deep understanding of life and fired intensity have inspired me to see beyond "the box"—not to mention the countless times she took charge of the children, allowing me to focus on the manuscript. May God help us grow old together in continued happiness.

I acknowledge with joy my dear children, Abraham Rahamim, Salha Gila, Shkediah, Moshe Yehuda, and Tiferet Emunah, for their constant, unconditional love. They must have been wondering what Abba was doing all that time on the computer. May God always bless them and protect them in their divine Way.

I acknowledge with respect my mother (now almost *always* referred to as "Grandma") and my father of blessed memory, Abraham ben Zerifeh, whose constant love, support, and insistence upon the primacy of education have shaped my being. May God grant "Grandma" long life, unfaltering good health, and determination, and grant my father *a"h nahat ruah*.

I acknowledge with fondness my sister, brother-in-law, and their family, all my in-laws and their families, whom we love to be with, and look forward to the next excuse to visit, whether in Israel or abroad.

ACKNOWLEDGMENTS

I acknowledge with reverence all the rabbis, dear friends, and educators who have guided me along my Path. May God multiply their teachings.

I acknowledge with thanks all those who contributed their insights, advice, friendly encouragement, writing skills and more towards the publication of this book. Specific thanks goes to: Rabbi Yaakov Beasley, Rabbi Shalom Berger, Director of E-communities at the Lookstein Center at Bar Ilan University, Dr. Gabriel Danzig, Rabbi David Fohrman, author of *The Beast that Crouches at the Door*, psychologist and playwright, Sara Halevi, Dr. Michael Kagan, author of *The Holistic Haggadah*, Shlomit Ben-Michael, Rabbi Jonathan Mishkin, author of *Think of It This Way*, Yaacov Peterseil of Simcha Media Group and the entire support staff, HaPaytan Dr. Avi Shmidman, Rabbi David Silverberg, my editor Sorelle Weinstein, Rabbi Reuven Ziegler, editor of the Virtual Beit Midrash and of a number of books by Rav Soloveitchik, and Dr. Yael Ziegler, author of *Promises to Keep*.

INTRODUCTION

There is no subject so old that something new cannot be said about it.
≈ Fyodor Dostoevsky

Considering the Bible has been around a long time, one would imagine that if there was something worthwhile to say, it has already been said. Why, then, yet *another* book commenting on Genesis?

For some, the classical eleventh-century commentator, Rabbi Shlomo Yitshaki, Rashi, is the final word when dealing with Biblical commentary. Yet, for others, the world of Biblical exegesis is endless and timeless. The nineteenth-century Italian commentator, Rabbi Yitshak Samuel Reggio, deals with this idea in the introduction to his work, *Beiur Yashar*[1] and lists no fewer than 148 commentaries known to him (back in 1821) that have been compiled since Rashi's time. He also illustrates that many traditional commentaries provide vastly different—and, at times, contradictory—understandings of the Biblical text. I will not speculate as to the current count of post-Rashi commentaries nor make any feeble attempt at assembling an up-to-date anthology. It is clear that there are new daily insights into, and understandings of, the Bible, as Rashi's grandson (Rabbi Shemuel Ben Meir, also known as Rashbam) observes in his own commentary.[2]

Based on the number of post-Rashi commentaries, Reggio concludes:[3]

---

1   Reprinted and published by Yosef Shlomo Harari, Jerusalem, 2004.
2   Rashbam commenting on Genesis 37:1.
3   Reggio, *Explanation of the Torah* (2004 ed.), pg. 22 of the introduction, end of his response to the first claim.

1

If the ancient geniuses who explained the Torah left room for those coming after them to call their own, this will clearly prove that no person can complete this task. By corollary, the ability and license remains for every person to contribute his share in what he was enlightened about the eloquence of the Torah...For since the gate is open, anyone can pass through; the insignificant just like the great.

I have decided to pass through this gate.

Jacob's Family Dynamics is a literary Biblical commentary that demonstrates how Jacob's character traits and early life experiences leave a visible mark on the ensuing formation of his family dynamic. His innate and learned characteristics not only influence his relationship with immediate family members, but also leave a lasting impact on future generations.

In future volumes of this work, Jacob's family dynamics continue to be examined, and a thorough analysis of the remaining chapters in Genesis unravels the lingering mysteries of the Joseph saga.

Within these pages, I undertake a thematic analysis of the text, an approach that is innovative in a number of different ways:

The use of a theme as the basic unit for textual analysis can require covering large amounts of text. In contrast, commentaries that have merited appearing in most editions of elucidated texts of the Bible are those that approach the matter on a very narrow basis. For example, popular commentators such as Rashi approach the text on a word-by-word basis or occasionally comment on one verse at a time. This critical development, which has largely shaped the nature and substance of studying Bible, is partly a product of the casual nature attached to reviewing the Biblical narrative, such as during the weekly public reading at synagogue, as well as printing considerations. In remedying this situation, I strive to address issues thematically while following the order of the text.

Modern scholarly works dealing with Biblical narrative as literature have met with much success and enthusiasm. The works of Robert Alter, Meir Sternberg, Nahum Sarna, Michael Fishbane, Aviva Zornberg and others have all contributed greatly to this exciting genre of Biblical exegesis and have greatly influenced my work. As already mentioned, the analyses in this book attach themselves to running themes regardless of the position within any traditional unit. However, I do not view this book merely as "a collection of essays on selected texts"[4] meant to offer "inductive possibilities for readers interested in developing for themselves a similar reading method."[5] Rather, this book implements the robust literary and analytical tools that modern scholarship has made available and illustrates the newfound power that this analytical, literary approach creates. This is not a "collection" of essays, but rather a calculated, continuous flow of analysis adjoined to the text and one may read this work regardless of whether he or she has a desire to develop a similar reading method.

To some extent, this book represents a unique hybrid of approaches. By way of example, one might best identify Chapter One's psychological analysis of the Biblical characters with the work of Aviva Zornberg. Chapter Two draws more upon the literary techniques and close readings of Robert Alter, while Chapters Three and Four bring to mind Meir Sternberg's textual scrutiny in determining "who knows what and when." Throughout this work, I attempt to wrest meaning from the text that will explain the biblical characters' motivation and mindset, and follow their development through the entirety of the narrative.

There are occasions where I reference Midrashic and other traditional material and subsequently provide alternative and/or contradictory explanations. At times, my suggestions may involve erasing the colorization of character intended by the Midrash. For those to whom such an approach may seem heretical on a religious level, I again refer to Reggio's introduction,[6] where he admits to a similar style. Reggio securely documents a fundamental difference between interpretation of religious law and interpretation of dictum. He demonstrates that so long as the new interpretations of the Bible do not impinge upon the practice of religious law, one is free to interpret passages of the Bible in any manner that makes sense. He further explains that the goal of Midrash was not to explain the storyline (*peshat*), but rather to provide homiletics (*derash*), and a reader interested in properly understanding the storyline is not bound by homiletic interpretations. This is further elucidated by the Talmudic dictum: "*Ein hamikra yotse midei peshuto*—The verse does not lose its storyline reading."[7]

---

4   See David M. Gunn and Dana Nolan Fewell, *Narrative in the Hebrew Bible* (Oxford: Oxford University Press, 1993), Preface, pg ix.

5   Ibid.

6   Ibid., pgs. 23–30 in response to the second claim.

7   B. Talmud *Shabbat* 63a, *Yevamot* 11b, 24a.

Indeed, even Rashi acknowledges the legitimacy in providing explanations of *peshat* that differ from and contradict its Talmudic homiletical-*derash* counterpart. By way of example, Rashi, commenting on Exodus 6:9, provides the Talmudic explanation of the passages there and then writes: "And this homiletical understanding [Midrash] does not reconcile well with the text for a number of reasons…therefore, I say, reconcile the text according to its storyline reading [*peshuto*)] an eloquent accounting of events, and let the homiletical understanding be sermonized, as it says, 'Is not My word like fire, says the Lord, and as a hammer smashes a rock' (Jeremiah 23:29). Just as this rock explodes into multiple fragments, so too the words of Torah divide into multiple fragments."[8]

Finally, in reading this work, one may imply or find negative descriptions of the patriarchs and other revered Biblical characters. From a religious perspective, some may take umbrage at such implications or descriptions, preferring to elevate these venerated figures to superhuman status. While the superhuman approach is well-documented in traditional sources, there are also many other traditional sources which seek to humanize these beloved figures, and even those that do not shy away from leveling criticism against the patriarchs.[9] Just by way of example, the Talmud (B. Shabbat 10b) declares that one should not favor one son over another, pointing to the catastrophic consequences of Jacob's favoritism towards Joseph. Clearly, this statement depicts Jacob as a negative role model from whom to learn what *not* to emulate with regard to parenting.

Such an approach is not tantamount to disparagement of the patriarchs;[10] one cannot accuse the authors of the numerous statements in the Talmud of such an indictment. On the contrary, one might contend

---

8   The literature is replete with discussions of defining *peshat* and *derash* and of various other techniques and approaches in developing the multiplicity of textual meaning. I clearly cannot undertake to fully explore this fascinating topic in the Introduction, and merely focus on briefly illustrating the legitimacy of this well-documented phenomenon. For further reading see, Michael Fishbane, *The Garments of Torah, Essays in Biblical Hermeneutics* (Bloomington and Indianapolis: Indiana University Press, 1989).

9   For a collection of such references, see the MA thesis paper of Gilad Sasson, *Pokdei Avon Avot-yehasam shel hazal lehetei haavot*, Bar-Ilan University, where he also suggests historical-sociological reasons for the shift in outlook on the sins of the patriarchs amongst Tannaitic and Amoraic authors.

10   See also Rabbi A.Y. Kook, *Ma'amerei Hareiyah*, pg. 509.

that the more human the patriarchs, the *greater* their character. As they become more human, their lives are more accessible to the reader and create a stronger connection to reality than they could if portrayed as superhuman figures. The narratives of the patriarchs reveal a *development* of their characters. To deny the patriarch's development would be to sentence them to life-long stagnation. Their personality flaws or misdeeds provide further opportunity to illustrate the principles of specific divine retribution for evildoings and sin[11] and highlight their distinction from the whimsical, haphazard behavior of the pagan gods.

Giving the characters' credence as human beings leads us to discover veritable worthiness in what otherwise seems a morally precarious situation. It leads us to recognize the delicate balance of competing values encountered by the characters that a superhuman reading may dismiss. For example, questions like, "Why was Jacob passive and silent about Dinah's rape by Shechem?" or "How could Jacob use his family as a 'human shield' by sending them directly into the ominous path of Esau and his men?" imply a certain failing from what we expect of a Biblical character. A superhuman approach would negate such an implication and would justify the character's action or inaction in order to learn the relevant life lesson. The humanizing approach, however, accepts the implied failing, but goes on to analyze and understand why the character chose such action or inaction. In certain instances, the humanizing approach can transform impulsive condemnation of a Biblical character into tolerable resolution or even reasoned commendation.

The humanizing approach allows the reader to form an intimate bond with the narrative, while the superhuman read seeks to establish a level of perfection towards which to strive. The human element brings readers back to the Bible repeatedly to experience the characters' dramatic, real-life choices, while the superhuman approach draws readers to the text to be inspired once more by the perfection of the characters' personal attributes. Thus, from a religious perspective, both approaches have validity and can operate in parallel, each appealing to a different audience.

---

11   For examples of sources stating that the patriarchs sinned, see Isaiah 43:27 and Rashi *ad loc.*, Rabbi Moses Ben Nahman (hereinfater: Nahmanides) commenting on Genesis 12:10 and 16:6, Rabbi David Kimchi (hereinafter: Radak) commenting on 16:7 and Rabbi Isaac Arama (herinafter: Akeidat Isaac) Gate 25, *Vayetse*, answering question 3.

Further, from a literary viewpoint, there is no evidence that the Biblical narrative intended to portray the patriarchs in myth-like proportions, as would be the conclusion regarding many characters in works of Greek mythology. Indeed, this may be a defining difference between the origins of Israel and those of the Greeks, in that the origins of Israel describe ordinary people living extraordinary lives, not extraordinary people living imaginary lives. Therefore, whether judging by the content of the narrative, Biblical figure or within the broader historical context, viewing these characters as earthly humans is perfectly valid.[12]

I have not made any attempt at elucidating the lessons one can or should glean from the textual analysis. Nor do I try to delve beyond the level of the narrative which represents only one of the many dimensions of Torah learning, as pointed out in the Zohar (*Parashat BeHa'alotekha* 152a): "Therefore, the narrative in the Torah is the garb of Torah. One who thinks that this garb is the Torah itself and that there is nothing else should have his spirit blown out from him and he will not have a portion in the world to come."

This work offers a new interpretation of the narrative and appreciates the rich texture comprising the garb of Torah. The lessons and deeper levels of understanding which the Torah seeks to impart with these narratives are left for each spiritual and lay leader and for every individual to deduce for themselves and for their community.

It is my hope that *Jacob's Family Dynamics* will lift the habitual blinders that have subdued the full power of the text. While exploring this new area of study, one will be better equipped to follow the development of Biblical personalities and themes, thereby galvanizing renewed insight into the human condition. With the release of this new energy into Biblical studies, the natural flow of the narrative will be able to fill its destined space.

Gad Dishi
Alon Shevut, Israel
May 2009

---

12   See Gunn and Fewell, *Narrative in the Hebrew Bible*, pg. 2: "First, narrative constructs a verbal world that imitates and centers on *human characters* [emphasis in original] (or personifications), their speech and actions, their relations and desires, their ideas and institutions."

CHAPTER ONE

The Fire-Straw Dynamic:
The Early Struggle for Space

Character cannot be developed in ease and quiet. Only through experience of trial and suffering can the soul be strengthened, ambition inspired, and success achieved.

&ep; *Helen Keller*

It is Rebekah, Jacob's mother, who is usually considered responsible for encouraging Jacob to cloak his identity as his brother Esau in order to receive his father Isaac's blessings.[13] However, let us revisit this understanding. The text records:

> And Rebekah said to Jacob her son saying: "Here I heard your father speak to Esau your brother saying: 'Bring me venison[14] and make me delicacies and I will eat and I will bless you before God before my death.' And now my son, heed my voice as to what I am commanding you. Go now to the flock and take from there for me two good kid goats and I will make them delicacies to your father as he loves. And you will bring to your father and he will eat so that he will bless you before his death." And Jacob said to Rebekah his mother: "Here my brother Esau is a hairy man and I am a smooth man. Perhaps my

---

13 For example, see Rashbam 25:28 and Leon Kass, *The Beginning of Wisdom* (New York: Free Press, 2003), pgs. 389–403.

14 All references to venison are meant to refer to animals hunted in the wild.

father will feel me and I will be a mocker in his eyes and I will bring upon myself a curse and not a blessing." (27:6–12)[15]

Rebekah gives Jacob complete detailed instructions. She describes the entire sequence of events as one smooth progression. ("Heed my voice… take…two good kid goats…and you will bring…and he will bless you before his death.") Yet Rebekah provides no instructions or guidance whatsoever with regards to the main point of the deceit, namely, the masquerade. It is worth rereading the opening verses quoted above to sharpen this point in the reader's mind.

Having read the verses again, one must wonder what Rebekah is thinking. Does she really believe that Jacob can simply waltz in with her homemade meal (not venison), proclaim to be Esau, and receive Esau's blessing? Does she think that Isaac being blind implies a deficiency in his intelligence?

As readers, we know that even after the masquerade is afoot, Isaac expresses numerous reservations about the identity of the man before him and hesitates before granting the blessings. Isaac explicitly questions the identity of the disguised Jacob no less than three times, inquires how he made it back so quickly, feels his hair, listens to his voice, kisses him, and smells his clothes before finally granting the blessing.[16] From the above, it is clear that Isaac has good command of his faculties. Rebekah, a product of Haran and wife of Isaac for no less than sixty years, should know better. She should at least mention *something* about Jacob's need for a disguise and inform him that she plans to utilize the goat skins and Esau's fine clothes as necessary props for Jacob's performance.[17]

These difficulties force us to rethink Rebekah's role in Jacob's deceit and adopt a new understanding of the blessings episode. A close reading of the verses indicates that Rebekah simply advises Jacob to take two kid goats

---

15   All references to chapter and verse will refer to the book of Genesis unless otherwise indicated. All references to Alter's translation refer to the translation as it appears in Robert Alter's *The Five Books of Moses,* London: W.W. Norton & Company, 2004. First edition. Throughout the book, I adhere to Alter's style and spelling for names of people and places. In some cases, in order to capture a particular nuance in line with the thesis presented in the main body of the text, I made use of my own translation.

16   See 27:18–27.

17   See 27:15–16.

so that she may prepare them as Isaac loved. Rebekah never suggests Jacob *replace Esau*. In line with her upbringing in Haran,[18] Rebekah merely wants Jacob to take advantage of the opportunity to get blessed by Isaac as well. Rebekah makes no mention of the deceit because it was never her intention that Jacob masquerade as Esau. She wants Jacob to walk in with her food and tell Isaac that his son *Jacob* has arrived to also receive a blessing before his death.

Sadly, Jacob cannot even fathom that his father would bless him as he would Esau, and thus never entertains the notion, as his mother intends, that he identify himself *as Jacob*. He fails to hear the nuance in his mother's command: "And *you* will bring to your father and he *will* eat" and "he *will* bless *you* before his death" (27:10).

It is only after Jacob shares his concerns with his mother about her suggestion that Rebekah becomes aware of his train of thought. Special attention should be paid to locate the point in the text below where she becomes an active participant in the identity theft. The continuation of the text cited above reads:

> And his mother said to him, "Upon me your curse, my son. Just heed my voice and go take for me." And he went and he took and he brought to his mother, and his mother made delicacies as his father loves. And Rebekah took her elder son Esau's fine garments that were with her in the house and put them on Jacob her younger son, and the skins of the kids she donned on his hands and the smooth part of his neck. And she put the delicacies, and the bread she had made, in the hand of Jacob her son. (27:13–17)

It is only after Jacob retrieves the goats, and Rebekah finishes preparing the delicacies, that she subsequently adopts and assists Jacob's idea of the masquerade. Rebekah's silent acquiescence and mind switch may even imply her agreement with Jacob's assessment of the situation. Nonetheless, Rebekah is not fully at peace with the plan. She remains silent about Jacob's suggested deceit and seems reluctant to adopt Jacob's perception of his father. She wants Jacob to be blessed as Jacob and for him to feel that he is worthy in his own right of his father's blessing. As further proof of Rebekah's reluctance to go ahead with the plan, one notes that she does

---

18   This point will be explored in Chapter Two.

not alter her initial order that Jacob bring her two kid goats. Had she really wanted to assist in the deceit she may have chosen a different animal from the wild that was closer to venison. In addition, she supplements the meat with her own home-made bread, which is never mentioned in Isaac's request or in her initial description of the menu she is to make for Jacob to bring to Isaac. Given her alliance with Jacob, she should have especially avoided providing something like the home-made bread, that is a product of her own handiwork. These points further reinforce the idea that Rebekah is not in favor of the deception. Her providing home-made bread is an expression of her hope that Isaac will discover the truth as to which son is really before him.[19]

Rebekah is disappointed with the ensuing outcome and comes to grips with the reality that Jacob's perception of his father, her husband, is correct. She pays dearly for her participation in the plot as she is forced to bid her beloved and favored son a final farewell as she and Isaac subsequently send him to Haran.

Understanding the Family Dynamic

Given the above reality, a number of new questions arise: In what kind of family environment is Jacob raised? What is it about Jacob's personality, and about Jacob in his family dynamic, that possesses him to masquerade as his brother Esau in order to receive his father's blessings?

The answer lies in Jacob's perception of the family dynamic and of Esau's monopoly of Isaac's blessings. These perceptions are textually supported as the narrative aligns the Jacob-Rebekah and Esau-Isaac relations with the fitting epithets. Jacob is described as "her" son and she "his" mother (see 27:6,8,11,13,14,17). Esau is described as "his" (Isaac's) son and Isaac called Esau "my" son (see 27:1,5,20,21,24,25,26,27). This textual grounding implies some justification of Jacob's inability to see himself as "his"—Isaac's—son. Thus, while the initiative for Jacob to obtain a blessing is Rebekah's, it is Jacob's idea to replace Esau and take his by deceit.

---

19   See 27: 3–4, 17, and especially, 33. In verse 33, Isaac mentions his eating "from all" the foodstuffs which apparently triggers his realization that it was Jacob who was there earlier for he then proceeds to confirm the blessing and informs Esau that Jacob was there (compare Isaac's ignorance in verse 33 to his knowledge in verse 35). Thus, the home-made bread does help Isaac discern Jacob, albeit too late to accomplish Rebekah's goals.

Yet, it would be unfair to categorize Jacob's deceit as a dastardly plot of deviousness. Jacob's masquerade is not borne out of malicious envy of Esau or out of a dark coveting of Isaac's blessings to be acquired at any price. Rather, Jacob's psychological state and home environs lead him to believe that, as opposed to Esau, he is unworthy and unloved by Isaac. As will be discussed below, Jacob desires to be closer to Isaac and, in his fear that his father's death is imminent, wants, at least once, to feel loved and blessed by his father. Isaac's dynamic with his sons leaves Jacob feeling that the only way to achieve that closeness is to adopt Esau's identity as his own. With this new understanding, Jacob's deceit is thus transformed from what some might see as an abhorrent, immoral manipulation of his blind father into a heartbreaking, desperate exigency to obtain his dying father's elusive love.

As the above powerfully illustrates, attempting to understand Jacob's home environment and family dynamic requires that one not only track Jacob's life as an individual, but as a member within his family unit. The Biblical account of Jacob provides the reader with an abundance of information about his beginnings. The text lures the reader to accompany his life's development from before his birth until after his death in an intricate weaving of events encompassing a complete and rich life cycle. By relaying all this information to the reader, the text informs us that in order to better understand Jacob's life, one needs to recognize Jacob's mindset and his surrounding family circumstances.

In doing so, certain illogical understandings of critical episodes will need to be re-examined toward developing a new, thematically coherent approach, as is the case above. Yet, even after understanding all the above, one still wonders: What was it that led to the Rebekah-Jacob, Isaac-Esau alignments to begin with?

On Parents and Children

The answer to this question requires us to return to Jacob's early years. As noted, the text supplies many pieces of information regarding Jacob's family. Aside from passages mentioning his parents and brother, we also learn of his paternal grandparents, Abraham and Sarah, his paternal uncle, Ishmael, and later, his maternal uncle, Laban.

The tension in his grandfather's home as a result of familial favoritism caused a split along parental lines. Grandmother Sarah was zealous about Isaac taking his proper place in the family and insisted on ousting Hagar and

Ishmael from the house, while grandfather Abraham was reluctant to expel Hagar and Ishmael. Divine intervention allowed Abraham to overcome his doubts and carry out the expulsion as Sarah desired (21:12). Whether the details of God's involvement were relayed to Isaac, Jacob, or anyone else, is difficult to surmise. Nonetheless, Jacob is born into a family where the connection between his father and his father's half-brother is actively severed by his grandparents. With this precedent of favoritism and separation of brothers already in place, Isaac and Jacob's behavior, as will be shown, is better understood by the reader.

Favoritism and separation are not phenomena confined to Jacob's grandparents' home. Jacob, too, grows up in a home where each parent allies himself with one child. Isaac loves Esau, Rebekah loves Jacob. The verse reads: "And Isaac loved Esau because venison was in his mouth and Rebekah loves Jacob."[20] When studying this verse in contrast to other recorded episodes of favoritism, one notices a linguistic oddity. In comparing Jacob's loving Rachel "over" Leah, the text records: "And he loved also Rachel over Leah"—*miLeah* (29:30) and in comparing Jacob's loving Joseph "over" all his brothers, the text records: "And his brothers saw that their father loved him over all his brothers"—*mikol echav* (37:4). In Isaac's favoring Esau, one notices that Isaac is not recorded as loving Esau "over" Jacob—*miYaakov*—but simply that: "And Isaac loved Esau because venison was in his mouth" (25:28), without any reference to Jacob at all.

This oddity reveals a deep insight into Isaac's psyche. By omitting the relative term of Isaac loving Esau "over" Jacob, the text informs us that Isaac's love for Esau is not relative to his feelings for anyone else. Indeed, the text attributes Isaac's love for Esau to the external factor of Esau's bringing him venison. As such, Isaac does not contrast his love for Esau "over" his love for Jacob, but rather contrasts his love for the son who brings him venison "over" the son who does not. The textual absence of Jacob in that verse implies that Jacob is not inherently excluded from Isaac's love. Thus, Isaac's love for Esau is not favoritism for Esau qua Esau. When Jacob, later disguised as Esau, brings Isaac venison, such love is forthcoming to Jacob as well as he becomes the new provider of venison.[21]

---

20   25:28. See Shmuel Klitsner, *Wrestling Jacob: Deception, Identity, and Freudian Slips in Genesis* (Urim Publications: Jerusalem, 2006), pg. 52, discussing the asymmetry in verb tense.

21   For a similar idea, see Rabbi Chaim Ben Moses Ibn Atar (hereinafter: Or

Isaac's favoritism creates a unique father-son dynamic which is responsible for molding the brotherhood dynamic between Jacob and Esau. Since Isaac's preference for Esau will have far-reaching ramifications, it is worthwhile analyzing the underlying cause of the favoritism.

I Know That Smell

Moses Ben Nahman (hereinafter: Nahmanides)[22] comments that when Esau supplies venison, this is not an occasional occurrence. Rather, comments Nahmanides, Esau's venison comprises the entirety of Isaac's diet.

Why Isaac's voracious appetite for venison? A look at the binding of Isaac on the altar (22:1–19) provides meaningful clues. At that event, as Isaac's trauma reaches its apex, he realizes that his father does not intend to sacrifice an animal on the altar, but that his father intends him to be the sacrifice. Abravanel[23] argues that this realization only occurs to Isaac once he is already bound and placed on the altar. At that moment, Isaac endures many harrowing minutes of uncertainty. Abraham hears the heavenly voice instruct him not to harm the lad, but the divine voice is directed only to Abraham. It seems doubtful that Isaac, too, knows the life-saving content of that divine message. All Isaac may have heard was his father's oral reply to a phantom voice: "Here I am."[24] Thus, Isaac still does not know he has been saved even when Abraham proceeds to obtain a substitute ram.

Hahayyim) commenting on 25:29.

22 Commenting on 25:28.

23 Parashat *Vayera* immediately preceding his commentary to 22:11.

24 22:11. A complete study of Isaac lies beyond the scope of our discussion, but it is worth noting here that Isaac's ignorance of the entire divine plan and subsequent retraction plays a significant role in his life. It is for this reason that God reiterates explicitly to Isaac both in Gerrar (26:3,5) and in Beersheba (26:24) that Isaac's blessings are forthcoming because of Abraham's adherence and subjugation to God. God here alludes to the fact that He orchestrated the binding at Moriah and that Isaac should therefore hold his father blameless. The language of 26:5 —"*Eqev asher shamah Abraham bekoli*–Because Abraham has listened to my voice" (Alter trans.)—is almost identical to God's comments to Abraham following the dénouement of Isaac's binding in 22:18: "*Eqev asher shama'ata bekoli*–Because you have listened to my voice" (Alter trans). (See also Reggio, commenting on 26:5, who notes and references the Binding of Isaac.) For years, Isaac reels from his near-death experience and questions his father's motivations. The revelations in Gerrar and Beersheba are meant to inform Isaac of the divine role in the binding at Moriah. Only after receiving the divine assurances in Beersheba not to be fearful

A close reading of the text supports the notion that Isaac remained in the dark for many long moments. The text states:

> And He said: "Do not send your hand to the lad and do not do anything to him for I now know that you are God-fearing and have not withheld your son, your only son, from Me." And Abraham lifted his eyes and saw and, here, a ram was caught in the brush by its horns and Abraham went and took the ram and offered it up as a burnt offering instead of his son. (22:12–13)

Since Abraham does not desire the ram to escape from the bushes, it would seem to follow that he secures the ram *prior* to unbinding Isaac. Abraham then removes Isaac,[25] and immediately offers the ram.

From Isaac's perspective, therefore, the possibility of being killed remains real until the ram is offered in his stead. It is only then that the finality of Abraham's change of direction and Isaac's personal salvation are internalized. For Isaac, the burning of that ram is what signifies his being saved. Forevermore, that smell and taste remains associated with the life-saving gift he receives once down from the altar. It allows Isaac to relive the elation of being spared and being alive. Isaac harbors positive feelings for anyone who succeeds in recreating that feeling for him. Thus, Isaac's love for Esau stems from a very deep place within Isaac—and it serves as the catalyst for a potent, emotional bond between them.[26]

---

and that God was also with him does Isaac build an altar and call out God's name. No sacrifice is brought upon the altar (see Klitsner, *Wrestling with Jacob,* pg. 48), as the altar represents the altar of Moriah and the non-sacrifice of Isaac years earlier. (See Rabbi Don Yitshak Abravanel (hereinafter: Abravanel), commenting on chapter 26, answering question 5.) It is Isaac's prayer that it remains empty. According to Isaac's reasoning, since his father was prepared to kill him, he will act towards Abraham as if he were in fact dead. No further contact is recorded between them during Abraham's life. Since he associates his father with death, it is only in death that he is prepared to deal with his father and arrives to bury him together with Ishmael who may have felt the same way.

25 Isaac is bound separately from the altar. The text states that Abraham bound Isaac and then "placed him" (22:9) on the altar above the logs. This allows for his removal to occur while he is still bound without dismantling the altar and his being present during the ram's burning on the altar.

26 This understanding would also help explain why Jacob's vegetarian attempt to win over

Coming to Grips with the Truth

The text ascribes the venison as a reason for Isaac loving Esau. The bringing of venison renders the relationship between Isaac and Esau as conditional love. This would imply that before Esau brings home his prey, Jacob and Esau are on an equal footing in Isaac's eyes. It is only as they grow older that they drift apart and deepen the parental alliances between them.

The status quo of Isaac favoring Esau continues uninterrupted until Jacob misappropriates the blessings. Afterwards, Esau is recorded as hating Jacob over the blessing that "his" father blessed him (27:41). The "his" pronoun leaves room for a critical ambiguity.[27] It can refer to Esau or Jacob, i.e., Esau hates Jacob because it is "his"—Esau's father, the father who loves and favors him, who gives Jacob the blessing. Yet, it can also mean that Esau hates Jacob because he fears that the blessing is given to Jacob out of an acknowledgment that Jacob has now won Isaac's love and is now "his," Jacob's father—even perhaps to the exclusion of Esau.

To Esau, the loss of the blessing to Jacob represents a loss of his father's love. Isaac asks Esau for a special hunt, since hunting represents the special bond between them. Jacob's usurping his blessing confirms Esau's fear that Jacob is trying to replace him. This dread has been festering ever since Jacob is born holding on to Esau's heel, symbolically representing his desire to pull Esau back into the womb (permanently?) and emerge (first) himself. At this point, Esau needs his father's blessing in order to confirm his role in the family *vis-à-vis* his father.

When Esau initially fails to obtain Isaac's blessing, Esau's world begins to crumble. Upon discovering that it was Jacob who took his blessing, Esau cries out about Jacob's name and refers to the sale of the birthright. For Esau, the two events are not linked merely by the tactics employed, but, on a much deeper level, by what the two events represent to him *vis-à-vis* his relationship with Isaac. Jacob's usurping the blessings replaces him before his father as firstborn, just as the sale of the birthright intended, rendering him

---

Isaac's love by preparing soup as Or Hahayyim suggests would have failed. Cf. Alter, *The Five Books of Moses,* pg. 131 note on 25:29. After developing this theme I saw it mentioned in Klitsner, *Wrestling with Jacob,* pg. 43. Nonetheless, as my development is more textually based and necessary for the remainder of the work, I have left it in its original form.

27   See also Klitsner, ibid., pg. 79, who identifies the ambiguity over which blessing it was—Jacob's dressed as Esau or Esau's—that causes Esau's anger to flare.

superfluous. In Esau's mind, Jacob has succeeded in eliminating Esau from the competition for parental love and attention by assuming his identity.

Moreover, Esau sees that Isaac now loves Jacob as well because he too has brought him venison. Isaac declares his inability to retract the blessings given to Jacob while masquerading as Esau: "For you, then, what can I do, my son?" (27:37).[28] At this moment, Esau realizes that his father's love, which he cherishes, is nothing more than a love of venison. Esau wakes up to the reality that he is just a means to an end. He is nothing special on his own. He can easily be replaced with some shaggy goat skin and a good meal. When Isaac does not express remorse, and later even endorses the blessings to Jacob,[29] Esau's worst fears materialize. Esau's monopoly on venison and his father's love is now broken.[30]

That this is Esau's mindset can be evinced by noticing Esau's language when insisting on a blessing and his subsequent weeping and crying. He exclaims: "Have you not kept back a blessing for *me—lī*" (27:36). Esau yearns for the special blessing a father grants to his favorite son. When Isaac shows further reluctance, Esau knows that he has been living a lie. In desperation, he calls out to his father to at least equate his standing with that of Jacob and bless him as well. The harsh reality of his not being special, and to such an extent that he literally needs to beg his father to bless him, reduces Esau to tears: "And Esau said to his father, 'Do you only have one blessing, my father? Also bless me, my father.' And Esau raised his voice and cried" (27:38).

Esau is so bewildered by this turn of events that he seeks to rationalize and attribute his father's emotional switch to something other than venison. Ironically, it is Rebekah who provides Esau with the sorely-needed illusion. Immediately prior to the passage dealing with the blessings, the text informs us of the Hittite wives that Esau takes and that these wives are a source of grief to Isaac and Rebekah (26:34–35). The location of these verses seems out of place. Later, the text laboriously details the genealogies of Esau which also includes his wives, thus rendering their mention prior to the blessings episode superfluous. Similarly, after the blessings, Rebekah complains to

---

28   Alter's translation

29   See 27:33, "also blessed will he be."

30   Naftali Zvi Yehuda Berlin (hereinafter: Netziv) commenting on 25:28 makes a similar observation when commenting on Isaac's love for Esau: "Indeed, in the end of his (Isaac's) days the love was reversed (from Esau to Jacob)."

Isaac regarding the wives of Esau so we know that they are a cause of grief. Why does the text bother to record these facts immediately prior to the blessings episode when the information was to be relayed in a different form later on? What connection exists between Esau's taking Hittite wives and the blessings episode?

Upon close scrutiny, the only added value of these verses is that they inform us that the wives distress both Rebekah *and* Isaac. Were we to be left only with the post-blessing passages, the cause of grief to Isaac could not be definitively gleaned from the text. As such, the critical piece of information the text needed to record prior to the blessings is that Esau's wives deeply disturb Isaac. This piece of information is now utilized by Esau to explain Isaac's strange behavior and emotional reversal. Rebekah, in trying to save Jacob from Esau, urges Isaac to send Jacob to Paddan-Aram to seek a non-Hittite wife. Isaac agrees and blesses Jacob once more before he departs. Esau exploits the juxtaposition of events to connect them causally.[31]

Esau then attempts to win back Isaac's love by marrying a non-Hittite wife himself. After taking a new wife, and with Jacob no longer in the picture, Esau can attempt to resume living his lie. It is worthy exploring how Esau feels staying home once Jacob is commissioned to Haran. In having Jacob expelled from home for his misdeeds, Esau essentially succeeds in permanently eliminating his brother from the competition for parental love and attention.[32]

---

31 Nahum M. Sarna, *The JPS Torah Commentary: Genesis* (Philadelphia: JPS, 1989), pg. 196, note on 28:6–8, understands the causal connection to be explicit in the text: *When Esau saw*—"Realizing that his marriage outside the kinship group and his alliances with native women had contributed to his loss of the blessing, Esau now tries to repair the situation." In reality, the connection between the women and the blessing is non-existent and is only now conjured up by Rebekah as an excuse for Jacob's exit. It is Esau who hunts out a logical reason to psychologically assuage his loss that implies the connection. Textually, Esau's marriages are adjoined as "bookends" for the scene (26:34–35 and 28:8–9) and are thus part and parcel of the blessings scene as they set the stage for the psychological crutch as explained above.

32 Similarly, Cain's misdeeds lead to his expulsion from his parental home—the face of the earth: "For here today you have chased me from the face of the earth" (4:14). As opposed to Cain's fratricide as a means of eliminating his brother, Esau merely threatens to kill Jacob. Later, Joseph's brothers also succeed in eliminating Joseph in a long-lasting manner from the parental home when they nearly kill him by leaving him in the pit in the desert. From these examples, the primal urgency to be the beneficiary of parental favor is potentially lethal and emotionally charged. However, despite the high

Esau no doubt revels in finally having his own "room" without having to worry about Jacob.

However, Esau's new sense of security is short-lived when Isaac does not revert to his former self. He fails to denigrate Jacob's actions and Esau comes to realize that the mechanical act of bringing venison lies at the heart of the matter. For Esau, things will never be the same again. With the seeds of doubt firmly planted in his mind, Esau is forced, over time, to come to grips with the truth.

The Tent Dwellers

While the text ascribes Isaac's love of Esau to the venison, Rebekah's love for Jacob is textually unqualified. Yet, while unconditional, the text perhaps still hints at a reason for its development. The text records that each parent loves the child who demonstrates the stereotypical behaviors associated with his or her gender. Isaac favors Esau who is described as a hunter and Rebekah favors Jacob who is described as a "tent-dweller"—a homebody.[33] Rebekah is also described as a tent-dweller, "And Isaac brought her to the tent of Sarah his mother."[34] Thus, Rebekah's love for Jacob may be rooted

---

stakes to supplant the beloved sibling, the coveted love is not forthcoming. In the cases of Cain and Joseph's brothers, the success of the not chosen child/ren in eliminating their brother not only fails to garner them exclusive parental love and attention, but boomerangs to create further distancing from their parent/s. Jacob replaces his favoritism for Joseph with that for Benjamin, as evidenced by his reluctance to allow him to descend with his brothers to Egypt. Cain's permanent removal of his brother also fails to garner parental love as Adam decides to have a third child whom he tellingly names Seth: "For God has given me a different child, *in place of Abel*, for Cain killed him" (4:25). Thus the void created by the removal of Abel is not emotionally filled by Cain but by Abel's substitute—Seth. These textual similarities call upon the reader to surmise that Esau's primal urgency to be recognized in his own right and monopolize his parents' love and attention, especially from his mother, should similarly fail.

33   See Rav Joseph Bekhor Shor commenting on 25:27 and referencing 4:20 from where he deduces that Jacob was not a homebody, but rather a shepherd—a trade that remains his occupation until the end of his life. This would reinforce the idea of Jacob preferring the status quo, as will be developed shortly. As pointed out in the main body of the text, whether or not there is a reason for Rebekah's preference, the parental split remains the same from the children's perspective.

34   24: 67. Her replacing Sarah also correlates with her favoritism of Isaac's younger son over Isaac's elder son, just as Sarah favored Abraham's younger son over Abraham's elder son.

in a certain sense of identification with Jacob as a fellow "tent-dweller," adding a dimension of depth to their affectionate bond.

This special bond is put to the test when Jacob hesitates to masquerade as Esau. Jacob is not only anxious about approaching Isaac because he fears the future fulfillment of a possible curse. He is anxious that Isaac will view him as "*meta'teyah*" (27:12)—that his father would make fun of him. Isaac's curse would represent more than the loss of the blessings or a curse to be materially poor or the like, but would signify a loss of any chance of receiving love from Isaac. Jacob desires the blessings as a means of growing closer to Isaac by being the one to provide Isaac food—the role that is set aside for Isaac's favorite son, Esau. Only after Rebekah reassures him does Jacob undertake the challenge. At this point, Jacob feels that, if caught, Rebekah, as a result of their special bond, would take responsibility for the ruse and clear Jacob of any blame. In addition, Jacob reasons that not fulfilling his mother's wishes would lessen Rebekah's love for him, and he would then stand to lose the love of both his father *and* his mother. It is only with this in mind that Jacob's sense of risk and reward tells him that it is now emotionally worthwhile to go forward. When Jacob succeeds in securing his father's blessings and later receives other blessings before exiting to Haran, he leaves home feeling loved by both his parents even though he is essentially being sent away.

On Brotherly Dynamics

Regardless of the reasons behind the favoritism, the closeness between sibling and parent prove to be a central issue throughout the lives of Jacob and Esau, as seen when dealing with the blessing episode. However, as deep and potent the factors of favoritism and parental love are, the brotherhood of Jacob and Esau takes shape from other factors as well. In fact, their brotherhood begins before they are even born and before these parental alliances are formed.

Still while in the womb they struggle, "And the children clashed together within her and she said: 'Then why me?' and she went to inquire of the Lord,"[35] (25:22) and, upon inquiry of the Divine, Rebekah

---

35 Alter's translation.

is told that: "two nations from your innards will be *separated*."[36]

The Midrash[37] picks up on this theme and depicts the desire for separate physical spaces when expounding upon the wrestling of the brothers in Rebekah's womb. The Midrash relates the in-utero wrestling to a symbolic struggle where Jacob desires to exit at places of worship to God while Esau desires to exit at various locations of idolatry worship. According to the Midrash, therefore, Jacob and Esau each desire their individual and different space. They realize that they cannot, and should not, occupy the same space and therefore do not vie for the same area outside the womb. Indeed, a simple, non-Midrashic, understanding of the in-utero wrestling is that there is not as much room in the womb for two fetuses as there is for one. They do not want to share the same space. As shall be seen, it is this struggle for space, which begins before birth, that serves as a formative and driving force throughout their lives.

The struggle for space is also illustrated by comparing the dual descriptions that the text ascribed to Jacob and Esau: "And Esau was a man knowing the hunt—a man of the field and Jacob was a simple man—dwelling in tents (25:27)." The first part of their descriptions refers to their personal character (simple versus knowing the hunt) while the second part is more indicative of their physical habitats (a tent-dweller versus a man of the field). From the description of their physical habitats, a portrait emerges where despite their being

---

36   25:23. The unique word choice for womb—*meayikh*—meaning innards as opposed to the more common word—*rehem*—implies that the separation does not merely refer to the physical separation from the womb but that temporally from the time they were in Rebekah's innards—*mimeayikh*—from the time they were in your innards—they will seek to separate. See also Reggio commenting on this verse stating that as the twins will be different in their natures they will have to separate one from the other. A similar divine emphasis on Jacob's spreading out and separating from Esau can be seen in 28:14: "And your seed shall be like the dust of the earth and you shall burst forth to the west and the east and the north and the south." (Alter's translation.)

37   Genesis Rabbah, Section 63:6.

members of the same household, Jacob and Esau grow up separately. Esau occupies his own vast space out in the field while Jacob sits enclosed in tents.[38]

Jacob's simplicity is contrasted with Esau's knowing the hunt. The parallel suggests that Jacob's personality does not allow him to become a hunter and vice-versa. Indeed, even when Jacob becomes a man of the field while working for Laban, he grazes animals rather than hunts them. As Netziv notes,[39] Jacob not only yearns to be alone, but to be safe. The cruelty, dangers, risks, and instability of the hunter are not his lot. Hence, the driving personality trait that fuels Jacob being a tent-dweller and his need for separateness is his inborn *aversion to risk*.

In this light, Jacob's grasping Esau's heel is not an expression of Jacob's desire to be first, as Esau interprets it, but rather an attempt to hold on to Esau for security as Jacob fears coming into the world. The grasping is in violation of the need to separate and can only endure for mere moments before they separate after birth.

As Isaac grows older, he calls his son Esau to arrange the proper atmosphere and setting in which to bless him before he dies. Jacob desires the blessings not only as a means to grow closer to his father but because they also represent additional security for his future, and thus dovetails with his desire for stability.

---

38   This need for space also helps one understand the lifestyle that Jacob adopts in his later tirade with Laban. There he mentions that he exhausted himself watching Laban's sheep day and night. "I was there in the day—the parching heat ate me, and ice—in the night" (Alter's translation) (31:40). Also, when Leah hires Jacob for the night in lieu of the *dudaim* she trades to Rachel, Jacob is described as coming home in the evening, i.e., already after dark: "And Jacob came from the field in the evening" (30:16). The impression is that Jacob does not spend much time with his family. He prefers to be alone. Jacob thus allows his need for space, which he acquired and perhaps needed while growing up with Esau, to extend to other areas of his life. As will be pointed out later, when Jacob proceeds to Haran and grazes Laban's cattle, Jacob is provided with more than ample opportunity to fulfill his need for space alone.

39   Commenting on Deuteronomy 33:28.

In furthering the idea of Jacob's risk-averse pragmatism, one notes that when Rebekah instructs Jacob to bring food to his father to receive a blessing, Jacob's aversion to risk leads him to analyze the situation from an emotional risk-benefit point of view, as discussed above.

Later, Jacob's scheming against Esau can only be accomplished with the help of Rebekah, whose keen sense of opportunities is refined while at the home of Laban. On his own, Jacob sells stew/soup for Esau's birthright. The sale entails no risk as he sells the passing benefits of a bowl of soup for the permanent stature of firstborn with whatever rights that confers upon him. Even this sale is playing it safe for Jacob as he favors saving up for later. He is worried,[40] and wants to provide for his future. He insists that Esau swears so as not to risk a later retraction. Jacob's focus on the future frames his thoughts and directs him to weigh the consequences of multiple competing values and factors in any given situation.

Esau, in contrast, is an aggressive risk-taker whose precarious existence precludes thinking beyond the present. This idea is borne out by Esau's statement: "Here I am about to die and why does this one ask me for the birthright?" (25:32) As Rabbi Abraham ben Meir ibn Ezra (hereinafter: Ibn Ezra)[41] explains, Esau enters the killing fields each day with the knowledge that he may die while doing so. He is a hunter. He is constantly "about to die" and so the need for the pension plan which the birthright represents is useless to him.[42] Esau's response to Jacob's request for the birthright reflects this dichotomy as his focus is only on his present predicament. The verb usage relating to Esau's eating (gorging) and Esau's behavior also reflects a

---

40   Indeed, Jacob is recorded as being or acting fearful numerous times during his life. He fears being cursed by Isaac; he is frightened by the vision of God upon exiting Beersheba; of raising his claims against Laban regarding the conjugal switch; of Laban stealing his daughters away from him after twenty years of service; of Esau destroying him and his camp; of the nations destroying him and his household after the massacre of the City of Shechem; of sending Benjamin to Egypt; of the sight of the money in the brothers' satchels; of possibly not seeing the newly-discovered Joseph before he dies; of descending to Egypt and of being buried in Egypt.

41   Commenting on 25:32.

42   This assumes that the birthright grants an advantage in the inheritance upon Isaac's death.

focus on the present and of satisfying the present desire without thinking about the future ramifications of his action.[43]

Their innate personality clash is, therefore, the reason why they need to be separate and why their togetherness represents a meeting of fire and straw, as described below.[44]

Fire and Straw

The separation between Jacob and Esau is not only a way to avoid conflict, but also is necessary to ensure the boys' respective survival. In the book of Obadiah,[45] the idea of necessary separation is clearly symbolized when referring to "the house of Jacob as fire and the house of Joseph a flame and the house of Esau as straw."[46] When one adds straw to a fire, the straw is not only consumed but becomes the fuel for the flames. Once the straw is incinerated, the fire itself is in danger of being extinguished.[47] The fire-straw description further crystallizes that it is the innate character of the brothers that do not allow for their cohabitation.

Having noted the need for separation between the brothers, one can better understand the dynamics displayed when the two meet. The first recorded interaction between them is when Esau returns tired from the field and Jacob ostensibly negotiates the birthright for a bowl of his stew.[48]

---

43 See also Alter, *The Art of Biblical Narrative* (NY: Basic Books, 1983), pg. 45.

44 See also Reggio commenting on 25:23.

45 Which is the traditional *haftara* reading for this section of the text.

46 Obadiah 1:18.

47 While the metaphor in Obadiah is clearly meant to be one-sided as indicating the ultimate victory of the house of Jacob over that of Esau, taking the metaphor to its end yields the mutual danger of destruction described above.

48 Despite the simple reading of the text implying otherwise, Rashbam (25:30) explains that the stew is not the barter for the birthright. Rather, Jacob pays for the birthright, and the stew is merely the impetus for Esau to close the deal. A technical reading of the text also supports this understanding as it states at the end of verse 33: "And (Esau) sold his birthright to Jacob" while reserving recording "And Jacob gave to Esau bread and lentil stew etc." for verse 34 as a separate occurrence. Thus, the full stop between the verses describing the sale and the next verse's giving of the stew coupled with the switch in verb usage from "sold" when referring to the birthright to "gave" when referring to the food implies that they are legally two separate acts. In addition, Jacob's inclusion of bread that Esau does not ask for conveys the sense that while Jacob is insistent on receiving the birthright formally he is not treating the barter in an exacting manner. The mysteriously-added bread will resurface when

Once the exchange is complete, the interaction is transformed into quick and succinct actions leading to separation, as demonstrated by the multiple verbs the text records in rapid succession: "And he (Esau) ate and drank and got up and went and despised the birthright."[49] The interchange with Jacob makes Esau so uncomfortable that he keeps company with Jacob to a minimum and promptly leaves. Indeed, the brothers are not recorded as eating together, but rather Esau eats and drinks alone.[50]

The next recorded incident where the two meet, or almost meet, is when Isaac later desires to bless Esau, and Jacob usurps Esau's blessings. There, the event almost proves disastrous because of the near-miss collision of the two personalities.[51] The text relates (27:30): "And Jacob barely had left the presence of Isaac his father that Esau his brother came back from the [his] hunt."[52] So close are the two to colliding that, according to the Midrash,[53] Jacob indeed exits Isaac's area of the tent, sees Esau coming, and backtracks to hide behind the door until Esau enters. When Esau enters, Jacob makes his second and final exit literally behind Esau's back. Thus, while the catastrophic collision of fire and straw is averted, the proximity of the two at that one point situates the "straw" close enough to the "fire" for things to "heat up" to the point where Esau is ready to kill Jacob: "And Esau said to himself: 'The days of my father's mourning will draw near and I will kill my brother Jacob'" (27:41).

Similar to their separation at birth, Jacob's usurping of Esau's blessing leads to yet another, and even greater, physical separation of the brothers that lasts for over twenty years. In contrast to what occurs at the usurping

---

Rebekah provides the foodstuffs for Jacob's impersonation of Esau. It is perhaps this constancy of having bread that Jacob seeks to perpetuate when he asks God to provide him bread to eat and clothes to wear (28:20).

49 25:34. See also Alter, *The Art of Biblical Narrative*, pgs. 42–45, where the rapid succession of verbs is understood as indicative of Esau's "uncouth dispatch" of the birthright.

50 Cf. 31:54 where Laban and Jacob are recorded as eating together as a seal to their pact.

51 See Sarna, *Genesis*, pg. 189, note on 27:1–28:9: "All four members of the family participate, but only in pairs. Neither Jacob and Esau nor Rebekah and Isaac appear together; they dare not confront each other."

52 Alter's translation.

53 Genesis Rabbah 66.

of the blessings, where it is Esau who leaves to bring venison and thereby creates space for Jacob to enter in his stead, this time it is Jacob who leaves in order to give Esau his space at home.[54]

Curiously, throughout the years of Jacob's stay in Haran, there is no record of Esau tracking Jacob down or even visiting his uncle Laban. Indeed, when Jacob finally leaves Laban's home, Jacob and Esau's reactions indicate that this is the first time they were meeting in over twenty years. Due to their not seeing each other for so many years, Jacob needs to inform Esau of his acquisitions and to introduce his wives and children to Esau (32:5, 33:5) and the entire exchange is laden with references to the usurping of the blessings that occurred twenty years earlier (32:21, 33:10, 11), such that the impression is that they are picking up from where they left off.

It is interesting to note why it is, given Esau's hatred of Jacob and desire to kill him, that Esau does not pursue Jacob during this prolonged period of time. After all, Esau knew of his brother's whereabouts. He hears Isaac send Jacob to Paddan-Aram,[55] and Laban is just as much Esau's uncle as he is Jacob's to allow Esau access to his home.[56] Therefore, why doesn't Esau follow Jacob to Laban's house to execute his plan?

Furthermore, it is Rebekah's initiative to send Jacob to Paddan-Aram.[57] Why does Rebekah opt for separation between the brothers to prevent a possible calamity when that would also mean losing contact with her favorite son? She could have opted to keep Jacob at home and track Esau's movements from up-close or to adopt any other possible precautionary tactic. Alternatively, she also could have taken a more proactive stance and, in keeping

---

54 Ironically, while Jacob requires separating from Esau for his own physical and emotional well-being, Jacob also feels a need to hold on to a part of Esau throughout his life for a sense of security. At birth, this is accomplished by holding on to Esau's heel. Yet, in the long run, the only way Jacob can safely accomplish this is by incorporating part of Esau into his own personality. His desire to become Esau and gain security drives him to obtain the birthright and the blessings. Jacob's physical masquerading as Esau leaves a residual role reversal between the brothers, with Esau "staying home" and Jacob becoming a "man of the field" in Haran. The theme of "space," therefore, spills over from the physical to the relative role each brother fills, whether as "man of the field" or as "firstborn."

55 See 28:6.

56 See Abravanel answering questions 17 and 18 at the end of *Toldot*.

57 See 27:43,46.

with her Sarah-like resemblance, urge Isaac to expel Esau despite any misgivings Isaac may have, in the same way that Abraham expelled Ishmael.

In order to answer these questions, one would benefit from analyzing these matters in terms of Esau's and Jacob's need for their own "space." When Jacob takes Esau's place before Isaac he violates their need for space and begins to assume Esau's characteristics as a man of the field. Rebekah understands that if the boys' spaces were to converge, if Jacob plays out his residual role reversal as a man of the field in the fields of Esau, the danger is great that the "straw" would be devoured and soon after the "flame" extinguished.

Friction or Fusion

Rebekah realizes that in the womb, the two opposing energies of Jacob and Esau are forced to occupy the same space, which results in a struggle. Their innate tendencies are akin to the repelling forces of similar magnetic poles. They must be apart by nature. As they approach each other, they shoot apart from each other. The closer they get, the more powerful the repelling force.

For Jacob and Esau, the opposite danger also exists. Should one of them succeed in shifting energies/personalities they could be fused together as two opposite magnetic poles. Each would lose their identity and cease to exist as individuals. Indeed, modern studies suggest that "strong inter-twin dependence will repress individual personality development, and though twins can support each other in many way, some mental health problems may be exacerbated by twinship, the main risk factors being high inter-twin dependence and pronounced submissiveness."[58] Other studies discuss the fusion or partial fusion of identity between idenical twins.[59] In the Biblical case of Jacob and Esau, whether identical[60] or non-identical twins, Jacob's decision to remain geographically apart from Esau reflects Jacob's need to be separate from Esau, to develop his own personality, and to avoid such fusion or submissiveness. As the literature suggests, the fusion that can arise between twin siblings results from the co-twin being the human being who

---

58 Abstract of Inter-twin relationships and mental health: "Review of the literature and Clinical Experiences" by Irma Moilanen, published in Nordic Journal of Psychiatry, 1987, Vol. 41, Issue 4, 1987, pgs. 279–84.

59 For example, see "On Being a Twin: How the View may Differ for Each of the Pair" by Lilly Dimitrovsky, published in The Journal of the American Academy of Psychoanlysis and Dynamic Psychiatry, 1989, Vol. 17, pgs. 639–653.

60 As Reggio suggests when commenting on 25:23.

is most constantly present in the twin's range of perception during the years of his growth. By neutralizing this avenue of contact, Jacob better assures and preserves his own sense of self.

Yet, when Jacob crosses the very boundaries he erects and becomes Esau, Esau's fury erupts. As the blessings represent an overlap between Jacob and Esau's characters seeking, respectively, future security and instantaneous gratification, the danger of the brothers' identities fusing together becomes a real concern. When Jacob temporarily assumes Esau's identity, the feared fusion of identities begins and leaves a residual Esau-like quality imprinted on Jacob's character. It is thus not only the threat of being *replaced* but of being *subsumed* by Jacob that fuels Esau's wrath. Remaining apart philosophically thereby becomes a prerequisite for existential security.[61]

The overlapping of physical and psychological space, of the concern over the fatal fusion of their identities, is an issue that will recur frequently between Jacob and Esau. Even though it must have been very difficult for her, Rebekah understands her sons' need for space and their fire-straw dynamic, and urges Jacob to go to Laban's house to avoid the conflict. Thus, Rebekah's attitude further reinforces for Jacob the idea that space and physical separation bring safety.

Jacob, who has grown up with this message *vis-à-vis* Esau, further internalizes the point. He personally experiences the equation of physical avoidance bringing safety as Esau does not chase him to Laban's home. Thus, at the end of the fourteen years, Jacob opts to stay by Laban and maintain a physical distance from Esau, as his becoming a "man of the field" by Laban further precludes his return home without colliding with Esau.

Rebekah and Jacob are not the only ones to realize the fire-straw dynamic. Esau chooses to stay at home while Jacob traveled to Laban's fields. Once given more of his own space at home and preserving his hunting grounds as his own, Esau no longer feels the need to kill Jacob. Esau benefits from not only added physical space, but also psychological space, from Jacob. In this way, Esau is able to preserve his identity as his own. Thus, the separation is voluntarily assumed and promoted by all the parties involved.

---

61   This would be especially true if, as Reggio suggests, Jacob and Esau were identical twins. In such case, each brother's need to differentiate themselves from his brother as an individual (and garner parental attention) would be that much greater.

The lack of recorded conflict between Jacob and Esau during their early years is thus a result of a natural and self-imposed separation. With a model of separation already in place from their grandparents' home and their father's childhood, such resolution is an acceptable mode of behavior. For Jacob, though, his separateness becomes a learned *modus operandi* for avoiding conflict and (not) dealing with family, as will be demonstrated.

As a case in point, when Jacob moves on to Laban's home, he recreates the same dynamic with Laban as he had with Esau. They even refer to each other's kinship using the same term that also means brother—"*ach*."[62] His occupation as shepherd in Haran provides him with physical distance from Laban as he tends to the sheep in the field alone. Later, their flocks are physically separated by a three-day journey. As they grow horizontally and the space between their camps is diminished, the sons of Laban insinuate that Laban should take back Jacob's wealth as his own. This misidentification of ownership is a call to commingle the divergent camps and, as a result, requires Jacob to leave and effectuate a separation from Laban. As with Esau, Jacob espouses a fire-straw dynamic with Laban as well and seeks to avoid a collision of "fire" and "straw."

However, in this instance, Laban chases Jacob claiming that Jacob stole his *terafim*. For Jacob, any intermingling of possessions is a violation of maintaining the requisite space between camps. As space equals life, the violation of space equals death, and Jacob issues the death penalty to the unknown thief who violates the space between their camps (31:32). Should Laban find anything of his amongst Jacob's camp, the only solution would be to eliminate that point of connection where the "fire" was consuming the "straw," and thereby contain the damage from the rest of the camp.

Jacob's projection of the "fire-straw" dynamic onto Laban demonstrates that failure to resolve issues in one's past inevitably results in the same problems recurring again, albeit in a new context. It is a message that Jacob internalizes, for after he separates from Laban, and establishes a border to prevent any future violation of space, he later initiates contact with Esau with an eye toward final reconciliation and a complete clearing of their past.

---

62   See 29:12 and 29:15.

Chapter Two

The Materialistic World of Haran

Try not to become a man of success but rather to become a man of value.

                      ‭꙲ *Albert Einstein*

The Grip

Jacob's risk-averse pragmatism, as explored in the previous chapter, teeters toward a skewed emphasis on reward when he arrives at Haran. For Jacob, the land of Haran represents more than just a safe haven from Esau. Haran becomes a land of opportunities: the opportunity to find love, to find a wife, to have children, and above all, to make money—lots and lots of money.

Haran's tyrannical hold grips Jacob so long as he remains within its physical borders. As will be seen, once Jacob physically leaves Haran, the stranglehold is relaxed. However, despite the strict geographical divide, the repercussions of Jacob's time in Haran continue to cause a ripple effect throughout his life. Let us begin our exploration of this phenomenon from when Jacob begins his journey to Haran.

Jacob travels to Haran via the land of the Easterners. The East is the direction people have been traveling away from since the beginning of Genesis: The people of the Tower of Babel[63] and Abraham[64] travel away from the

---

63 11:2. The fact that the people are moving in the "right" direction is reported prior to their thwarted attempt to build a tower that displeases God.

64 11:31–12:6. Abraham's journey from Mesopotamia to Canaan is a generally westward direction. Indeed, geographical progress in the Bible may be seen as movements towards the Promised Land.

East. Similarly, the text reports Abraham sending his children from Ketura "*eastward*—to the land of *the East*" (25:6), which signifies their not carrying forth his line.[65] In contrast, Jacob journeys *towards* the land of the sons of *Kedem*—of the East (29:1). This geographic regression corresponds with Jacob's personal regression,[66] which can be attributed to his usurping Esau's blessings. The very word for East—*kedem*—carries with it the meaning of "predecessor"—*kodem*—which reinforces the idea of regression.

Jacob no sooner arrives at Haran when he is struck by the sight of a well and three flocks of sheep: "And he saw and, look, there was a well in the field, and, look, three flocks of sheep were lying beside it, for from that well they would water the flocks"[67] (29:2). Jacob's focus on the sheep is so great that the text notes how the identity of the flocks and shepherds are intertwined: "And when all the flocks were gathered there, *they* would roll the stone from the mouth of the well and would water the sheep" (29:3). The text omits any reference to the shepherds but implies their presence. The text describes the flocks of sheep as "*a'darim*" and proceeds to record that "they" roll the rock and water the flocks and that it is to "them"—*lahem*—that Jacob inquires: "My brothers, where are you from?"(29:4).[68]

---

65   Jacob's going eastward may thus have been a source of solace for Esau, who perhaps viewed Jacob's eastward travel as indicating that Jacob will not carry forth Isaac's line. This would provide an alternative reason for why Esau did not pursue Jacob to Laban's home.

66   The idea of traveling eastward carrying a connotation of personal regression is also illustrated by Cain's leaving the presence of God after killing his brother and dwelling *east* of Eden (4:16).

67   Alter's translation.

68   The usual term for shepherd, "*ro'eh*," appears shortly thereafter in 29:9 when describing Rachel's occupation. Therefore, the word *a'darim* ostensibly cannot be construed to mean shepherds. However, see Amihud Glazer, *Amudei Hod* (Hebrew) (Jerusalem: Feldheim Publishing, Jerusalem 2008), pgs. 37–38, who contends that the word *a'darim* refers to the shepherds and that they do not merit their usual title in this instance as they are not shepherding but "lying around." While only attempting to resolve the local difficulty of the dual *adarim-ro'eh* usage in ch. 29, Glazer, apparently unknowingly, has discovered one of the true definitions of the Hebrew word *eder* in the plural *adarim*. Throughout the Bible, defining *adarim* as a group of animals leads to difficulties. For example, see Judges 5:16, "Why did you sit among the sheepfolds to hear the whistling of the *adarim*?", where the definition of *adarim* as shepherds is clearly superior. However, in other instances, the word *adarim* must mean a group of animals as in Ezekiel 34:12, "As a *ro'eh* seeks out

This seemingly clumsy textual presentation makes it sound as if Jacob is speaking with the flocks of sheep and not the shepherds.

Apparently, Haran has this magical hold over everyone in its midst, and has its sway over the inhabitants well before Jacob's arrival. Even before investigating the current scene, one recalls the episode of Abraham's servant arriving at the (same?[69]) well years earlier. In that episode, Abraham sends his servant to procure a wife for his son Isaac from Haran. The servant arrives at the time that the women of the town are out drawing water. He prays to God to provide him with the woman destined for Isaac, and devises a test to ascertain that the woman is the one God has chosen. The destined woman, when asked to water the servant, would offer to water him and then his camels. When Rebekah arrives at the well and indeed offers to water him and then his camels, the servant gives her a golden nose ring and two bracelets. Rebekah informs her family, including her brother, Laban, of what has happened. Laban welcomes the servant warmly while remaining focused on the wealth that the servant brought with him (24:29–30). Indeed, the jewelry and camels are designed to wow the candidate and her family to close the wedding deal and the servant's display of wealth excites Laban to such a great degree that he begins to run towards the servant.[70]

---

edro—as a shepherd seeks his flock," where the simultaneous dual usage of *ro'eh* and *edro* forces the latter meaning as a group of animals. The use of *adarim* in the Pentateuch is strictly confined to Genesis and may reflect certain chronological, geographical, or dialectal nuances. The text's word choice of *adarim* in discussing Haran, a word that carries the meaning both for the animals and for the shepherds, further reinforces the blurred distinction between people and things in Haran, as I further demonstrate in the main body of the text.

69 While the well is a known type scene for the introduction of the heroine and as a sign of fertility, the geography of the scene and its involving an overlapping family member—Laban—invites the inference that it is the same well. Alter's inference that this well, reported as being in the fields, cannot be the one located outside the city, as reported in Genesis 24, is not conclusive. True, the verse states that "from *that* well they would water the flocks" (29:2), apparently contrasting it to other wells from which people drink. Yet, the environs surrounding the city may be fields and the water source of the well may provide the necessary irrigation of such fields as well as drinking water for the nearby residents. There would be no better location to have a field than in proximity to a well and close to one's home, and it would be quite ironic if the materialistically inclined inhabitants of Haran would fail to arrange the dual usage of such natural resources.

70 The Sages are critical of Laban on this point. See Rashi 24:29: "Why did he run

Looking back, Rebekah's impressive show of kindness in offering water to the servant and the camels takes on a new light. Traditionally, the proffering of water is viewed as an act of kindness. Rebekah's impressive behavior is certainly to be lauded. She undertakes a difficult task without any explicit understanding that she is to be rewarded for her deeds. However, in offering to draw water and water the camels, Rebekah may have been providing her services rather than performing an act of kindness. Rebekah has already identified the camels as belonging to the "man" whom she addresses as "my master" (24:18). She offers to draw water and water the camels. She, much like Laban, also runs. She runs to the well (24:20). She runs to tell her family what has happened (24:28). The arrival of a convoy of camels headed by an out-of-town lord represents an opportunity to make money. The speed in carrying out the task is designed to deter any others from participating and diminishing her possible prize. Indeed, she doesn't refuse the servant's offer of a nose ring and bracelets, claiming that her intention is only to perform an act of kindness.

The test set out by the servant, then, is not necessarily designed to identify kindness, but to find a woman who is clever enough not to let a good opportunity pass her by. Indeed, the textual references almost preclude the test being associated with kindness.[71] The word *hesed*—kindness—is used by

---

and for what did he run? When he saw the nose ring (29:30), He said 'this man is rich' and he eyed his wealth." Ostensibly, at that point, the possibility that the "man" and his camels would need to be put up for the night could allow Laban to profit nicely as innkeeper if the "man" proves to be as generous to him as he is with Rebekah. Hence, Laban runs to ensure that the "man" does not go elsewhere. The later request by Laban that the servant stay a couple to ten days is more than just a delay tactic. Laban wants to run up the bill for the servant's stay over a longer period of time. Note 24:55 where Laban states that after the couple to ten-day period the servant may leave. There, Laban uses the word "*telekh*"—you—in the singular—that can be read as referring to the servant leaving alone without Rebekah, and implying Laban's focus on the servant's stay.

71 See Meir Sternberg, *The Poetics of Biblical Narrative: Ideological Literature and the Drama of Reading* (Indiana: Indiana University Press, 1985), pgs. 131–152, where he points out that the servant's test is not designed to test character, but to identify the woman chosen by God for Isaac. It is only later that the servant describes to the family how the drawing of water was a test of character. My suggestion above is that the servant did have a character test in mind from the start, but that the trait sought was opportunism rather than kindness. The servant later fashions the trait to be that of kindness when relaying the details to the family.

the servant numerous times (24:12, 14, 27, 49), all in relation to God or the family performing kindness to his master Abraham. The word is never associated with Rebekah's acts of drawing water. Rebekah's astuteness indicates to the servant that she is the type of woman who would agree to travel to Canaan and marry the promising prospect of Abraham's heir—the unnamed Isaac.

In this vein, one needs to recall that Canaan has already been struck by famine during Abraham's days and the dependence on scattered rains did not make Canaan an attractive place of residence. Indeed, another famine sets upon Canaan in the days of Isaac and Rebekah (26:1). The servant's concern regarding bringing the woman specifically to Canaan is emphasized in his conversation with Abraham and reiterated to the family. To Abraham the servant posited, "Perhaps the woman will not want to come after me *to this land*" (24:5), and to the family he truncates his concern to, "And I said to my master, 'Perhaps the woman will not come after me'" (24:39).[72] The servant therefore sets a test which will provide Isaac with someone who knows how to take initiative and seize an opportunity.[73]

The grip of Haran has thus already taken hold of Rebekah and Laban many years earlier, and Abraham's servant plays that weakness perfectly for his own ends.[74] The servant, apparently aware of the influential sway of Haran, comes equipped with the wealth of his master and a determination to leave as soon as possible in order to avoid being swept up in the seductive embrace of Haran philosophy. Indeed, Abraham's warning not to have his son return "there"—"Watch yourself, lest you bring my son back *there*" (24:6)—may have been indicative of foreknowledge about how difficult it is to break free from such influences.

By the time Jacob arrives on the scene, a new element is introduced to the well. Perhaps even as a result of Rebekah's alacrity, and her holding a monopoly over Abraham's servant's generosity, a large boulder is placed over the well requiring *all* the shepherds to roll it off together. This ensures that no one can repeat what Rebekah achieves alone without the others having fair chance to approach the newcomer and provide their services. However,

---

72 Alter's translation.

73 It is this ability to seize an opportunity that allows her to steer Jacob towards receiving his own blessing from Isaac.

74 For a magnificent close reading of the episode (24:1–67), see Sternberg, *The Poetics of Biblical Narrative*, pgs. 131–152.

in this instance, the goal is not to gain the newcomer's wealth, as he has none, but to "acquire" the newcomer himself.[75]

Rejected Brotherhood

> And Jacob said to them [*vayomer lahem Yaakov*]: My brothers, where are you from?
> And they said [*vayomeru*]: We are from Haran.
> And he said to them [*vayomer lahem*]: Did you know of Laban son of Nahor?
> And they said [*vayomeru*]: We knew.
> And he said to them [*vayomer lahem*]: Does he have peace?
> And they said [*vayomeru*]: Peace, and here, Rachel his daughter is coming with the sheep. (29:4–6)

Jacob's first interaction in Haran is telling. He approaches the shepherds addressing them as "my brothers."[76] The shepherds' replies are terse, even bordering on rude. They are barely civil. Jacob's repeated attempt at dialogue is seemingly rejected for no apparent reason. Yet, in relaying this dialogue, the text provides the reader with a key insight that will help shed light on many of the interactions in Haran.

Jacob is repeatedly recorded as speaking *to them*—"*vayomer **lahem**.*" The shepherds' responses are blurted out in no relation to Jacob as respondent. They are not recorded as speaking *to him*, as would have textually paralleled Jacob's speech. Their speech is recorded as *vayomeru*," rather than

---

75   See Alter, *The Five Books of Moses*, pg. 153, note on verse 10, where the stone is symbolic of a blockage of Rachel's fertility that is represented by the well itself. This symbolism would reinforce the idea that a hero at the well would again capture the fair maiden as a wife for a prize and help her become fertile. Yet, while Jacob's arrival at the well is typical for the type-scene for a betrothal, it is odd that Rachel seems to be the only female candidate present to make the most of the situation. Viewing the episode as an opportunity to "acquire" Jacob as a worker better explains the presence of male shepherds along with Rachel at the well scene. Since this scene does not juxtapose Rachel to any other female, it should not be seen as a pure betrothal type scene, but rather as the townspeople's attempt to acquire Jacob.

76   29:4. Jacob's search for brethren after severing ties with his biological brother foreshadows Joseph's later quest for the same. As discussed previously, Jacob will soon identify Laban as his next brotherly figure.

"*vayomeru* **lo**." The shepherds are relieved to direct him to Rachel with whom he should continue the conversation. The textual cue alerts the reader from the outset that, in Haran, people do not relate to each other as people. Their focus is on money and possessions. Note the immediate shift in verbosity in the next verse when the topic of conversation switches to sheep instead of Laban:

> And he said [*vayomer*]: Here, still the day is long. It is not time to gather in the herd. Water the sheep and go graze.
> And they said [*vayomeru*]: We cannot until all the flocks have gathered and the rock is rolled off from the opening of the well and we water the sheep. (29:7–8)

Jacob adopts the local parlance quickly and speaks in an undirected fashion. He no longer speaks *to them*. The text abruptly changes from the formulation of "*vayomer* **lahem**" to "*vayomer*." Jacob's critique on the locals' shepherding practices prompts the shepherds to provide Jacob with a complete answer to his query. They do not simply respond by saying: "We cannot." Jacob succeeds in drawing out the shepherds by switching the topic of conversation from inquiring about the welfare of an individual and trying to connect to another human being, to talking shop.

Person, Place, and Thing

> And it was when Jacob saw Rachel daughter of Laban his mother's brother and the sheep of Laban his mother's brother, Jacob confronted and rolled the rock off the opening of the well and watered the sheep of Laban, his mother's brother. And Jacob kissed Rachel and raised his voice and wept. (29:10–11)

Jacob's eyes are then drawn to Rachel, the daughter of Laban, his mother's brother, and to the sheep of Laban, his mother's brother, when he feels the impetus to roll the rock off the well. The text's redundancy of attributing Rachel's genealogy to Laban as well as lining up the sheep with their owner is meant to set up an equation. It is not Rachel's beauty which captivates Jacob at this point, but the sheep she accompanies. Indeed, Rachel's beauty is only described in the text eight verses later when Jacob has already been working for Laban for over a month.[77]

The shepherds, too, do not acknowledge Rachel for her beauty, but because she comes "with the sheep" (29:6). At this juncture, Jacob sees Rachel and mentally categorizes his current relationship to her. At the same time, he is also eyeing the sheep and mentally setting up the identical relationship between them and himself. And if the equivalence is not sufficiently stinging, the text proceeds to describe that Jacob favors the sheep over Rachel and first waters "the sheep of Laban, his mother's brother" (29:10) instead of Rachel.[78]

It is only after Jacob has finished giving water to Laban's entire flock that he now turns to relate to the person—to Rachel. "[He] watered the sheep of Laban, his mother's brother. And Jacob kissed Rachel" (29:10–11). In what might have been an attempt to compensate for his indifference, Jacob kisses Rachel to emphasize his relationship to the person whom he ignored.[79] Jacob

---

77   Cf. 24:16. This is to be contrasted with Rebekah's beauty, which is depicted immediately upon Rebekah's arrival at the well. Similarly, we are only told that Jacob loves Rachel nine verses later, when Jacob has already been working for Laban for over a month. This textual distancing tapers the luring and romantic "love at first sight" reading that naturally arises with a cursory read.

78   Indeed, the equivalence becomes complete when one realizes that Rachel's very name actually means "a female sheep."

79   Jacob kissing Rachel at this juncture may dovetail with Jacob's being sexually impetuous as evinced in his comment for coming unto his wife seven years later. (See the first opinion of Midrash Rabbah 70:12 opining that the kiss at the well is a romantic one.) However, Nahmanides, Rabbi Levi ben Gershon (herinafter: Ralbag), and the second opinion in the Midrash cited above deem the kiss at the well to be a cordial one. Some surmise he kisses her hand, clothes or shoulder. Abravanel (chapter 28 answering question 8) hints that he truly kisses her romantically and then tries to cover up his embarrassment by emphasizing his familial relation. The willingness of Rachel to be kissed romantically would indicate her desire to be swept off her feet by the powerful stranger. Her later turning to Jacob for children would fit with her perception of the prince charming who has wed her. However, Alter, *The Five Books of Moses*, pg. 153 note on verse 11, obviates the need for conjecture about the kiss. Alter quotes Nahum Sarna as noting the wordplay of *vayishak*—and he kissed—with the word *vayashk*—and he watered. Taking the wordplay as a possible reading would have Jacob watering the sheep prior to watering Rachel, thus reversing the order of priorities the servant of Abraham succeeded to set out with Rebekah when he asks only to water himself

cries.[80] He realizes how he has ignored Rachel, and is filled with remorse. How could he have wasted time watering sheep instead of first speaking with Rachel, with whom he may have fallen in love with at first sight?[81] His desire to connect with Rachel is so strong that he identifies himself at length to her as the brother of her father and tells her he is the son of Rebekah.

After Rachel runs to tell her father Laban, and Laban in turn runs towards Jacob,[82] Jacob relates to Laban "all these things" (29:13). He perhaps explains to Laban the overwhelming urge he has at the well to roll the rock and water the sheep or boasts of his strength at the well in order to hint at his utilitarian value should Laban allow him to stay. Laban, perhaps seeking to head off any anticipation of reward Jacob may have for watering the sheep, identifies with Jacob's awareness and reassures him that he is "just like him,"[83] and that he is his relative. In other words, that was nothing special and family members are expected to do such things for free.

---

and only afterwards does Rebekah volunteer to water the camels. This reading highlights the disregard for the person in deference to the sheep and would, in turn, give rise to Jacob's cry. It would also better parallel the prior events at the same well while avoiding the need to explain the mysterious kiss.

80 29:11. Jacob's "lifting his voice and crying" is reminiscent of Esau's lifting his voice and crying in 27:38 when asking his father for a blessing of his own. In both cases, the character is experiencing a moment of self-awareness with existential ramifications.

81 See Rashi 29:11 where Jacob's crying stems from his inability to win over Rachel with money as he is penniless. As will be seen, the principle cited by Rashi of "The poor is as good as dead" applies with full force in Haran. The thrust of the crying, therefore, stems from his inability to be with Rachel. Similarly, the Midrash attributes Jacob's crying to his foreseeing that Rachel is not going to be buried with him and in line with the ideas mentioned above, reflects the idea that Jacob's crying stems from his inability to be with Rachel. (See Genesis Rabbah 70:12.)

82 Laban's running may have had possibly similar motives as outlined for Rebekah and Laban earlier. See also Rashi 29:13: "He thought he was laden with money." However, as pointed out earlier, Rachel's and Laban's running may have been to secure Jacob from going elsewhere. Alternatively, Rachel's running is a result of her being swept off her feet at the well and falls in love with Jacob at first sight. However, as time progresses and Jacob first marries Leah, Rachel becomes bitterly disenchanted. Jacob's later harsh retort to Rachel's desperate request for sons utterly and tragically crushes her true first impressions of Jacob's wholehearted and genuine love.

83 "Atzmi ubsari" refers to an identity with the person. Cf 2:23.

Jacob subsequently stays for a month by Laban and works without pay.[84] As Jacob does not want to be consumed by materialism to such an extent that he values things over people, as he did at the well, he is reluctant to even ask for any pay beyond his room and board.[85]

Laban, however, cannot endure the pure familial relationship with Jacob. After all, Laban is a long-time veteran of Haran philosophy. He cannot allow Jacob to receive room and board gratuitously as a relative, and to work/help with his herds on a voluntary basis. In such a situation, Laban would not be in a position to demand anything of Jacob, because Jacob would only be herding flocks as a familial favor. Laban needs to shift the dynamic to exert control. Laban thus creates a new compromise position. Laban states: "Is it because you are my brother that you will work for me for free?! Tell me what your wage is" (29:15).[86]

Laban informs Jacob that he acknowledges his kinship relation,[87] but that Jacob can still be recompensed for his work. For Jacob, Laban's proposal offers him the opportunity to be freed from the grip of pure materialism, since he would have to work in order to possess sheep. In contrast, during the scene at the well, Jacob is not responsible for taking care of the sheep and does not work for pay, but simply waters the flocks because he is obsessed with someone else's sheep.

Laban's seemingly generous position of asking Jacob to state his wage was, in reality, Laban's first step towards "acquiring" Jacob. Laban would now be Jacob's employer, and Jacob would need to perform satisfactorily in order to remain with the family. Laban deftly changes his role from being

---

84   The word "va'avadtani" in 29:15 seems to indicate the past tense. See Rashi, ibid., and see Alter, *The Five Books of Moses*, pg. 154, note on verse 15.

85   Perhaps this is in fulfillment of his request from God for bread to eat and clothes to wear 28:20. Perhaps Jacob is already aware of the influence of Haran on these matters and is praying to return in peace to his father's home untarnished by such negative influences.

86   The word for "It is because"—"hakhi"—as introducing a question serves as a throwback to Esau's outcry upon learning that Jacob usurped his blessings. See 27:36. Aside from these two instances, the word "hakhi" does not appear in the Pentateuch. The message of both is one of disbelief. Thematically, just as Esau cries not to be denied his rightful blessing, so, too, Laban does not want to deny Jacob his rightful wage.

87   Hence, Laban uses "brother" to express the colloquial understanding of family. He is also echoing, perhaps cynically, Jacob's earlier reference to him as "brother."

Jacob's "brother" to being his employer, and this transformation is the reader's first cue to the skewed metamorphosis of human relations in Haran. The following transformations are soon to follow as the subsequent verses deal with the mutation of people into a fungible means for barter payments that ultimately leads to the switching of sisters and the granting of maids as Jacob's wives.

Crossing Party Lines

> And Laban had two daughters: The name of the older one was Leah and the name of the younger Rachel. And the eyes of Leah were soft and Rachel was beautiful in form and looks. And Jacob loved Rachel and he said: "I will work for you seven years for your younger daughter Rachel." (29:16–18)

It is at this juncture that the text alerts us to Rachel's beauty and Jacob's love for her. In his eagerness to ensure that he is not blinded and obsessed by the lure of materialism, Jacob decides that the best reward for his herding would be a significant relationship with a person. He opts to remain destitute. He loves Rachel and still seeks to make amends for ignoring her earlier in deference to Laban's sheep. There could be no better choice than Rachel with whom to form a relationship. Nonetheless, despite Jacob's well-meaning intentions, his position objectifies Rachel as a means of barter, which utterly sabotages and undermines his true feelings.[88] Jacob unwittingly follows Laban's lead and succumbs to transforming a human-familial relationship into a monetary equation. Thus, in Haran, a person is a "thing"—a commodity to possess.

The Give-Take Relationship

> And Laban said:[89] "It is good to *give* her to you than I would *give* her to another man, stay with me." And Jacob worked for Rachel seven years and they were in his eyes but like a few days in his love of her (29:19,20) …

---

88   This objectification will also boomerang against him when Rachel and Leah will also treat him the same way in the episode of the *dudaim* (30:15–16).

89   The sincerity of Laban's offer will be explored in Chapter Three.

And it was in the evening and he *took* Leah his daughter and brought her to him and he came unto her.[90] And Laban *gave* her Zilpah his maid to Leah his daughter a maid. And it was in the morning and behold—she is Leah. And he said to Laban: "What is this that you have done to me? Did I not work by you for Rachel—and why did you deceive me?"[91] (29:23–25)

Jacob is recorded as working—slaving away—for Rachel for seven years. His love for her makes the time fly by. When the requisite period comes to an end, Jacob makes the following demand from Laban: "Give me my wife (*hava et ishti*); for my time is done, and let me come unto her (29:21)."

Aside from the unrefined manner of speech at the end of his statement, for which the Midrash[92] attempts to compensate, the beginning of the sentence is no less problematic. Jacob wants Laban to "give" him his wife. Thus, despite Jacob's desire to distance himself from the world of giving and taking, his mode of thinking and speaking reveals that he has internally espoused the Haran philosophy.[93]

Yet, even more indicative of Rachel's objectification is the fact that she is not mentioned by name. Jacob does not ask for "Rachel" or "my wife Rachel." Jacob wants to "have" a wife and come unto her. The personal element of the relationship has been removed and has seemingly degenerated into the satisfying of a physiological need. This perhaps alerts Laban to Jacob's state of mind and supports Laban's plan for a successful switch between the daughters. In fact, Laban later echoes back this anonymous reference to Rachel when he informs Jacob that if he works an additional seven

---

90   29:23. The presentation and then partaking of that which is brought recalls Jacob presenting Isaac with the food and drink when usurping the blessings which also follows a curt command by Isaac to "serve me and I will eat from my son's game." Cf. 27:25.

91   I will deal with the actual switch at length later on. Currently, my focus is on the acts of giving and taking mentioned throughout the episode.

92   Midrash Rabbah, *parsha* 70:18 and see Rashi ibid.

93   The unique term Jacob uses for "give me," "*hava,*" is poignantly hurled back at Jacob by Rachel later: "*Hava li banim*—Give me children—and if not I will die" (30:1), when she, too, objectifies children as "things" she must have. In these contexts, the word "*hava*" seems to carry a certain sense of entitlement behind the giving as opposed to the more gratuitous giving embodied in the word "*ten.*"

years, Laban would give him also "this one": "Complete this week and we will give you also *this one* for the work that you will work with me another seven more years " (29:27).

Finally, Jacob's further slip into Haran's grip can be gleaned from the possessive nature of Jacob's statement: "Give me *my* wife." Jacob is utterly caught up in the philosophy of Haran of material possessions. While Jacob remains insistent that he earn his possessions, the world of giving, taking, and possessing become Jacob's lexicon and later plays a major role in his family formation, as will be explained below.[94]

The key words of "giving" and "taking" are pervasive throughout Jacob's stay with Laban. As shown above, they reflect the give-and-take of sales negotiations even when referring to people and relationships.[95] Below is a brief synopsis of the "give-take" phenomenon in list form:

1. And it was in the evening and he *took* Leah his daughter and brought her to him. (29:23)
2. And Laban *gave* her Zilpah his maid. (29:24)
3. And Laban said: It shall not be done in our place to *give* the younger before the eldest. (29:26)
4. Complete this week and we will *give* you also this one. (29:27)
5. And Jacob did so and completed this week and he *gave* him Rachel his daughter to him as a wife. (29:28)
6. And Laban *gave* to Rachel his daughter Bilhah his maid to her as a maid. (29:29)
7. And she said: For God heard that I am hated and He *gave* me also this. (29:33)
8. And she said to Jacob: *Give* me—(*hava li*) children and if not I will die. (30:1)
9. And she *gave* him Bilhah her maid as a wife. (30:4)

---

94   As I proceed in quoting the text, I will highlight the use of these key elements while not necessarily commenting on each.

95   Another distinctive text where these words are seen as key words is in Genesis 23 regarding the sale of the Cave of the Machpelah field from Efron to Abraham. The significant difference is that the subject of the negotiations in Jacob's case does not only refer to things but to people and relationships as well. Associated theme words throughout the Jacob episode are "steal," "wage-reward," "sale," "money," and "work," where these terms do not always refer to things but to feelings and people.

10. And Rachel said: The Lord has judged me and also has listened to my voice and He *gave* me a son. (30:6)

11. And Leah saw that she stopped birthing and she *took* Zilpah her maid. (30:9)

12. And she *gave* her to Jacob as a wife. (30:9)

13. And Rachel said to Leah: *Give* please/now to me from your son's *dudaim*. (30:14)

14. And she said to her: Do you belittle that you *took* my husband? (30:15)

15. That you *take* also my son's *dudaim*. (30:15)

16. And Leah said: The Lord *gave* me my reward. (30:18)

17. For I *gave* my maid to my husband. (30:18)

18. *Give* me my wives and my children. (30:26)

19. And he said: State your wage and I will *give* it. (30:28)

20. And he said: What will I *give* you? (30:31)

21. And Jacob said: Do not *give* me anything. (30:31)

22. And he removed that day the spotted and speckled he-goats and all the brindled and speckled she-goats, every one that had white on it, and every dark-colored one among the sheep, and he *gave* them over to his sons. (30:35)[96]

23. And Jacob *took* for himself moist rods. (30:37)

24. And the sheep Jacob kept apart: he placed them (*gave* them) facing the spotted and all dark colored in Laban's flocks. (30:40)[97]

25. And he heard the sons of Laban saying: Jacob *took* all that our father has. (31:1)

26. And you (*atena*—a wordplay) knew—that with all my strength I slaved for your father. (31:6)

27. God has not let him do me harm (lit. God did not *give* him to do me harm.) (31:7)

28. And God saved your father's flock and *gave* to me. (31:9)

29. And he *took* his brothers with him. (31:23)

30. What is with me and *take* for you. (31:32)

31. And Rachel *took* the *terafim*. (31:34)

32. And Jacob *took* a stone. (31:45)

---

96   Alter's translation.
97   Ibid.

33. And they *took* stones. (31:46)

34. And if you *take* women in addition to my daughters. (31:50)

The general "give-take" obsession escalates into "stealing" as Jacob attempts to escape the world and influence of Haran. Below is the list of the appearance of the key word "steal":

1. And Rachel *stole* the *terafim* of her father. (31:19)
2. And Jacob *stole* the heart of Laban. (31:20)
3. What did you do and you *stole* my heart. (31:26)
4. Why did you conceal your quick exit and you *stole* me. (31:27)
5. Why did you *steal* my gods? (31:30)
6. For I said lest you *steal* your daughters from being with me. (31:31)
7. And Jacob did not know that Rachel *stole* them. (31:32)
8. What was *stolen* by day (31:39)[98]
9. And *stolen* by night. (31:39)[99]

These lists clearly demonstrate that everything in Haran is translated into a quid pro quo. There are no favors or sustained familial cordiality. Rachel and Leah refer to the children God gives them as "things."[100] Similarly, Jacob refers to his wives and children as "things" that Laban should give him in order to leave[101] (30:26).

Yet, the extreme of the give-take mode of existence is no more evident than in the context of the conjugal setting. Marital relations are reduced to bartered goods. Leah and Rachel, as wives, are turned into subjects of barter for Jacob's work. Later, Reuben finds *dudaim* in the field and gives them to his mother Leah. These flowers, believed to have an influence on fertility, are then bartered to Rachel in lieu of a night of marital relations with Jacob.

---

98 Ibid.

99 Ibid..

100 29:33, 30:18. Indeed, the entire competition between the sisters portrays the children as items to accumulate.

101 Similarly, Jacob has no recorded interaction with his children at all. His first recorded speech to any of his children will tellingly be his harsh rebuke of Simeon and Levi after the massacre of the people in the city of Shechem.

Bilhah and Zilpah are also given and taken in marital settings by Rachel, Leah, and Jacob.[102]

As Jacob attempts to leave the world of give-and–take and return to Canaan, the "possessions" already bartered for are thrown back into question. Unless continuously fed, the cycle of give-and-take ends with each party feeling they are the last to give without taking in return. For example, although Laban "steals" seven years of Jacob's life, the sons of Laban, probably ignorant of this, intimate that Jacob has stolen all his possessions from their father. Further, although Laban provides a husband, maid, room and board for them, Rachel and Leah feel their father is responsible for consuming their monies, and Rachel steals her father's *terafim*. Yet further, although Laban ultimately provides Jacob with two wives, a job, and room and board, Jacob is recorded as stealing the heart of Laban. These charges give rise to self-righteousness from each party. Whether legitimate or not, each perpetrator feels as if s/he is the victim. Thus, as Jacob and his family continue their journey to Canaan and Laban and his "brothers" catch up with them at Galed, it is the fate of the entire chain of barter exchanged since Jacob's arrival that are at risk, and not simply the missing *terafim* that Rachel stole.[103]

This and That

The give-and-take existence breeds the desire for amassing more and more wealth of all types. This idea of constantly wanting more, of having this and wanting *also* that, is exemplified in the text by the repetitive use of the word "*gam*," meaning "also." The word appears nine times in the span of 38 verses which deal with Jacob's stay in Haran.[104] The next eight times the word appears over the next four chapters corresponds to each character and their relinquishment of their pursued goals. The following chart outlines the occurrence of the word "*gam*":

---

102 As maids, they are legally considered chattel, but as they elevate their status from maids to Jacob's full wives, one would have expected a different linguistic nuance to reflect their new relational aspect.

103 Indeed, Laban's charge included his daughters and the children as well as the sheep, as his later comment evinces (31:43).

104 See 29:27; 29:30; 29:33; 30:3; 30:6; 30:8; 30:15 and 30:30. See also Avivah Zornberg, *Genesis—The Beginnings of Desire* (Philadelphia: JPS, 1995), pg. 186, note 13.

Verses Related to Jacob's Stay in Haran	Verses Using Gam After Leaving Haran
1. Finish out the week of this one and we shall give you also the other (***gam et zot***). (29:27)	1. And there was to me an ox and a donkey, a sheep and a slave and a maid …And the messengers returned to Jacob saying, "We went to your brother, to Esau, (***vegam***) and he is also traveling to greet you." (32:6–7)
2. And he also came unto Rachel (***gam el Rachel***). (29:30)	2. And you shall say, "We belong to your servant Jacob, it is a tribute sent to my Lord Esau, and, here, he is also (***gam***) behind us." (32:19)
3. And he loved also Rachel over Leah (***gam et Rachel***). (29:30)	3. And he commanded the second one as well (***gam***) (32:20)
4. For God heard that I was hated and gave me also this one (***gam et zeh***). (29:33)	4. also (***gam***) the third (32:20)
5. Here is my maid, Bilhah, come unto her and she will birth on my knees and I will also (***gam***) beget sons from her. (30:3)	5. also (***gam***) all those that were going after the flocks, saying, "Like this statement shall you speak to Esau when you find him" (32:20);
6. And Rachel said, "God adjudicated my case And also (***gam***) heard my voice and He gave me a son." (30:6)	6. And you shall say, "Also (***gam***), here, your servant Jacob is behind us." (32:21)
7. And Rachel said, "In mighty struggles I have struggled with my sister and I also held my own (***gam yakholti***). (30:8)	7. And Leah, (***gam***) too, and her children drew near and bowed down. (33:7)
8. Do you belittle that you took my husband that you take also my son's *dudaim*? (30:15)	8. The midwife said to her, "Fear not, for this one, (***gam***) too, is a son for you." (35:17)
9. And now, when will I also (***gam***) do for my household. (30:30)	

Fittingly, almost all the references that are cited after Jacob leaves Haran speaks of the character relinquishing control and severing their connection from the subject of their desires. Jacob transfers animals to Esau's control; Leah and her children bow down to Esau as master; and Rachel dies at childbirth. The hypnotic effect of the philosophy in Haran is thus limited to its geographic borders as the characters psychologically let go of their obsessions.

Looking back, Rebekah employs the "this and also that" signet of Haran when she seeks to impress the servant of Abraham by telling him: "Also hay also provender, we have a lot, also a place to lodge" (24:25). In fact, the word *gam* appears nine times in the Rebekah-servant narrative.[105] The repeated references there to the camels—"*gemalim*"—can also be seen as further wordplay on this theme.[106]

All of the above help define the framework for the fallout between Jacob, Laban, Laban's sons and Laban's daughters/Jacob's wives. As the narrative proceeds, the debates surrounding who owns what, who takes what, and who should be giving what will spiral into the need for Jacob to leave.

On Employers, Employees, and Livestock Incentives

> And Laban said: "It shall not be done so in our place to give the younger before the firstborn. Complete this week and we will *give* you also this one for the work that you will work with me another seven more years." And Jacob did so and completed this week and he *gave* him Rachel his daughter to him as a wife. And Laban *gave* Rachel his daughter Bilhah his maid to her as a maid.[107]

Despite Jacob's seven years of work, and silent compliance for seven more, as indicated by the verses above, Laban considers Jacob's marriage to Rachel as a "giving," as the future work is still pending. From Laban's

---

105 24:14, 24:19, 24:25 (three times), 24:44 (two times), 24:46 (two times).

106 One does not find the word "*gam*" anywhere else in the Bible in such high concentration as it appears in relation to Haran.

107 29:26–29. The textual emphasis both here and above (29:24) about the intent of Laban's gift, i.e., that they were to be maids for Leah and Rachel, underscores what really happens later when the terms of the gift are broken and the maids are given as wives to Jacob during the sisters' competition over children. This may also explain why they seemingly keep this fact a secret from Laban and Laban later unknowingly seeks for Jacob to declare that he will not take any additional wives in addition to his daughters. Jacob remains silent on this point and does not respond to Laban, as he already wedded other women. This, in turn, leads to a renewed effort by Laban to redefine the terms of the pact. See 31:50–51.

perspective, he is gratuitously giving Jacob his daughter, as opposed to Jacob earning her hand in marriage.

The divergence of views between Laban's and Jacob's sense of entitlement intensify over time. The dynamic is all-too familiar even in today's modern world. An employer takes on an untrained, unskilled, penniless worker and offers him an opportunity to learn a trade and earn a wage. As the years pass, the employer gives the trusted employee increased responsibilities. The employee, while grateful for the opportunity, does not think that the employer is doing him a favor by giving him additional responsibilities. The employee feels and knows that he is working hard for the wages he earns. He also is aware of how much of an asset he is to the employer. A sense of entitlement creeps into his thinking as he awaits a raise in salary, or at the very least, an acknowledgement of all his efforts. As more time passes, the employee feels that he should be made a partner, and should be given significant shares in the business.

The employer's perspective, however, is radically different. He congratulates himself for finding and training such a valuable employee. Thanks to his keen insight and excellent managerial skills, the employee is realizing his full potential. The employer feels that the employee should forever be indebted to him, and in fact should be grateful to receive a salary at all. After all, the employer can replace him at any moment with someone else. As time passes, he allows the employee to take on more responsibility as a reward to himself for doing such a good job as an employer. The employer now has less to do. The employer feels that he "made" the employee into the person he has become, and as such, deserves respect, admiration, and even subservience.

Imagine now that the employee marries the employer's daughter(s). The employer expects even greater respect, since he is not only the man's employer, but also his father-in-law and grandfather to the employee's children. Further suppose that this same employer provides free room and board for fourteen years, and undertakes the maintenance of the employee's home and pays for childcare. As a result, the employer may even come to expect free labor in return for his generosity. Thus, the cycle continues while the dichotomous positions could not become more polarized.

Given all the above, the conflict seems inevitable. As such, at the end of fourteen years of labor on behalf of Leah and Rachel, without any acknowledgement or gratitude for all his hard work, one would expect that Jacob would be all too happy to leave the home of the man who tricks him into wasting seven years of his life:

"Send me and I will go to my place and to my land. Give me my wives and my children, that I worked you for and I will go for you know my labor that I labored for you." (30:25-26)

Indeed, Jacob begins by initiating a conversation with Laban and requests that Laban "give" him his wives and children, for Laban is fully aware of the work that Jacob has done for him. While the latter vague reference of "you know the service that I have done for you" may be a veiled reminder of the years of service forced upon Jacob due to the conjugal switch, the former initiative to leave Haran has Jacob asking Laban to "give" him what he has already worked for. Jacob thus couches his request in terms that Laban would understand. If he is planning on leaving, it certainly wouldn't hurt to speak in Laban's language and request that Laban "give" him what he has already earned.[108]

Jacob's opening indicates that, despite his being penniless, he is intent upon leaving. Perhaps Jacob is confident that his local connections will secure him a good job as someone else's shepherd. In any case, Jacob's later response to Laban's offer reveals that matters are much more complicated than one would assume. Jacob does not dismiss any offer from Laban out of hand. Jacob's penniless state and call to be a responsible father makes even Laban a viable option for employment.

In addition, Laban seemingly provides Jacob with the acknowledgment he sorely wants to hear. Laban attributes his wealth to God, but on account of Jacob: "And Laban said to him, 'If I have now found favor in your eyes, I have divinated and God *has blessed me* because of *you*'" (30:27).

However, as opposed to Jacob's formulation ("*You* know my labor that I labored for you"), Laban's acknowledgment of being blessed because of Jacob falls far from the mark because Laban attributes this insight to the

---

108 Akeidat Isaac, answering question 9 on part two, surmises that Jacob is fearful at this point and is concerned that Laban would claim that his granting of his daughters as wives to Jacob would only be valid so long as Jacob remains with Laban. Jacob, therefore, couches his request from Laban's possible perspective that he would be "giving" them to Jacob at this point.

fact that he makes use of divinations[109] to arrive at this conclusion. In other words, Laban does not acknowledge that this is his personal belief and observation, but rather that of the deities.

As he does not get the acknowledgment he seeks, Jacob remains silent.

Laban then offers a different lure. He asks Jacob to state[110] his "*sakhar*"— "reward" and he will "give" it. For Jacob, this response is also far from adequate. While the reward aspect would indicate Laban's admission to Jacob earning his wage, the "giving" aspect detracts from such an offer.

Jacob then responds to both these points:

> And he said to him: "*You* know how I labored for you and how your flocks were with me.[111] For you had few before me and it has *burst into many* (*va'yifrotz*) and God blessed you on my account and now— when will I also *make* for my house."(30:29–30)

Jacob challenges Laban's contention that it is only through the divinations that he acknowledges Jacob to be the source of his success. Jacob stresses: *You know*. Jacob then proceeds to point to simple math. Before Jacob's arrival, there is few. After Jacob works, there is a lot. Jacob makes reference to his being with the flocks and singles himself out as the only one who has anything to do with them. Thus, whatever happens to the flocks is his doing only, with the help of God.

---

109 Nahmanides (31:19) and Ibn Ezra (30:27, 31:19) point out that Laban uses the *terafim* to obtain this information. They posit that these are the same *terafim* that Rachel later steals. The symbol of the *terafim* as gods indicating the wealth and prosperity of the family has been pointed out by Alter, *The Five Books of Moses*, pg. 169, second note on 31:19. However, Alter rejects the translation of *nihashti* (30:27) as referring to divination and instead translates it as: "I have prospered" based on the Akkadian cognate. I prefer upholding the translation of divining as it explains the apparent redundant reply of Jacob, as will be explained shortly.

110 Laban's word choice of "*nokva*"—"state" your reward can be seen as wordplay on *nekeva*— "female." Laban is hinting that whichever woman Jacob would now want to work towards getting, Laban will provide. The poetic form of "and I will give"— "*ve'etena*"—can also be read as *ve-etenah*—"and I will give her," thus furthering the wordplay.

111 Given Jacob's later statement of being with the flocks day and night (31:39, 40), I believe Jacob's statement here of the flocks "being with him" constantly is meant to be taken literally.

Jacob then addresses Laban's second offer. He states that he wants to "make" for his household. He is not interested in payment or even reward, as Laban suggests. He simply wants to create new equity for his household.

Laban understands that Jacob wants to replicate the blessing Laban experiences for himself.[112] He realizes that Jacob owns nothing in his own right. Jacob needs Laban to provide the "little" from which to make many.

Laban then asks Jacob: "What can I *give* you?" (30:31)

Again, Laban's use of the word "give" indicates that he misses the point of Jacob making and earning his keep.

Jacob responds that Laban will not "give" him anything, and then asks Laban to enter what, in essence, becomes a partnership. The text records Jacob's proposal as having Jacob pass through the flocks.[113] As a second step, any speckled goats and any brown sheep would be set aside for Jacob.[114] In addition, the sheep that are to be Jacob's are given over to "his" sons.[115]

---

112 Thus, we find Jacob saying: When will I "also" make for my household in 30:30. Jacob's use of the word "*gam*"—also—highlights the Haran influence prevalent in his proposal.

113 This passing through seems to indicate a covenantal passing through as in 15:17 or as an evidentiary support to the deal struck, as in 21:29–30. In this case, 30:32, the verb for "passing" is conjugated in the singular as referring to Jacob while the verb for removing is in the third person, ostensibly referring to Laban. The joint activity, therefore, is what will create the partnership.

114 Jacob also allows for a third step where Laban would on some later date, *beyom mahar*—translated as "in the days to come" (See Alter, ibid., pg. 163 verse 33), examine his wages. As this stage never occurs, Jacob's later exit and "stealing" provides grounds for Laban's pursuit to conduct precisely such a search for anything that belongs to him. The literal translation of *beyom mahar* as "on the morrow" is to be rejected as it would incorrectly imply that the only day that Jacob needed to pass inspection and possess solely brindled, spotted, and speckled sheep would be the day following the agreement. Were this to be the case, Jacob would ostensibly be entitled to any type of sheep after the morrow inspection and his later manipulation of the rods and his relaying of the dream to his wives where God manipulates the type of sheep that would be born would then be superfluous.

115 An important question is: Are these Laban's children, as Alter, *The Five Books of Moses*, pg. 166, note 1 explains, or are they Jacob's? If they are Laban's children, the later statement of the sons of Laban claiming that Jacob has taken everything belonging to their father would indicate their proximity to the flocks of Jacob and their witnessing the growth firsthand. If "his" sons refer to Jacob's children, it would imply that Jacob's children are put in charge of the family wealth from a very young age. Reuben is no older than six and a half at the time, and the others

By the terms of the partnership, Laban becomes owner of all the white sheep in the flock, thereby getting his name—"*Laban*"—meaning white.

Following the description of the partnership and its aftermath, the text confirms that Jacob does indeed do the same for his household as he does for Laban: "And the man *burst forth (va'yifrotz)* very, very much[116] and he had a lot of sheep, maids and slaves, camels and donkeys" (30:43). Indeed, the text records the sons of Laban saying that Jacob has *made* this entire honor from their father's belongings.[117]

Yet, despite the new partnership, the underlying tensions between Jacob and Laban persist. What is earned and deserved, and what is taken and stolen? The sons of Laban perceive that the "little" capital investment made by Laban, which Jacob nurtures and invests wisely until it becomes "very, very much," is given to Jacob gratis. At that time, Jacob has not yet done any work for Laban beyond his pledged dowry, and Laban gives, what appears to the sons, to be an unwarranted advance on his paycheck. In their eyes, *all* that Jacob has amassed is taken from their father. Their claim, as Jacob will astutely impute to Laban, encompasses more than just the sheep. It also includes the wives and the children.[118]

In contrast, from Jacob's perspective, the initial flocks awarded to him may actually have been Jacob's idea of compensation for the seven years that he worked for Laban unjustifiably. The language Jacob uses when setting out his proposal is that the original set of animals be set aside "and it will be my wage" (30:32). This phrase could just as easily refer to a wage for work already done as it could to work yet to be done.[119]

---

are even younger. Nonetheless, it would be more logical that Jacob's sons would herd and guard their father's flocks, rather than Laban's sons herding and guarding Jacob's flocks while Jacob was herding and guarding Laban's. This onerous task for such young children would no doubt leave a lasting impression on them. Their father's stress on the sheep's welfare, even at the expense of taxing his own young children, may leave them feeling that the sheep's welfare almost rivals their own. Jacob's preoccupation with the sheep's welfare recurs a few times in the narrative, most poignantly after hearing the news of the rape of Dinah and in his sending Joseph to his brothers in Hebron.

116 This echoes the text's attestation of the growth of Laban's sheep in 30:30: "*vayifrotz larov.*"

117 This echoes Jacob's desire as set out in 30:30 to *make* for his own household.

118 This point will be more fully developed in Chapter Five.

119 If referring to wages for past labor, the future work would be for the rights to the offspring of these animals.

In choosing this linguistic ambiguity, the text attests to how Jacob harnesses his Haran-like philosophy in order to administer justice. Part of Jacob's drive to possess "this and that" is motivated by the desire for compensation as a result of the seven additional years of work that Laban demanded for Rachel. In a sense, it can even be said that the Haran philosophy exerts a positive influence over Jacob, whose drive for materialism spurs him to obtain justice.[120] Furthermore, such positive influence is exhibited when Jacob's desire to maintain his wealth motivates him to adhere to the divine command to leave Haran before the sons of Laban encourage Laban to confiscate things/people from him.

Jacob calls Rachel and Leah "to the field, to his sheep."[121] He calls the meeting by the sheep as he intends to test the waters regarding their loyalty to their father. He wants them to be aware of the flocks they stand to lose should they side with their father.

Jacob explains to his wives that their father's face has changed. He tells them that they are fully aware of how hard he has worked for their father. Jacob may be referring, as he attests later, to the many late nights he slept with the sheep and away from his wives.[122] Jacob then fabricates that Laban has toyed with him and switched his wages ten times.[123] The women then respond, in material terms, declaring that they view themselves as sold chattel. At the same time, their paranoia and warped perception on the world of possessions cause them to believe

---

120 Indeed, Jacob states: "And my righteousness will bear witness for me" (30:33). The word for righteousness—"tsidkati"—is from the same root as the word for justice—"tsedek."

121 31:4. In ascertaining their loyalties, Jacob mentions Laban being their father four times in six verses and pits that against his father's God being with him. Interestingly, as the hold of Haran continues to grip Jacob, Jacob does not even mention his desire to return home to see his father. It is ironically only the materialistically-gripped Laban who later imputes Jacob's quick exit as being motivated by a desire to see his father.

122 See Alter, *The Five Books of Moses*, pg. 160, note to 30:16, who suggests that Jacob did not frequent Leah's tent much at all and did not take turns between the wives. The inference from the later tirade where Jacob claimed he stayed with the sheep day and night would further imply that he did not spend many nights with any of his wives.

123 See the beginning of Chapter Five for an explanation of Jacob's fabrication and see there Abravanel's suggestion that the dream he relays to Leah and Rachel never occurred.

that Laban has eaten away at *their* money and that everything that has been saved from their father belongs to *them* (to the exclusion of Jacob?) and their children: "Do we still have any share of inheritance in our father's estate? Haven't we been considered as strangers to him as he sold us and certainly has consumed our monies? For all the wealth that God saved from our father is ours and our sons. And now, all that God said to you—do" (31:14–16).

In response to this warped sense of ownership, the narrative goes out of its way to demonstrate where the truth lies. Describing Jacob's exit, the narrative reads: "And he led all his flock and all *his possessions* that *he acquired*, the livestock that *he purchased*, which *he purchased* in Paddan-Aram, to arrive at his father Isaac, towards the land of Canaan."[124] By using the singular masculine form of "acquired"—*asher rakhash*,[125] and the singular pronoun suffix for "*his* possessions" and "*he* purchased," the text sides with identifying the wealth with he who helped produce it—Jacob.

The Showdown

Following Jacob's exit and Laban's pursuit, the two parties vigorously argue atop Mount Gilead. Significantly, the thrust of Jacob's argument surrounds his relationship to Laban. Jacob continuously speaks of his history throughout the period at Laban's home (31:38, 41). He points to his long years of dedication by Laban and his disbelief at the sheer lunacy of Laban's claims. Jacob, who is now free of Haran's materialistic grip, succeeds in reclaiming the emphasis on human relationships. Laban, however, intending to return to Haran, remains entrenched in the Haran mindset and focuses solely on the issue of possessions. As far as Laban is concerned, Jacob's years of labor and all relational aspects are irrelevant to the discussion.

Jacob concludes his final volley by stating: "My suffering and the *toil of my hands* God has seen, and last night He determined in my favor." (31:42)[126]

Nonetheless, Laban attempts to maintain the moral high ground and further insists: "And Laban answered and said to Jacob: 'The daughters are my daughters, and the sons are my sons, and the sheep are my sheep, and everything that you see is *mine*.'"(31:43)

---

124 31:18. Also see Alter, *The Five Books of Moses*, pg. 169, note to 31:20.

125 This is to be contrasted with the plural form as used by Abram and Sarai's exit in 12:5 "*asher rakhashu*"—that they acquired.

126 Alter's translation and see Alter, *The Five Books of Moses*, pg. 174, note to 31:42.

Although the debate remains unresolved, a pact is reached whereby each party is to remain in their respective geographic area, with Laban ceding control over his daughters and grandchildren to Jacob.

As Jacob and his family cross over the newly-drawn demarcation line between Jacob and Laban towards Canaan, the mysterious grip of Haran loosens its hold on all of Jacob's "newly acquired" family, allowing them to reevaluate their skewed emphasis on possessions, as illustrated above. This shift in perspective is best illustrated when Jacob releases his animals and wealth to Esau after they reunite and reconcile their past. As part of that reconciliation, Leah and her children bow to Esau as master. This bowing symbolically represents Leah's relinquishing control over her children and their symbolically entering the dominion of Esau as master. As Jacob travels onwards in Canaan, Rachel tragically dies while birthing Benjamin, thus symbolizing Rachel's perforce release of her obsession to outdo her sister and have more boys.

Despite being free from the spell of Haran, there will always remain periods in Jacob's life when materialistic concerns hold sway over him. The legacy of Haran leaves Jacob not only striving to maintain an emotional status quo and avoid risk, but also to maintain the status quo of his wealth.[127]

---

127   As the narrative continues, Jacob encounters personal and familial tragedies that also include certain financial dimensions. They include the prospect of losing his newly acquired field and his sheep when dealing with Shechem as well as weighing the proposed economic benefit offered to marry off Dinah. To recall, and as will be fully discussed later on in Chapter Eight, Jacob settles near the city of Shechem and Dinah is raped by Shechem. In trying to cover up the affair and marry the girl he loves, Shechem offers to pay any price for Dinah's hand in marriage. Simeon and Levi, Dinah's brothers, massacre the town and the other brothers pillage the city. They partly attribute their father's silence to his desire to possibly acquiesce to Shechem's wishes in order to gain financial advantage. This explains the brother's allusion to harlotry where the laying is to be compensated by money. Otherwise, their stinging analogy lacks internal logic. Such a scenario, of allowing a family member to be raped for pecuniary gain, had an ancestral precedent to draw from, as Abram remains silent as Sarai was raped by Pharaoh, while seemingly seeking to gain financial advantage. See 12:10–20. Jacob's children also identify with their father's monetary obsession, as is evinced by their pillaging the City of Shechem and as seen in Judah's later comment about the need to profit from Joseph's disappearance, "What gain is there if we kill our brother"? (37:26).

Jacob's stay in Haran thus not only influences his outlook on materialism, but also shapes his views on family and the family's view on money. Unfortunately, Jacob's stated desire to Laban to "also make for his house," that is, to make money for his family's sake, thus returns to haunt Jacob, as monetary aspirations contribute to the ultimate breakdown of his family unit.

CHAPTER THREE

The Conjugal Switch

To cheat oneself out of love is the most terrible deception; it is an eternal loss for which there is no reparation, either in time or in eternity.

                         ✍ *Soren Kierkegaard*

And Laban had two daughters: The name of the older one was Leah and the name of the younger Rachel. And the eyes of Leah were soft and Rachel was beautiful in form and looks. And Jacob loved Rachel and he said: "I will work for you seven years for your younger daughter Rachel." And Laban said: "It is good to give her to you than I would give her to another man, stay with me." And Jacob worked for Rachel seven years and they were in his eyes but like a few days in his love of her. And Jacob said: "Give me my wife for I have fulfilled my days and I will come unto her." And Laban gathered all the men of the town and had a drinking feast. And it was in the evening and he took Leah his daughter and brought her to him and he came unto her. And Laban gave her Zilpah his maid to Leah his daughter a maid. And it was in the morning and behold—she is Leah. And he said to Laban: "What is this that you have done to me? Did I not work by you for Rachel—and why did you deceive me?" (29:16–25)[128]

---

128   To recall, Rebekah leverages Isaac's dislike of Esau's Hittite wives and arranges an elegant escape for Jacob from Esau's vengeful wrath over the usurped blessings. As a result, Isaac and Rebekah dispatch a compliant Jacob to Haran to find a non-Hittite wife. Once in Haran, Jacob is adopted by his uncle Laban and Jacob begins

The ten verses above encapsulate one of the most powerful experiences that forge Jacob's family dynamics. Jacob works for seven years in anticipation of marrying Rachel, but on the wedding night, Laban presents him instead with Leah. Jacob discovers the switch in the morning and asks Laban to explain his actions.

The duping of Jacob seems incredulous and requires exploration. Understanding how Jacob fails to notice the switch will help explain his state of mind and reaction the morning after.

How Could Jacob Not Notice the Switch Until Morning?

1. Timing

> And Laban gathered all the men of the place and made a drinking feast. And it was in the evening and he took Leah his daughter and brought her to him (Jacob) and he came unto her. (29:22–23)

The text relates that there is a drinking party and that later in the evening, even immediately before the conjugal act, Laban brings Leah to Jacob. Therefore, the amount of time that Jacob is actively fooled, between the initial moment of the switch and the conjugal act, is minimal—perhaps only minutes. The time period following the conjugal act until morning is less problematic as one may assume that after a drinking party and having relations, Jacob is asleep.[129]

2. Darkness

In addition, the text emphasizes that Laban brings Leah to Jacob in the evening, after the party. The reference to it being "evening" suggests that it is the dark of evening that contributes to a successful switch. The text further lends support to this suggestion by contrasting Jacob's nighttime ignorance with his morning enlightenment. The insinuation is that the morning light allows for Jacob's correct identification of the woman in his bed, which the dark of night prevented.

---

to work as his shepherd. After a month of service, Laban approaches Jacob to state his wage and the above verses describe the disturbing aftermath.

129 See Or Hahayyim commenting on 29:23 who also mentions these points.

3. Lack of Reference

The reference to "evening" also suggests that Laban deliberately brings Leah to Jacob in the evening. The inference is that the bride-to-be, whether Rachel or a disguised Leah, is not present at the party. It is only *later* that she is presented to Jacob. This idea is further supported by the text which relates that only the "men of the place" attend the party—the men—but neither the intended bride nor any other females are present.

Therefore, even if Jacob had any misgiving in the night, the lack of an earlier image of how Rachel the bride was supposed to look that evening contributes to Jacob's failure to recognize Leah. Since both Rachel and Leah do not attend the party, Jacob lacks a frame of reference for identifying the woman in the dark tent.

4. Jacob Is Inebriated

The text also informs us that the celebration takes the form of a "*mishteh*"—a celebration where drink is served. In that case, it is not unreasonable to assume that the bridegroom takes part in the drinking, thereby impairing his senses. The text does not record Jacob as being drunk as is recorded with Noah (9:21), or as inebriated as Lot (19:31–37), who does not know with whom he lies. However, the inference of drinking, even if not to the point of being "drunk," could impair Jacob's senses, making it easier for Laban to perpetrate the switch.[130]

5. Vocal Impressions

The Sages of the Talmud[131] go to great lengths to explain how Jacob is fooled. To assuage our natural doubts, the Talmudic Sages, and more fully developed in the Midrash, emphasize in precise detail Rachel's role in advancing the deceit and preserving her sister's dignity. The Midrash even goes so far as to suggest that Rachel is under the conjugal bed filling in vocally whenever a verbal reply to Jacob is necessary.[132] In that case, hearing Rachel's voice while visually in the dark would help explain Jacob's failure to identify Leah. This Midrashic gap-filler is also attempting to draw a parallel

---

130 See also Josephus, Ant. 1.19.7 where the darkness and drink are mentioned as the cause for Jacob's failure to discern: "as being both in drink and in the dark."

131 *Megilla* 13b, *Baba Batra* 123a and quoted by Rashi commenting on 29:25.

132 Petihta—Lamentations Rabba—end Parshia 24.

between Laban's deceit of Jacob and Jacob's deceit of Isaac, where Jacob's voice belies his disguised physical appearance.

6. A Mask

Later in the text, the Bible will startle the reader with yet another tale of someone having relations with a woman without recognizing her identity. Judah later has relations with his widowed daughter-in-law Tamar without knowing that it is her (38:14–19). He remains ignorant of this fact for a good amount of time beyond the next morning. In drawing parallels with the story of Judah and Tamar, as will be fully discussed in a future volume of this work, Netziv[133] comments that Tamar is not recognized by Judah because she covers her face even when having relations with him. If covering one's face during relations is a widely practiced custom of the time, it could well be that Leah is observing the same convention. Indeed, Shmuel David Luzzato (hereinafter: Shadal)[134] quotes a source that this is indeed the tradition of the time. Furthermore, the wedding rituals of the time may have called for the bride to apply excessive make-up on her face or wear an exotic headdress, thus making it even more difficult to discern fine facial features. As such, even if Jacob could see in the dark, the covering of her face with either cloth or excessive make-up would further disguise her true identity.

7. Leah's Modesty

Abravanel[135] explains that Leah is so modest that Jacob doesn't recognize her when he has relations with her. In other words, Leah has been out of sight until now. Therefore, it makes sense that on the wedding night Jacob does not recognize Leah. This would also explain why Leah is not present with Rachel at the well when Jacob first arrives. It is not befitting Leah's standards of modesty to be involved in such work. Only Rachel is recorded as working with the sheep.[136]

---

133 Commenting on 38:14.

134 Commenting on 29:23, see also Kass, *The Beginning of Wisdom*, pg. 426 who presumes this to have been the case. Rabbi David Zvi Hoffman also comments on 29:23 and parallels this case to Rebekah's scarf in 24:65.

135 Parashat Vayishlah answering question 4, ch.33.

136 However, this is not necessarily the case. Rachel and Leah may have had a rotating work schedule between them.

However, the difficulty with attributing Jacob's ignorance to Leah's modesty is that while Jacob may not have recognized Leah, he should at least have been able to recognize that she was not Rachel, for Rachel's modesty did not prevent her from being seen by Jacob.

8. The Double-Switch

In addition to the points mentioned above, the text relates that Laban gives Zilpah to Leah as a maid (29:24). This point is mentioned after Laban gives Leah to Jacob and prior to the morning revelation that a deception has taken place. The verses read:

> And it was in the evening and he took Leah his daughter and brought her to him and he came unto her. And Laban gave her Zilpah his maid to Leah his daughter a maid. And it was in the morning and behold—she is Leah. (29:23–25)

Why does Laban, or at least the text, interrupt the nighttime deception with the information of Laban's giving Leah a maid? Rashi comments that the granting of Zilpah is an essential part of the trickery.[137] Laban not only switches the brides but also their maids. Rashi suggests that Zilpah was originally Rachel's maid and given to Leah on her wedding night in order to further deceive Jacob into believing that Laban has brought him Rachel as agreed.[138] Thus, this double-switch, of the brides and their maids, contributes towards convincing Jacob that the woman presented to him in the dark tent is indeed Rachel.

---

137 29:24 in Mossaf Rashi.

138 This explanation, however, meets up with difficulty as the text specifically identifies both Zilpah and Bilhah as Laban's maids (29:24; 29:29). Nevertheless, Abravanel (commenting on Vayetse chapter 29 answering question 7) and Akeidat Isaac (answering question 5 on this section) later develop this point further in explaining the naming of Zilpah's first child—Gad. The text records Leah calling him "*Bagad*"—betrayed. The Masoretic reading transforms this betrayal into two words "*Ba Gad*" meaning "good luck came." Abravanel and R. Isaac Arama, however, believe that Zilpah's son was named "Bagad," meaning betrayed, because of Laban's deception when he switches the maids.

9. The Twin Hypothesis

Jacob's failure to identify Leah could also be attributed to the fact that Leah and Rachel are identical twins. This assertion is problematic, however, in light of the following text which states: "Leah's eyes were soft and Rachel was of beautiful form and looks" (29:17).[139] This is usually taken to mean that Rachel is more beautiful than Leah.[140] Leah's only noteworthy feature is her soft eyes. However, the commentaries[141] attribute this softness to excessive crying, so one could say that if not for Leah's crying, she and Rachel are identical from birth.[142]

The "morning" may have allowed Jacob to discern the subtle difference between Leah's "soft" eyes and Rachel's. As there are no other distinguishing marks between them, it is only in the light of morning that he can perceive this difference. Thus, the possibility of Rachel and Leah being twins remains a viable explanation for Jacob's inability to distinguish one sister from another.

Jacob's Reaction

Having explored the possible reasons for Jacob's inability to recognize Leah, we can now turn our attention to Jacob's reaction the following morning.

> And it was in the morning and behold—she is Leah. And he said to Laban: "What is this that you have done to me? Did I not work by you for Rachel—and why did you deceive me?"(29:25)

---

139 See Or Hahayyim commenting on 29:17 who views this verse as explicitly distinguishing the appearances of Rachel from Leah.

140 Another argument against presuming that the sisters are twins is that the text makes no mention of this important information. However, the text does not always satiate our desire for information even if we, as readers, deem such details vital. For example, the text does not record the conversation between the brothers and Joseph following the revelation of his true identity to them, and instead suffices with the following information: "And afterwards his brothers spoke with him" (45:15). As readers, we would have expected a word-for-word transcript of what appears to be the most important conversation between the characters.

141 For example, see Rashi and Alsheikh commenting on 29:17.

142 See Sharon Ruback, "*Shetayim Hen Shenitkasu Bitse'if*", [Hebrew], in *Beit Mikra*, Vol. 183, no. 4, Tamuz-Elul 5765, pgs. 366-390, pg. 375, ftn. 36, who cites *Sefer HaYashar* (edition of Rav Joseph ben Shemuel), Berlin, 5683, Parashat Toledot, pg. 93 which explicitly states that Rachel and Leah were twins and see also Genesis Rabbah 70:15 for further equations between Leah and Rachel.

Jacob lodges three separate claims against Laban.

PART 1. "*Ma zot asita li*—What is this that you have done to me?"

This query expresses Jacob's utter disbelief when he discovers Leah. How could Laban do this to him?[143] The switch is preposterous, immoral, even criminal. The outrageousness of the matter echoes similar questions posed to Abraham by Pharaoh and Avimelekh upon their discovery that Sarai/Sarah is not Abraham's sister, but his wife. To recall, Abraham, then still named Abram, migrates to Egypt because of a famine in Canaan. As he and his wife, then still named Sarai, approach Egypt, Abram requests that Sarai claim she is his sister rather than his wife. Abram is afraid that the Egyptians will lust for Sarai and kill him in order to take her as their wife. When they arrive, Pharaoh receives word of Sarai's beauty and orders her to be taken as his wife. God plagues Pharaoh until Sarai is restored to Abram, but not before Pharaoh takes Abram to task over the incident:

Pharaoh exclaims: "*Ma zot asita li*—What is this that you have done to me?" (12:18)

Similarly, when Abraham moves to Gerrar, he repeats a similar incident as he informs the inhabitants that Sarah is his sister and not his wife. King Avimelekh sends for her to be taken as his wife and God prevents him from touching Sarah. Avimelekh restores Sarah to Abraham but declares: "*Me asita lanu*—What have you done to us and what have I done wrong to you that you have brought upon me and my kingdom a great sin? Actions that shall not be done you did with me" (20:9).

Avimelekh[144] later has a similar experience with Isaac when Isaac declares Rebekah to be his sister. Upon discovery of the ruse, Avimelekh exclaims: "*Ma zot asita lanu*—What is this that you have done to us? One of the people almost slept with your wife and you would have brought upon us culpability" (26:10).

In all cases, the misidentification of a woman causing or almost causing a man to lay with her under false pretenses is morally reprehensible. The repetition of the same phrase "*ma zot asita li*" reinforces the idea that Jacob

---

143 Jacob's self-centered query does not ask how Laban could have done this to Leah and/or Rachel, but rather focuses only on the ramifications for him.

144 Possibly a different person than the one who dealt with Abraham, with the name Avimelekh acting as a common noun for ruler.

recognizes the moral reprehensibility of Laban's actions, and demands that it be addressed.

The linguistic parallels also call for an analysis of Jacob's ancestral dynamics. On that level, Jacob has already perpetrated and repeated the ancestral pattern of switching identities. While his ancestors encouraged their wives to assume the identity of sisters, Jacob assumes his brother's identity when usurping the blessings. On some level, a certain sense of ancestral poetic justice is delivered as Jacob, the progeny of the perpetrators, now becomes a victim and accuses others of switching identities—a crime of which he himself is also guilty. On a yet deeper level, the ancestral claim of wife-turned-sister is played out against Jacob as sister-turned-wife.

However, as opposed to the ancestral pattern, when Esau discovers the ruse he does not confront Jacob, as do Pharaoh and Avimelekh to Abraham, and as does Avimelekh to Isaac. Esau fails to ask, or is prevented from asking, Jacob: "*Ma zot asita li*?—What have you done to me?" Jacob never faces the full power of the moral argument the way that Abraham and Isaac experience its intensity. Jacob experiences no public embarrassment and does not need to make excuses for his behavior. At this point in his personal development, this lacking is Jacob's weak spot. As will be discussed, Jacob's non-confrontational approach with Laban is partially driven by a desire to avoid embarrassment. Had Jacob been taken to task for usurping Esau's blessings, he would have suffered embarrassment and the need to somehow excuse himself. Such an ordeal would have built a stronger sense of self-worth, as Jacob would gain the confidence to manage himself under stressful conditions. But since he is lacking this experience, he is not ready to fully charge Laban with his misconduct and even acquiesces to seven more years of labor for Rachel.

In addition, had Jacob been subjected to Esau's accusations, the ensuing dialogue between the two brothers could have resulted in a crucial turning point or a defining moment in the family's relationship. Jacob may have implicated Rebekah's role in the deception. Rebekah might have then discussed with Isaac the divine oracle given to her during her pregnancy (if she hadn't already)[145] and their favoritism towards their children. Jacob

---

145 See Abravanel commenting on Toledot 27 answering question five and six who espouses that Rebekah never told Isaac about the oracle as well as Nahmanides commenting on 27:4 who adopts the same position. Similarly, Rabbi Meïr Leibush ben Jehiel Michel Weiser (hereinafter: Malbim) commenting on 25:28 raises the

might mention the sale of the birthright from Esau. Jacob and Esau would then have been forced to settle matters amongst themselves and with their parents before Jacob's exit to Haran. Had the birthright and favoritism issues been resolved, Jacob may have been able to avoid a trip to Haran altogether and instead could have dispatched a servant to travel to Haran to pick a wife for him. However, since Jacob has not been forced to face these underlying familial issues, he continues to espouse the path of silence and innuendo, and it is this pattern that repeats itself when dealing with Laban and the conjugal switch.

PART 2. "Was it not for Rachel that I worked with you?"

Jacob's second charge against Laban moves away from the moral issue that would apply to all humanity to a more specific claim against Laban's personal and professional integrity. Jacob claims that they had a deal. In Haran, business is business. Jacob is relying on his understanding of his working agreement with Laban. The contract is clear, yet Laban is breaching the terms of their agreement. In this second charge, Jacob is asking Laban how he could do this to him in light of their agreement.[146]

PART 3. "And why did you deceive me?"

Jacob argues that even if Laban could excuse his actions, Jacob wants to know what motivated Laban to cheat him in the first place. Why couldn't Laban have been honest about the factors that compelled him into performing the switch?

---

possibility that Isaac does not know of the oracle. On the other hand, Netziv commenting on 25:23 identifies an ambiguity in syntax and hence in the meaning of the oracle such that knowledge of the oracle would be irrelevant as each parent could interpret the oracle as they pleased.

146 As with the moral claim, this charge also echoes back to Jacob's past. Jacob's wherewithal to usurp his brother's blessings is not only driven by his mother's reassurance but also by his sense of self-righteousness. Jacob had earlier purchased his brother's birthright. Esau's willingness to accept the blessings despite the sale allows Jacob to justify his actions. As Esau is in breach of the sales agreement about the birthright, Jacob would usurp the blessings to mitigate damages. Lacking the type of insider information that he received from his mother during the blessings episode, Jacob finds himself outmaneuvered in Haran. Laban succeeds in breaching their agreement without Jacob preempting the damage as he did with Esau.

Laban's Response

> And Laban said: "It shall not be done so in our place to give the younger before the elder. Complete this week and we will give you also this one for the work that you will work with me another seven more years." (29:26–27)

Laban's explanation suggests that he did not want to go through with the plot, but was left with no choice. Whether this statement is true or not is open to debate, but it opens up a new possibility for viewing Laban as less culpable of the sordid affair than traditionally thought. Accordingly, Laban can be seen as acting out of duress rather than malicious intent. It might have always been his intention to give Rachel to Jacob, but only after first giving him Leah.

Laban's seemingly ready reply referring to local custom also adds a dig at Jacob: "And Laban said: 'It shall not be done so in our place [pause]—to give the younger before the elder'" (29:26). Laban's pause, as suggested by the cantillations between "such things shall not be done in our place" and "to give the younger before the elder," allows Jacob to think that Laban's initial comment of "such things shall not be done in our place" refers to the way Jacob is speaking to Laban. It is only after the pregnant pause that Laban fills in the missing gap of what exactly it is that is not done in "our place."

Laban continues: "Complete this week and we will give you also this one for the work that you will work with me another seven more years."

After hearing this explanation and proposal, Jacob does not fly into a rage or demand that Laban give him Rachel immediately.[147] Laban's response is too honest for Jacob and takes him by surprise. Not only does Laban respond to Jacob's allegations, but he succeeds in placing the onus of responsibility on Jacob's shoulders. It is Jacob's suggestion to marry the younger before the elder that is the morally reprehensible act and in violation of society's norms of decency. Laban implies that such a suggestion cannot even be entertained as a possibility, and therefore could never have been the original intention of their agreement.[148]

---

147 See Or Hahayyim 29:25.

148 Laban's statement excusing his behavior based on the exigencies of local custom simultaneously evinces Laban's acknowledgment that what occurred is not in accordance with what Jacob thought of their earlier deal.

As for their agreement, as Or Hahayyim suggests, the giving of Leah does not preclude the giving of Rachel. Laban simply says that Jacob should wait the week and then "we[149] will give you also this one"—Rachel—as a wife. Thus, argues Laban, the intent of the original agreement is still intact.[150]

Laban's last point addresses his motivation for cheating Jacob. Laban wants Jacob to work another seven years for Rachel. Laban's honest answer is that he is cheating Jacob in order to receive another seven years of labor. Had Laban suggested during the first seven-year period that Jacob work another seven years in order to marry Leah, or had he initially quoted fourteen years for Rachel, Laban assumes that Jacob would have refused. *It is therefore evident that Laban is confessing that he is not simply complying with local custom and technically postponing the fulfillment of their agreement. That would not have required another seven years of labor.* Laban is unilaterally formulating a new deal. It is this added benefit to Laban as employer, and by his own confession, which points to him being the mastermind behind the switch. Indeed, as Laban does not even feign ignorance of the switch, Jacob's suspicion of Laban's prior knowledge is confirmed.

Jacob's Mindset

The text provides us with little information that sheds light on Jacob's thoughts after seeing Leah and prior to approaching Laban. From the textual proximity between the morning revelation and Jacob's speaking with Laban, the implication is that not much time has elapsed. Surprisingly, Jacob does not yelp upon his discovery of Leah,[151] or attempt to kick her

---

149   As Laban's wife is never mentioned in the text, the "we" Laban must be referring to is he and the townspeople. Laban's comment not only supports his excuse about local custom but also allows Jacob to entertain a conspiracy theory as will be detailed below. Laban's argument reduces their disagreement to when the seven years of work for Rachel come into effect. Jacob logically relies on them starting immediately after their original agreement while Laban claims they start after the seven years for Leah are completed, as would be dictated by local custom. Laban's automatic presumption of seven years of work for each of the daughters continues to uphold the "sameness" that Laban perpetuates for his daughters and that Laban forcefully projects onto Jacob's life.

150   However, as will be pointed out, the last part of Laban's retort demanding an additional seven years of work detracts greatly from this point.

151   Compare with Isaac's trepidation upon realizing he blessed someone other than Esau in 27:33.

out or divorce her, if a divorce would even be necessary in the face of the deception.[152]

Instead, Jacob simply expresses his surprise to Laban, and inquires as to why his uncle has deceived him: "What is this that you have done to me? Did I not work by you for Rachel—and why did you deceive me?" This would seem to imply that Jacob, who is surely upset, has calmed down, and is giving thought to his awkward position before approaching Laban.[153]

Already at this juncture, Jacob's behavior seems peculiar. Why wouldn't he express any wonderment immediately upon his discovery of Leah? Why does he automatically identify Laban as the culprit instead of berating Leah and/or Rachel? And why does he seemingly maintain his composure even when speaking with Laban?

While Laban's response, analyzed above, provides Jacob with one piece of conclusive information, one must wonder what else Jacob could have possibly been thinking immediately upon his discovery of the switch. As pointed out above, one is bewildered by Jacob's contained outrage when speaking to Laban. On the one hand, he does not simply return to work as if nothing has happened. On the other hand, why doesn't Jacob demand the immediate nullification of his marriage to Leah and/or demand an immediate marriage to Rachel? Why doesn't Jacob confront Leah and/or Rachel? Even if Laban is responsible for concocting the plan, he could not succeed without their joint cooperation. Rachel would need to agree to have Leah replace her, and Leah would need to voluntarily assume Rachel's role. Why not publicly charge Laban with the deceit perpetrated? How could Jacob remain silent and allow himself to be cheated out of seven years of his life? The betrayal cries out for redress.

---

152 See also Reggio 29:25.

153 As complex as the analysis below may seem, it is probably simpler for Jacob to juggle all these combinations than for the reader. As Jacob is aware of his own feelings and has spent seven years in Laban's home, the ability to size up who could have done this to him and why is surely more transparent to him than it is to us. On the other hand, the inquiries raised below must have been so much more emotionally charged and real for Jacob that all the possibilities must have swirled in his head like a raging tornado. Nonetheless, I concede that it is still possible that Jacob does not think through all of the raised possibilities, and simply approaches Laban instinctively with his well-reasoned complaint. Unquestionably, however, in the days and years to follow, Jacob would surely need to come to grips with each person's role in the switch and his relationship with each of them.

Why Didn't Jacob Publicly Charge Laban with the Deceit?

Fear of Humiliation

On a most basic level, Jacob must be extremely embarrassed. After seven years of intensive labor, the wedding night finally arrives. Jacob demands his bride from Laban saying, "Give me my wife for I have fulfilled my days and I will come unto her" (29:21). The language employed is direct and coarse and occupies much discussion amongst the classical commentaries.[154] After exhibiting such impatience and revealing his sexual desire for his bride, Jacob must surely be embarrassed that he does not notice the switch until morning.

Furthermore, were Jacob to publicly accuse Laban of the conjugal switch, not only would Jacob be humiliated in front of his family, but before the townspeople attending the party—most probably the locals whom he has to face on a day-to-day basis.[155]

Therefore, charging Laban with deceit would bring Jacob's personal embarrassment out in the open along with all the public humiliation associated with the charge. Naturally, Jacob would prefer not to admit publicly that he is the victim of deception.

Would Anyone Believe Him?

Jacob's silence is also fueled by the fear that nobody would believe him. If Jacob were to directly challenge Laban in public, he would need to prove the following points: That he had an agreement with Laban to marry his daughter; that they agreed that that daughter would be Rachel; that the issue of local custom was never referenced; that the deal was for seven years of work; that Leah is not presented to him properly on the wedding night; and that he managed to have relations without realizing it was Leah. Add to this the possibility that

---

154 See, for example, Rashi, Or Hahayyim and Nahmanides commenting on this verse.

155 The Abravanel commenting on 29:20, answering question 1 and 2, reinforces this point by commenting that Laban only throws a party for the wedding between Leah and Jacob but not for the later wedding between Jacob and Rachel. Laban's reasoning, comments the Abravanel, is that were Jacob to attempt to divorce Leah it would be a disgrace before all those who attended and would thus serve as a deterrent against such action. Laban realizes that he would not need to provide such a deterrent with Rachel, and therefore decides to dispense with the festivities and save money.

Laban may lie on any or all of the above points, or use his seniority in Haran, and the chance of Jacob being believed decreases yet further.[156]

Denial

In order to internalize the possibility that Laban is capable of carrying out such a preposterous deed, Jacob would need to view Laban as a fiendish, scheming cheater. Jacob would naturally prefer to avoid attaching such a description to Laban. For even if Jacob entertains doubts about Laban, he cannot easily forget that it is thanks to Laban that he has a roof over his head, a safe haven from Esau,[157] a job in Haran and that it was Laban himself who encouraged Jacob to state his wages in the first place. Jacob would rather seek an excuse, any excuse, to help him explain Laban's malfeasance. Once Laban provides such an explanation, Jacob does not have to entertain the idea that Laban, his uncle and now father-in-law, is a devious and dishonest man trying to take advantage of him at every turn. The possibly apologetic tone psychologically helps Jacob accept Laban's excuse that local custom forces him to deceive Jacob. He can now blame the force of local custom. Human nature will go out of its way to help Jacob explain any other inconsistencies he may see—even the need to work seven more years for Laban in order to "pay" for Rachel.

---

156 Furthermore, even if the locals are inclined to believe him, since Laban is his uncle, they may presume it is a family affair and advise him to work it out between the two of them. Jacob, too, may be hesitant to air out the family's dirty laundry in public.

157 It should be pointed out that it is not at all clear whether Laban truly knew that Jacob was running away from Esau when he took Jacob into his home. When reading Jacob's introduction of himself to Rachel, Jacob mentions his relation to Rebekah. When Laban greets him, Jacob "tells him all these things" (29:13). It is possible that Jacob then informed Laban of all that occurred at home until he arrived at Laban's home. However, it could be that Jacob only informed Laban of all the things that occurred at the well. After all, if Esau were to pursue Jacob to Laban's home it would possibly endanger Laban and his family. Laban may decide to avoid such risk. In fact, the Abravanel (Vayetse chapter 31 answering question 6) asserts that Jacob never told Laban of his fleeing Esau. (Although Abravanel contradicts himself in commenting otherwise on Vayetse 28 answering question 8.) This point will prove important in later analyzing Jacob's overall family dynamic and the ability or propensity to keep secrets from family members over extended periods of time.

Facing Up to the Consequences

Jacob may also feel that as he failed to notice the switch, he must live with the consequences of his mistake. His goal now, in confronting Laban, is not to demand nullification, but rather to find out why Laban is placing him in such a position. Jacob sees his continued marriage to Leah as a duty and a responsibility as a result of his own doing.

Exploring His Other Options

Jacob also assesses his current predicament. He has been working for Laban for the last seven years. He has just become his son-in-law. In contrast to what we find at the end of the next seven years, there is no indication in the text that Jacob is even considering moving on. Jacob is currently penniless, and relies on his job as a shepherd for Laban's herds.[158] For Jacob, as a newlywed with added responsibilities, the idea of economic stability and familial support along with the prospect of having both Leah and Rachel as wives is an attractive and practical option.

In addition, Jacob realizes that if he decides to go for broke on his deceit claim, he may be forced to return home and face Esau. Such a confrontation at this point is not a viable option for Jacob. Rebekah has not called for his return—indicating that things have not yet cooled down with Esau—and Jacob has not received a divine command to return home, as he later receives.

Keeping His Eye on the Prize

Jacob loves Rachel. The most important thing to him is to marry Rachel. He has already worked seven years for her. He will not allow this setback to prevent him from accomplishing his goal. If Jacob publicly raises the claim of deceit, he runs the risk of Laban successfully defending his actions on the grounds of local custom. At that point, Laban can easily refuse to allow Jacob to marry Rachel forever by claiming to have fulfilled the agreement by giving him Leah as a wife. Jacob cannot risk losing his true love. He reasons that he must remain silent.

---

158 This aspect is reinforced when Jacob hears Laban's response to his inquiry about the deceit. Laban's response of working another seven years for Rachel creates a new option for seven more years of job security.

For Jacob, the best course of action is to approach Laban privately in hope of an amicable settlement. The final result of approaching Laban privately is that he obtains Laban's consent to marry Rachel. Jacob's love for Rachel will not allow him to take any risks that could jeopardize his chances of marrying Rachel.

Considering Leah and Rachel

Until now, the points I have analyzed mainly focus on Jacob's concerns for himself. However, Jacob is well aware that he is not the only person who would suffer if he were to publicly confront Laban. Jacob may also be considering the effects his accusations could have on Leah and Rachel.[159]

Jacob is aware that Leah would be devastated if he were to confront her father. Despite everything, Leah is still Jacob's first cousin, and the sister of the woman he loves. This too contributes to Jacob's silence.

As for Rachel, Jacob surmises that Rachel herself must be involved on some level in the deceit. Otherwise, she could have easily ruined Laban's plan. Presuming her participation is consensual, Jacob maintains the relationship with Leah in order to show his respect for Rachel's implied wishes of that moment.[160]

This also explains, in part, why Jacob does not confront Leah or Rachel for their role in the plot. Jacob may be attempting to spare their feelings. In addition, Jacob may naturally assume that Laban is the one who puts them up to it, possibly against their will, and that they are not in a position, emotionally or financially, to refuse their father.[161]

---

159 Admittedly, on other occasions, Jacob's self-centered responses, as with his response to Simeon and Levi after the massacre of Shechem or his reaction to seeing the monies from the satchels upon the brothers return to Canaan, reveal that Jacob may not have always factored in anyone else's feelings. However, at this point, Jacob has not yet harbored any negativity against others that would cause him to disregard their feelings.

160 It may even be seen as a sign of callousness or rejection on her part, even if only from Jacob's standpoint.

161 Jacob remembers that Laban is the one who brings him the would-be bride to the conjugal tent (29:23).

Why Didn't Jacob Divorce Leah?

Having analyzed why Jacob would not publicly charge Laban with the deceit, one must now ask why Jacob does not divorce Leah the morning after as a regular divorce case.[162]

Local Custom

Technically, were Jacob to divorce Leah, he would then be unable to marry Rachel because local custom requires Jacob to wait until Leah is married before marrying Rachel.

Preventing a Pecuniary Claim

In the times of the Bible, a person who caused a woman to lose her virginity, and did not remain married to her, would be deemed as someone who inflicted "damage," and would thus be required to compensate the victim accordingly.[163] Jacob knows that he does not have any personal assets and cannot pay his way out of the marriage to Leah. It is only after he works an additional seven years for Rachel that he begins to amass his personal wealth. By that time, his marriage to Leah is a *fait accompli* and Jacob fathers six sons and a daughter from her, thereby forming a familial composition that Jacob cannot legally or emotionally jettison.

Not so Bad

While later passages allude to Jacob hating Leah, we also read that when Jacob first marries Rachel a week after Leah that Jacob loved Leah (29:30): "And he came unto Rachel too and he loved *also* Rachel over Leah [literally, 'from Leah']." The implication is that while he loves Rachel, he *also* loves Leah as well—just less.[164] Prior to being with Rachel, Jacob may not have had a yardstick with which to compare his emotional attachment. At the point when the deception is revealed, it may very well be that Jacob

---

162 Clearly, there is a degree of overlap between these two matters and the current analysis should be seen as complimentary to what was presented above.

163 Compare with Deuteronomy 22:29 where the act also carries the inability to divorce the woman. This may also have been a local custom that Jacob fears would apply to him as well despite his claim of deceit.

164 Abravanel, on Vayetse answering questions one and two on chapter 29, reads this verse to mean that Jacob loves Rachel "from Leah"—in other words, his love for Rachel stems from and detracts from his love for Leah.

believes, or convinces himself, that he is in love with Leah just as much as he is with Rachel. It is only a week later, after being with Rachel as his wife, that he experiences the true meaning of love, and loves Rachel even more.

As Abravanel explains:

> And he also loved Rachel "from" Leah—because Jacob came unto Leah first and then Rachel. The comparison with Leah made Rachel more perfect and then Jacob had two loves for Rachel. The one, on her own merits without any comparisons, and this is the love that Jacob had previously for her and the second, by comparison with Leah, and that is what he now had after coming unto her after Leah.

Therefore, we understand that even after being with Rachel, Jacob still loves Leah and therefore does not feel the desire or need to divorce her.[165] This last point, in conjunction with others mentioned above,[166] help explain why even after marrying Rachel seven days later, Jacob does not, at *that* point, divorce Leah.

Understanding the Major Players in the Conjugal Switch

To help complete the montage of emotions, motives, and possible reactions surrounding the conjugal switch, it is imperative to analyze the emotional make-up of the other characters in the narrative. Such an understanding will greatly contribute to our grasp of the remainder of the narrative in Genesis dealing with Jacob's family dynamics. Until now, we have explored Jacob's mindset and what possibly raced through his mind at each juncture of the conjugal switch. I will now investigate these events from Rachel's perspective.

In an attempt to understand Rachel's feelings, the first question that comes to mind is: Why would Rachel assist or even passively allow the switch to take place?

---

165 When hatred later develops, Jacob's children make it too difficult to summarily divorce Leah. Also, Jacob's family history allows him to infer that having only one wife is not synonymous with domestic tranquility.

166 For example, Jacob's concern to spare and consider Leah and Rachel's feelings.

Why Would Rachel Cooperate in the Plot?

1. Considering Rachel's family dynamic, at least up until this point, it stands to reason that Rachel would cooperate with her father and sister because family is family. The clannish bloodline bond and the societal expectation of respect for her father provide firm footing for Rachel's complicity.

2. The text never records that Rachel loves Jacob as Jacob loved Rachel. The implication is that Jacob's love is unrequited. Therefore, Rachel can cooperate with Laban's plot without any emotional disquiet.

3. Rachel is acting in deference to her economically established father's wishes as provider over the then-indigent Jacob. Rachel and Leah later speak of Laban in terms of money and inheritance such that it is not far-fetched to attribute Rachel's motives to Haran-like financial considerations. Jacob's being penniless forbids Rachel from acting against her only source of survival.

4. Rachel seeks to preserve her father's dignity by keeping the plot secret and participating. Should Jacob discover the ruse, his outrage would undoubtedly disgrace Laban before the townsmen.

5. Rachel desires to stymie the effects any embarrassment her father would sustain from reflecting poorly upon her.

6. Rachel wants to preserve her sister's honor in the same way that she wants to preserve her father's honor.

7. Rachel seeks to gain her father's approval for a later wedding with Jacob—something that Laban probably withholds prior to Leah being married.[167]

8. If one presumes that Rachel *is* desirous of Jacob, she may believe that playing "hard to get," by cooperating in the ruse, will further endear her to Jacob, all the while knowing that Jacob will always be eager to marry her afterwards.

9. As mentioned earlier, Laban's later excuse about local custom may be a fabrication or it may be true. If such a rule of the elder getting married first is truly the local custom, Rachel too may be acting out of deference to the local custom.

---

167 This would be true regardless of whether Rachel truly loved Jacob or merely needed to marry him in order to be equals with Leah.

10. Rachel participates in the scheme in order to orchestrate a scenario where her married family life will be identical to her childhood family structure. Cooperating in the plot would result in having her sister live in the same house as co-wife and keeping her father and Jacob's father-in-law/uncle/employer in the next tent over. Such a set-up lessens the natural anxiety that accompanies marriage and moving out of the house.[168] This arrangement also explains the ensuing family dynamic, especially Laban's unflinching attitude that everything belongs to him. As his daughters never move away from his home, he continues to view them, their children and Jacob, as part of his expanded household, as opposed to their being an independent family.

Having explored the labyrinth of Jacob and Rachel's psyches, one turns to the next major player in the conjugal switch—Leah.

Why Would Leah Cooperate in the Plot?

1. Leah's motivation to execute the switch seems obvious. She would be able to marry Jacob while obeying her father's wishes. However, Leah's desire to marry Jacob is not entirely clear. The text does not record that she loves Jacob. Even later references only allude to her desire to have Jacob love her. Thus, it seems that Leah's desire to be married is a result of her inner longing to be loved by someone. If this is the case, perhaps her need stems from a void of such love from her father's home. While there is no textual evidence of her early relationship with Laban, her and Rachel's statement that Laban treats them as chattel exhibits a strain in her relationship with Laban that must have began earlier on. Therefore, one can conclude that Leah would participate in the plan in order to potentially access someone who will love her and be able to assist her to jettison Laban.

---

168 Although some may be all too happy to leave the family nest, Laban's manipulations perpetuate the fusion of this family ensemble as will be developed more fully later.

2. Leah wants to marry Jacob in order to avoid social disgrace. Leah is the elder daughter and local custom dictates that she should be married first. Based on local custom, the marriage is owed to her and therefore, she may not even view Rachel's help as a favor or the conjugal switch as immoral.

3. Leah may also experience difficulty finding a groom. As pointed out above, the text juxtaposes describing Leah as having soft eyes next to describing Rachel as good-looking with an attractive figure. One possible inference is that Leah is not as pretty as Rachel,[169] and that the only attractive feature to be contrasted to Rachel is her eyes. Being given the chance to marry Jacob is a ready solution to her worries.

4. Leah desires Jacob because her beautiful sister Rachel is supposed to have him, and she feels the need to keep up with or outdo her sister.[170]

5. Leah cooperates with the plot because of her admiration of Jacob's strength and loyalty. The news of Jacob's impressive show at the well surely does not go unnoticed, even though Leah did not eye-witness the event. Also, Jacob's seven years of labor reveal him to be a loyal and physically strong man.

To sum up, Leah not only cooperates in the plot out of deference to her father, but also because of her own self-interests.

Why Does Laban Go Through With the Switch?

1. Laban's motivation to dupe Jacob is more complex than meets the eye. Laban, as Leah's father, is concerned about marrying her off. He also would like to avoid any social faux-pas and prefers to have Leah be married first. As will be mentioned below, the locals may even have approached him to ensure that such would be the case. Laban, therefore, may be acting out of fatherly concern for his daughter and/or under pressure from the locals to follow local custom. Out of either of these motives, Laban's ultimate motivation is external

---

169 See Or Hahayyim commenting on 29:17.

170 This idea will be more fully developed later when discussing the competition between Leah and Rachel surrounding the issue of childbearing.

and thus lessens the severity of any personal charge against him. To further elaborate, Laban is forced by outside circumstances to act as he did even if the means employed are dishonest. Indeed, the pressure of local custom (if not pressure of the locals themselves) is the explanation that Laban gives Jacob after the fact. Jacob's silence after hearing Laban's explanation attaches some level of legitimacy to Laban's reasoning, even if Laban takes advantage of the situation to obtain seven more years of service from Jacob.

2. Another possibility on the other end of the spectrum, and one that is commonly presumed, is that Laban realizes that Jacob will stop at nothing to marry Rachel and therefore plans to dupe Jacob all along[171] in order to later offer Rachel to Jacob for another seven years of labor.

---

171 In trying to hone in on textual cues as to when exactly Laban hatches his plot, one should examine Laban's response to Jacob's early request to work seven years to marry Rachel. "And Laban said: 'It is good to give her to you than I would give her to another man, stay with me—*shva imadi*'" (29:19). The alternative grammatical form, the cohortative form, used by Laban for "stay with me"—"*shva imadi*" instead of the regular "*shev*" distinctively recalls a scene from the blessings episode with Isaac: "Who are you my son?" And Jacob said to his father: "I am Esau your firstborn. I have done as you have spoken to me. Arise now, sit—*kum na shva*— and eat from my game in order that your soul blesses me" (27:18–19). This, in addition to many others, serves as a textual reverberation of Jacob's deception and as part of the divine retribution for his usurping of the blessings. However, as Jacob was not privy to such textual culling of information, his mindset would need to be fashioned by his personal knowledge and experiences. The above appearances of the word *shva* are the only two appearances of this form of the word in the Pentateuch. This wordplay would indicate that just as Jacob knowingly deceived his father at that point, so, too, did Laban knowingly deceive Jacob at this juncture.

On this issue, the Targum (pseudo) Yonatan Ben Uziel on 29:19 adds that Laban responded "deceitfully" to Jacob already at this point, thereby introducing the plan of the conjugal switch from this very work proposal seven years earlier.

Laban's word choice of "*shva imadi*" can also be seen as a play on "*sheva midai*"—meaning seven short of being enough—possibly alluding to, or serving as a foreshadowing of, Laban's machinations. Indeed, the words "*imadi*"—with me and "*sheva*"—seven—appear together again when Laban offers Rachel to Jacob a second time: "For the work that you will work *imadi*—with me, another different *sheva*, seven, years" (29:27).

Under this assumption, Laban is a devilish and selfish fiend, whose reprehensible and premeditated actions are inexcusable.

Why Would the Townspeople Cooperate in the Plot?

The inference that the locals are involved in the deceit is counterindicated by the usage of the term "men of the place" as seen elsewhere in the Bible. The phrase "*anshei hamakom*," referring to the residents of a particular locale, appears only five times in the Bible. It appears twice when Rebekah pretended to be Isaac's sister in Gerrar (both in 26:7); it appears once here (29:22); and twice later when referring to the people near where Tamar encountered Judah (38:21,22). In each instance, questionable sexual encounters surrounded the "men of the place." In our attempt to ascertain the culpability or knowledge of the locals in the conjugal switch, this parallel would suggest that just as in the other instances, where the populace is unjustly associated with the type of people to be involved with such chicanery, so, too, the locals on the scene prior to the conjugal switch are also innocent of such aspersions. Laban simply gathers them for a drinking party that they attend without knowing what was to follow.[172]

However, despite such counterindication, the Midrash assumes that the townspeople know the bride is supposed to be Rachel and not Leah.[173] The Midrash states that the men attending the wedding party would sing "Lai, Lai, Lai" to indicate that the bride is "Leah" in order to stop Jacob from later objecting to the union once he finds out it is her. The locals would then counter Jacob's possible claim of deceit by stating that they had informed him of the true identity of the bride through their singing. By including the townspeople as part of the plot, the Midrash entertains a full-scale conspiracy theory against Jacob.[174] Jacob himself may also entertain the idea that they are part of the conspiracy and, as such, the locals would not even blink an eye at the switch in deference to local custom. But what would motivate the townspeople to cooperate in such a plot?

---

172 Looking back, Laban does not invite the townspeople to a wedding, but rather Laban "gathers" them in an impromptu fashion and has a drinking fest (29:22). Thus they did not know anything about the guests of honor but rather joined the merriment for a good drink. Reference also the negative connotation of the "*asafsuf*— literally, the gathered ones in Numbers 11:4.

173 Genesis Rabbah 70:19.

174 One finds similar conspiracy theories in the Targumim. See Targum of Palestine and pseudo Targum Jonathan Ben Uziel on 29:22

1. According to the Midrash, the townspeople desired Jacob's presence in the town and the blessing of material success that accompanies him. By participating in the plot, the townspeople ensure that Jacob stays in Haran for at least another seven years, while he works in order to marry Rachel.

2. The townspeople could also have been motivated by resentment. When Jacob arrives at Haran, he "shows off" by the well and single-handedly rolls off the stone that all the shepherds would roll together. He then gives water to the sheep of Laban, most probably ahead of the usual order established by the shepherds.[175] Jacob continues from that day on to care for Laban's sheep and undoubtedly runs into these shepherds daily. Jacob, in loyalty to his employer and his family, probably continues to afford Laban's sheep preferential treatment at the well. Therefore, prior to the conjugal switch, Jacob has upset the previous local custom of drawing water from the well.[176] The locals who formerly ran the show probably carry a grudge against Jacob. They also are watching his every move to find an opportunity to help settle the score. Laban's later excuse implies that the people of the town are the ones responsible for the switch. They are not willing to tolerate any further reversals of local custom. This would be the type of measure-for-measure revenge the locals would love to exact from Jacob and it transforms Laban's excuse from lame to believable. This theory also explains why Jacob does not turn to the local townspeople's sense of justice and moral outrage. Having a history of discomfort with the shepherds, Jacob could not now bring himself to call upon them for recourse.

3. The townspeople feel strongly about adhering to local custom without an eye towards revenge. When the upcoming marriage

---

175 Compare and contrast with Moses' behavior at the well in Midian (Exodus 2:16–18) where he changes the usual order of watering.

176 In viewing the well as symbolic of the female organ, Jacob's upsetting of the natural order by removing the stone prematurely (before the remaining shepherds arrive) corresponds with and foreshadows Jacob's premature desire to wed Rachel (as Leah has not yet been wed in accordance with local custom). See also Kass, *The Beginning of Wisdom*, pg. 427, who also identifies Jacob as one who defies custom.

becomes known, they may even approach Laban reminding him to adhere to local custom and marry off Leah before Rachel.[177]

Whose Idea Is It to Perform the Switch in the First Place?

After having delved into the depths of the characters' driving forces in participating in the plot, one need ask who, of all the characters, came up with the audacious and daring plan to begin with.

It is normally understood that Laban is the orchestrator of the switch as he is the one whom the text records as bringing Leah to Jacob on the wedding night and is the one who directly gains seven more years of Jacob's work as a result. As mentioned above,[178] some attribute Laban with dark machinations from the moment he closes the deal with Jacob a month after his arrival at Haran. However, simply because Laban's participation, as the one presenting Leah instead of Rachel, is an absolute necessity does not mean that Laban hatched the plan. Upon examining all of the possible motivations of all the different players, one may just as easily conclude that it is Leah who puts Laban up to such a scheme. She also immediately benefits from being married and being married to her sister's fiancé Jacob.

Supposing that Leah is responsible for orchestrating the conjugal switch, it would mean that her character is strong enough to manipulate Laban. From textual inferences one may make the case that Leah indeed has such a character. She stands up for herself when Rachel later asks for the *dudaim* and negotiates an extra conjugal visit from Jacob in consideration (30:14–16). Thus, Leah knows how to do business when necessary, even in regards to marital relations. Leah also joins Rachel in lambasting Laban, albeit not in his presence, for using them as items for sale when Jacob later consults with them prior to leaving for Canaan (31:14–16). She thus exhibits a disdainful attitude towards Laban that she can use to her advantage against him. In addition, she exclusively names almost all her children alone, as opposed to Abraham's naming of Isaac (21:3), Isaac's naming of Jacob (25:26), and Jacob's renaming of Ben-Oni as Benjamin (35:18), which perhaps indicates her domineering personality.

---

177 In this case, Laban's later excuse to Jacob referring to local custom may actually have been a true driving force behind Laban's actions, with Laban and Leah's personal gain from the switch only providing supplemental motivation to that of adhering to local custom.

178 Footnote 171.

Leah is also not recorded as herding sheep as is Rachel although her later birthing seven children in seven years would indicate that she was physically able. Abravanel[179] posits that Leah is not a shepherd together with Rachel because Leah is extremely modest and such a vocation is inappropriate for her character. Yet, perhaps Leah chooses not to be a shepherd for a different reason. Perhaps as the elder daughter, she puts her foot down with her father and gets her way. Perhaps it is not her modesty but her stern character that relieves her of familial duties.[180] Thus, it could be that Leah knows how to manipulate Laban, and it may be her strong character that deters Jacob from confronting her the morning after.

Another possibility in identifying the mastermind behind the switch is to suspect the townspeople. They may have initiated the switch by pressuring Laban to follow local custom in order to get even with Jacob.

Regardless of who is responsible for masterminding the plan, it requires the cooperation of the other parties in its execution. If Leah is the instigator, Rachel and Laban act out of deference to her. If Laban plans it, his daughters act in deference to him. If the townspeople or simply local custom are behind the plan, then all the parties act in deference to social pressures or physical threats from the locals.

In all cases, the plot is kept secret from Jacob. The larger the conspiracy, the more people are involved and the more clandestine the plot. However, the larger the conspiracy, the harder it becomes to maintain secrecy on such a large scale, and the more tenuous it becomes to maintain that such a plot is being carried out.

The significant difference between the various possibilities influences the very future of Jacob's family dynamics. If Leah or Laban are responsible,[181] Jacob would feel estranged from them and a great strain would be placed on the family. If the townsmen are the plotters, future business relations would be at jeopardy.

---

179 Commenting on Vayishlah chapter 33 answering question 4.

180 While quite tempting, this point is not conclusive. Leah may have herded Laban's sheep, but just not on the day that Jacob arrives in Haran. Perhaps she and Rachel work in shifts or on a rotation basis.

181 I am not entertaining Rachel's planning the switch. She has no motivation to do so except if one posits that she did not want to marry Jacob. However, as she marries him seven days later there is no apparent gain for Rachel by devising the switch. Attributing Rachel with motivations solely to help her sister is contradicted by the emotional aftermath as recorded in the text.

To avoid these points of awkwardness, Laban attributes the plan to local custom without insinuating any person or group of persons at all. Thus, while Laban deftly diffuses the practical ramifications, the matter is never conclusively resolved for Jacob and Jacob does not investigate further.

Truth versus Practicality

After charging Laban, Jacob hears Laban's response and new proposal. Jacob is not recorded as immediately accepting the offer. In contrast, Laban is recorded as immediately accepting Jacob's terms seven years later regarding the sheep. There Laban states: "Yes. Be it as you said" (30:34). Jacob's acceptance of Laban's current proposal is demonstrated by his future actions, as per the terms set out. As the text states: "And Jacob did so" (29:28). Jacob does not dignify Laban with a response but silently acquiesces to the new reality in which he finds himself. Jacob, based on the above analysis, realizes that raising the claim of deceit might feel right, but, in all practical senses, would not accomplish any of the goals that he desires. Also, as concluded above, Jacob is exhibiting extreme sensitivity to Leah and Rachel in following through with the plot. As will be seen later, this painful dynamic of emotionally charged impulses being weighed against a practical and sensitive response replays itself throughout key episodes in Jacob's life and contributes to his life frustrations.

The incongruity between what is right and true and what is prudent and practical grows more poignant once Jacob marries Rachel. Jacob's desperation to marry Rachel causes him to opt for being prudent. Once Jacob marries Rachel, this need no longer exists. Despite the remaining factors outlined above, which persist, Jacob can easily begin to convince himself that he should now speak his mind.

Every day, Jacob must face Laban with a smile. He guards Laban's sheep and the two perhaps share the same table. He must take orders from Laban regarding the sheep as his employer and he must show respect and deference to Laban as his father-in-law and uncle. The fact that seven years of his life are, in essence, stolen away from him can never be amended. As time moves on, the daily grind gnaws at Jacob.

The Scapegoat

As a result of his pent-up emotions and feelings of frustration, Jacob directs his bitterness towards Leah, who proves to be an easy target. Were he to vilify Laban, he would risk being ousted to Canaan. Were he to vilify

Rachel, Jacob would risk damaging his precious relationship with her. Marginalizing Leah leaves Rachel emotionally available and Laban friendly. As time passes, Jacob's emotional reversal towards Leah reflects his siding with the option that the switch primarily benefits Leah and perhaps is even the product of Leah's initiative. As we continue our examination of the matter it is important to keep in mind that we are now tracking Jacob's perspective of the events and that his perspective may not necessarily correspond with the reality of how the conjugal switch occurred. Laban may have been the actual mastermind behind the switch, but for Jacob, that conclusion is not emotionally convenient or not as emotionally comfortable as blaming Leah. Nonetheless, for Jacob, his perspective is emotionally very real and is what drives him throughout the narrative.

Jacob can tell himself that Laban, in his eagerness to marry Leah off, participates in the plot and then takes advantage to gain seven more years of labor. Rachel, too, only takes part in order to preserve Leah's dignity. Leah's participation is purely selfish and emotionally manipulative. By becoming his wife, Leah is not only forcing a one-time non-consensual laying upon Jacob, but also an emotional relationship that she is asking him to maintain for a lifetime. Thus, Jacob begins to place the blame squarely on Leah's shoulders, and associates his marriage to her with the deceit of the conjugal switch.

However, it is only after Laban allows Jacob to marry Rachel at the very beginning of the second seven-year period of work, that Jacob continues to rethink the entire situation. Jacob now reinforces his suspicions that Leah is the control center leading to the conjugal switch, with Laban only acting as her pawn. So long as Jacob needs to live with Laban, Rachel's father, on a daily basis, Jacob prefers to view Leah, and not Laban, as the true schemer.

Channeling all his pent-up frustrations and suspicions into the daily grind of seven years of labor creates a possibly explosive situation. Jacob and Leah are living with each other as husband and wife. Jacob never mentions his suspicions to Leah. Jacob continually avoids confrontation in deference to the practical considerations mentioned above, and because he fears the fallout that might occur between himself and Rachel and/or Laban and/or even Leah, for that matter. By doing so, Jacob's anger towards Leah grows, and since he has no direction to vent his pent-up rage and frustration other than inwards, the situation creates a cesspool of negative feelings towards Leah.

The importance of these observations cannot be emphasized enough. As the continual gnawing at Jacob's emotional innards over the conjugal switch begin to produce tension in his family life, the negativity will soon spread to Leah's children as well, as will be evinced in the coming chapters and volumes of this work. The conjugal switch not only robs Jacob of seven years of his life but also forces him to dilute his love, attention, and conjugal duties away from Rachel. Jacob's frustration is constant not only because Leah's presence is a physical reminder of the conjugal switch but also because he is constantly forced to share himself with Leah and her children instead of solely spending the time with the true love of his life—Rachel. Guided by practical concerns, Jacob strategically maneuvers in order to obtain Rachel as a wife, yet finds that the full expression of his love for her is forever stunted and suppressed by the presence of Leah and her children and by the inviolable fact that he wed Leah first. While Jacob succeeds in having Rachel physically, he will forever seek to have her emotionally, which, tragically, never occurs.

All of the above explains how Jacob grows from loving Leah to actually hating her. The text itself attests that when Jacob comes unto Rachel that "he loved also Rachel from/over Leah," which implies that Jacob does have a certain level of love for Leah. However, later, the text also attests to the hatred Jacob feels towards Leah as it prefaces her first ability to conceive by stating: "And God saw that Leah was *hated*."[182] The language employed by the text is quite telling. "*God* saw" that Leah was hated already before conceiving Reuben. In contrast, Leah is only recorded as feeling "unloved" as she names her child Reuben: "For now my husband will love me" (29:32), implying that until that point, he did not. It is noteworthy that even this feeling is only recognized by Leah at the end of the pregnancy with the naming of Reuben. Further, it is only after conceiving, carrying to term, and birthing and naming Simeon, that she fully acknowledges the feeling of hatred as she names her second son Simeon: "For God heard that I was *hated*" (29:33). As far as Jacob is concerned, he may not realize that his feelings are transparent, or if he does, he may feel justified in his righteous indignation. Surely Leah needs time to digest the reality that her husband, the father of their joint children, hates her. As she grapples with this emotionally abusive state of affairs, she will continue to focus on shifting attention away from herself, and onto their joint children, in hopes of remedying the situation.

---

182 29:31. God's objective identification of the emotion should weigh heavily for the reader in granting the word "hate" its full emotional muscle.

CHAPTER FOUR

The Currency of Jealousy

There is no reciprocity. Men love women, women love children,
children love hamsters.

                    ⇜ *Alice Thomas Ellis*

Leah's Struggle for Jacob's Love

Leah perceives that Jacob does not love her. In a desperate attempt to win her husband's love, Leah plans to bear children in the hope that Jacob's love for her would grow along with the growth of their family. For years, Leah repeatedly deludes herself into thinking that "*this* time," he will love her.[183]

Nevertheless, Leah's desire for Jacob's love cannot be attributed to a burning passion to be with Jacob. Indeed, the text makes no mention of her pining away for Jacob as it records Jacob loving Rachel. Instead, her desire for her husband appears to stem from her wish to attain a prize possession that she feels rightfully belongs to her. She is desperate to gain possession over something that her sister Rachel—ostensibly the prettier one—is supposed to have had first. As she married Jacob first, Leah feels that this should award her not only seniority but also emotional supremacy with Jacob. For Leah, possessing Jacob is the fulfillment of a lifelong dream of "one-upping" her sister, as will be discussed below.

---

183 The key words "now," "this time," and "this is the time" recur four times in the naming of Leah's six children (29:32, 34, 35; 30:20), and span over a period of about seven years.

87

Leah's possessive feelings for Jacob can be detected by her choice of language in referring to him. She consistently and steadfastly refers to Jacob as "my man" or "my husband." Before anything else, he is *her* husband. The word "my man" is itself a *leitwort* which is repeated four times in Leah's naming of the children.[184] With this in mind, Leah's bearing of children is not a fulfillment of Leah's desire to be a mother, but a manipulative means to secure Jacob's love while marginalizing her sister.

Equal Treatment

In turn, when Rachel sees that she has not conceived, she becomes jealous of Leah. The verse states: "And Rachel saw that she did not bear children to Jacob[185] and Rachel was jealous of her *sister*" (30:1).

The text does not simply record that "Rachel was jealous of Leah" but rather emphasizes the familial relation—Rachel was jealous of "her sister." This word choice is significant as it allows us to understand the reason behind her jealousy. Rachel is not jealous of her sister's ability to conceive because she desires to be a mother. In Rachel's eyes, children are not a means to obtain Jacob's love as they are for Leah, but rather children are important to bear because her sister has them. This point is driven home as Rachel is not jealous of Leah in her position of co-wife, but rather jealous of Leah as her sister.

Had Rachel and Leah not been married to the same man, the jealousy may never have developed, even if there had been a greater disparity in number of offspring between them. Rachel's very marriage to Jacob is important to her primarily because Leah is married to Jacob. In Rachel's world of equality, once both are married to Jacob, everything must remain equal.

---

184 29:32, 34; 30:18, 20. Leah's steadfastness in referring to Jacob as "her man" is in stark contrast to the textual references of Rachel being Jacob's wife to the exclusion of Leah. See 44:27: "And your servant my father said to us: 'You know that *my wife* bore me two children.'" 46:19: "The sons of Rachel, *the wife of Jacob*: Joseph and Benjamin" and 49:31: "There they buried Abraham and *his wife* Sarah, there they buried Isaac and *his wife* Rebekah and there I buried Leah." Thus, even on his deathbed, Jacob cannot bring himself to identify Leah as his wife.

185 The verse would have read more smoothly had it left out "to Jacob": "And Rachel saw that she did not bear children and Rachel was jealous of her sister." By including that she did not bear children "to Jacob," the text forces us to acknowledge that Rachel desires children specifically *from Jacob*, especially since her sister has already achieved this with Jacob.

When Leah receives a maid upon marriage, so does Rachel. Since Jacob works seven years for one of the daughters, he must work another seven for the second. Their father Laban institutes these elements of equal treatment, indicating that his parenting model is to grant each daughter the "same" of everything, and thus Rachel carries this model of equality into her married life.[186] Everything that Leah receives from Jacob, Rachel expects to receive as well. Subsequently, Rachel feels that if her sister has children, she, too, must bear children.[187] Thus, the children are the currency of their sibling rivalry.

Emotional Sparring

It is the desire to have everything "the same" as her older sister, including the same husband, that provokes Rachel's harsh statement when she approaches Jacob and demands: "Give me children and if not I am dead" (30:1).

Rachel's statement can be understood in a number of ways. On a literal level, Rachel's anguish brings her to suicidal thoughts. A more figurative reading would depict Rachel as being upset and distressed about not having children to the point where she may say extreme things she does not really mean.[188] Subscribing to this theory, Rachel expresses her desperation by dramatically playing the role of the victim in order to provoke sympathy

---

186 Interestingly, it is God who upsets the delicate balance of equality the sisters enjoyed. God's opening of Leah's closed womb while leaving Rachel's closed sets off the competition that Laban presumably succeeded in avoiding during their upbringing. Indeed, the text records the onset of Rachel's jealousy only at this point in their adult lives.

187 Indeed, the textual inference of Leah's barrenness prior to God opening her womb would indicate that the sisters were initially "equal" in their barrenness as well.

188 This phenomenon would not be new to Jacob who already heard his mother use similar tactics in manipulating Isaac to send Jacob to Haran (27:46): "If Jacob takes a woman from the daughters of Het like these, from the *b'not ha'arets*—the daughters of the land—what good to me is life?" On a subconscious level, Jacob may be hearing his mother's last recorded words and responding negatively to Rachel as a result of the feelings that he associates with that stressful time, or it may cause him to be wary of Rachel's manipulations as Rebekah manipulated Isaac. From a literary perspective, Rebekah's last words: "What good to me is life?" serve as a wonderful stage exit as these are her final recorded words in the Bible. Unbeknownst to Jacob, Rebekah also employs similar existential phraseology upon experiencing her painful pregnancy with Esau and Jacob: "And she said: If so—*why am I?*" (25:22).

and a reaction from Jacob.[189] Perhaps she is even trying to get him to take sides with her against her sister.

An even more liberal reading of: "And if not I am dead" would be to view Rachel as nagging Jacob with impractical requests and expecting him to fulfill her every wish in line with her "knight in shining armor" vision of Jacob that she espoused at the well years earlier.

Regardless of our interpretation of her state of mind, in all readings, Rachel's request is self-centered. "Give *me* children and if not *I* am dead." She does not yearn to bear children out of a desire to build a beautiful family together with Jacob, but rather to ensure that she has what her sister has. Jacob is the means to the end, and she therefore attributes the children only to herself, "Give *me* children."

Jacob is angered by Rachel's outburst and responds harshly: "Am I in place of God that prevented you from having children?" (30:2) His seemingly insensitive response refers to Rachel's barrenness as an immutable fact imposed by God.[190] Jacob's response is countered by another self-centered suggestion from Rachel who offers her maid in her stead for bearing the children: "Here is my maid, Bilhah, come unto her and she will birth on

---

189 See Nahmanides commenting on 30:1.

190 Yet, one must ask, why does Jacob get *angry* in the first place? Understanding Jacob's anger will allow us to understand his seeming insensitivity. Jacob loves Rachel more than Leah. His silence over losing seven years of his life is partially due to his feelings for her and maximizing his chances to marry her. Jacob feels he does everything to show Rachel his love and that she is oblivious to all his efforts. Without children, she doesn't seem to have the will to live. Jacob is not seeking to keep Rachel barren to preserve her beauty as some commentators suggest. (See Kass, *The Beginning of Wisdom*, pgs. 428–429.) He is utterly frustrated that his relationship with her is not enough for her and that she fails to acknowledge his love for her. She essentially demands that Jacob prove his love for her, but her request is not made in terms of years of labor. Rachel wants Jacob to guarantee her equality with her sister. Jacob is dumbfounded as he sincerely cannot repair her barrenness and resents that his love be tied to matters beyond his control. Hence, Jacob's anger and harsh reply results from his bitterness over Rachel's unrequited love and from her dramatic display demanding he give her/love her more.

my knees[191] and I will *also* beget sons from her" (30:3).[192] In other words, Rachel is saying: "Not just Leah (or not just you, Jacob) will have sons—but so will I."

Rachel's proposed substitution of Bilhah, the maid, cheapens Jacob's profound love for her to merely providing Jacob physical pleasure, suggesting that even the maid can satisfy him. This gesture simultaneously also cheapens her own relationship with Jacob, dismissing it as a mechanical means for her to bear children in order for her to keep up with her sister.[193] Jacob is a necessary participant and having children is the desired goal, but Rachel now implies that having *biologically joint* children is not important. What is important to Rachel is that her children are *legally* recognized as her own. This attitude sadly reinforces Jacob's feelings of rejection and, in the hopes of proving his love, or even perhaps out of spiteful anger, Jacob actually follows through on Rachel's suggestion.[194]

---

191 The phrase employed by Rachel to refer to Bilhah's childbearing literally implies that Bilhah will birth on her lap. This depicts a birthing position with Bilhah sitting on top of Rachel's knees leaning back on Rachel with the child issuing forth as if from Rachel's extended womb.

192 Rachel's approach is not original. Sarah had given her maid to Abraham to give birth in her stead. There the issue sought to be resolved is also a legal one albeit it being to provide a legal heir to carry on Abraham's line. Here, Rachel is perhaps harkening back to that event in her proposition and likening herself to Sarah. This identification suggests that Rachel would like her status as matron to be as uncontested as that of Sarah's. Abraham had granted Sarah matron supremacy despite Hagar's presence and her bearing Ishmael. Rachel wants matron supremacy despite Leah's presence and her bearing children. She would like her husband to care for her as Abraham had cared for Sarah. Indeed, the classical commentators, based on the Midrash, make the connection between Rachel's proposition to Jacob and that of Sarah's to Abraham. For example, see Rashi and Or Hahayyim commenting on 30:3. Taking this paradigm to its logical conclusion would have Rachel desiring Jacob to oust Leah and her children as Abraham ousted Hagar and Ishmael.

193 See Zornberg, *The Beginning of Desire*, pg. 210.

194 One must wonder if Rachel's offer was originally meant in seriousness or was originally only meant as banter to elicit Jacob's sympathy, and only later became reality.

Maintaining Equality

The text records how Leah proceeds to give her maid to Jacob as a wife when she no longer bears Jacob children. As pointed out by Akeidat Isaac,[195] the granting of Zilpah to Jacob as a wife is puzzling. Unlike Rachel, Leah is not barren and, ostensibly, there is no reason to offer her to Jacob as a wife.[196]

The sisters' sibling rivalry explains why Leah gives Zilpah to Jacob as a wife. While Leah does not *need* to give her maid to Jacob in order to bear additional children, she feels compelled to give her maid to Jacob simply because her sister has done so with her own maid.

The general idea of maintaining equality may be attractive to Rachel and Leah in that it seems to promote fairness between them and should ensure that Jacob treats them equally. If Leah were to allow Rachel to give Bilhah to Jacob as a wife, while she keeps Zilpah strictly as her maidservant, Leah would later wonder whether withholding Zilpah from Jacob contributed to her husband's continued disregard for her.

However, this approach is deceptive because while Leah blindly seeks to maintain equality, she does so without understanding the repercussions of the actions aimed at achieving that equality. The trickery behind Leah's very marriage to Jacob causes him to feel emotionally tumultuous and negative towards her. As a result, Jacob further favors Rachel. In granting Zilpah to Jacob as a wife, Leah attempts to regain Jacob's love and restore emotional equality but in reality accomplishes exactly the opposite. Unfortunately, in this situation, probably because she does not know of the quarrel between Rachel and Jacob, she further estranges Jacob by giving him Zilpah. Had Leah been able to break free of the equality model, she would have enhanced her relationship with Jacob because she would have demonstrated that while Rachel is competing with her to restore equality, she is only seeking his love. Once Leah offers Zilpah to Jacob as a wife, Jacob now feels that much like Rachel, Leah only views their relationship as a means for having children in order to compete with her sister.

---

195 Akeidat Isaac, Parashat Vayetse, Part two, question 5.

196 Based on the Midrash, R. Arama opines that the marriage compensates Zilpah and helps foster Jacob's positive feelings towards her, as Jacob did not have such warm feelings towards Zilpah. He further elaborates by stating that Jacob is duped at the conjugal switch because he sees that Zilpah, formerly Rachel's maid, is given to the bride on the wedding night. Thus, Zilpah is a reminder of the deception and this ancillary role fosters negative feelings between Jacob and Zilpah. This view is to be contrasted with Abravanel's view presented below.

What's in a Name?

In this regard, the name choice for some of the children is significant. Rachel names Bilhah's children, "Dan" and "Naftali," as she perceives that God judges her and rewards her with a son (Dan) in order to allow her to grapple/compete (Naftali) with her sister. She calls her own son "Joseph"—declaring "God should add to me another son" (30:24). Her choice of names thus embodies the contest Rachel is trying to win.

On the other hand, Leah's naming of Zilpah's Gad,[197] as well as the ideas behind the names of Reuben: "For God has seen me in my affliction for now my husband will love me," Shimon: "For God has heard that I am hated and gave me also this one," Levi: "Now is the time that my man will accompany me," and later, Issachar:[198] "God has given me my reward for I have given my maidservant to my man," and Zebulun: "This time my husband will inseminate me" embody her quest for Jacob's love.[199] Similarly, when Leah gives birth to her last child, a girl, she names her Dinah, meaning literally, her judgment, possibly as a retort to Rachel's naming of Dan years earlier. Leah may think that perhaps her previous attempts to win over Jacob's love failed because she only had boys.[200] Therefore, Leah's naming of Dinah reflects her desperation to capture Jacob's heart. This also explains

---

197 Abravanel posits that Leah actually called Gad—"Bagad"—or betrayed—as a reminder of Zilpah's role in the duping of Jacob. By reminding Jacob of Zilpah's role in the deception, she hopes to have Jacob shift blame away from her and onto Zilpah. Unfortunately, the opposite comes true. The more she reminds Jacob of the deception, the more his hatred of Leah is reinforced. Contrast with R. Arama's view above where the marriage sets out to help Jacob forget Zilpah's role in the deception and not memorialize it as Abravanel suggests.

198 As an interesting aside, the Hebrew for "Issachar" is spelled with a double "*shin*" consonant. In modern readings, one is silent. However, an old manuscript attributed to Ben-Naftali renders the Hebrew as "Yish-sakhar" meaning "there is reward" and explains the double "*shin*" consonant—one as a "*shin*" and one as a "*sin*." Rav Yoel Bin-Nun in *Pirkei HaAvot* (Tevunot Press, 2003), pg. 119, renders it as "Yisa-sakhar," meaning "he will carry reward" rendering the double consonant "*sin*" and "*sin*."

199 29:32–34; 30:10,18,20.

200 One may even read her naming of Asher as an expression of her wish for girls. She exclaims: "*BeOshri ki Isheruni Banot*" (30:13) meaning "in my happiness let me be made happy by girls." This is opposed to the more common understanding of: "Now I am happy because girls (other women) make me happy," that is, by praising me on my births.

why Leah no longer bears children after Dinah. Once the possibility of Jacob loving her through her/their children is exhausted, she no longer perceives the need to continue to bear children.

Of particular import towards understanding the depths of the rivalry is that the naming of Leah's son Issachar takes place after the text records that Zilpah had two children. Leah names Issachar stating: "The Lord gave me my reward 'sakhar' for I gave my maid to my husband" (30:18). Leah does not choose this name for Zilpah's first child (Gad) who was born earlier. It would have made more sense for Leah to recognize Gad's birth as being a reward for granting Zilpah as a wife to Jacob. In addition, Leah's naming Issachar by harkening back to an event (her giving of Zilpah to Jacob) that took place well over a year earlier seems quite odd.

A daring explanation might be that she actually is referring to Rachel rather than Zilpah when she mentions giving "her maidservant" to Jacob. Leah is naming her son Issachar because she feels that God is rewarding her for trading the *dudaim* with Rachel that she believes may allow Rachel to conceive and have children.[201]

Her degrading reference to Rachel as a "maidservant" would help explain Rachel's angst regarding her infertility. This verse hints that Leah belittles Rachel throughout in much the same way that Hagar belittles Sarah's matronhood after becoming pregnant (16:4) and as Peninah torments her barren co-wife, Hannah (1 Samuel 1:6).

---

201 As will be discussed below, Reuben finds *dudaim* in the field. These *dudaim* are associated with being fertile or used as an aphrodisiac. Leah agrees to transfer her rights to the *dudaim* to Rachel in lieu of receiving Rachel's rights to lay with Jacob that evening. The reward aspect would seem quite clear: since her trading the *dudaim* assists her sister in being able to procreate and have children, so too does she receive a reward with procreating and having children. Up until this point, in Leah's mindset, the way to get close to Jacob is to have "enough" children. Thus, trading the *dudaim* is her way of giving Rachel to Jacob. In Leah's eyes, such sacrifice deserves a reward.

It is no wonder, then, that Jacob never names any of the children born in Paddan-Aram.[202] Being manipulated by his wives, who compete with each other to bear children, leaves him feeling like a mere vehicle for carrying out their petty contests. It is only when Rachel tragically dies and the contest is clearly over that Jacob decides to strip away Rachel's naming of that child as Ben-Oni and names the child Benjamin (35:18).[203] Were Jacob to actively name his other children, it would have indicated his siding with one of the wives in the contest. Preferring to err on the side of caution, and avoid strife wherever possible, Jacob decides to exclude himself from any such alignment. As with the conjugal switch, Jacob attempts to exhibit sensitivity to the people around him.

Reuben's Interference

Immediately after the recorded birth of Asher, Reuben, as mentioned above, discovers *dudaim* in the field. As Reuben is no more than six years old at the time, it is not clear that he understands the traditional association of the *dudaim* with fertility or as an aphrodisiac. Reuben, therefore, collects *dudaim* and brings them to his mother because he must have seen her with them often. Leah's frequent use of *dudaim* may also explain her incredible rate of births (seven children in seven years with a reported "dry period" after the fourth). Reuben hopes to endear himself further to Leah by providing her with something that will make her happy. For Leah, the *dudaim* represent what she believes is the means of winning Jacob's love. Reuben's deliberate act of giving the *dudaim* to "Leah his mother" (30:14) instead of to his infertile Aunt Rachel presents Reuben as a dutiful son.

---

202 The text (29:34) sets out that he calls Levi by his name, but only because of the reasoning set out by Leah. Apparently, at that juncture, Jacob attempts to appease Leah and assure her that things will be different. However, because of the deeper unaddressed issues, this promised change does not come to fruition. Leah's later naming of Zebulun for "'this time' my husband will inseminate me" (30:20) reflects the same pining that Leah expresses in the births of Reuben and Levi that "now" or "this time" Jacob will love her. Therefore, Leah's praise of God at the birth of Judah should not be taken as a sign of reconciliation between Leah and Jacob or of Leah's giving up on obtaining Jacob's love. The analysis of the narrative throughout also dictates this conclusion.

203 This point supplements the full analysis I provide in Chapter Nine surrounding the renaming.

However, Reuben may also be self-motivated because he wants to endear himself to his father as well. Reuben hopes that if Leah is happier, then perhaps Jacob will be with her and with her children more often. It appears that Jacob projects his strained relationship with Leah onto her children. Jacob continually feels forced into a relationship with Leah just as he felt on the night of the conjugal switch. As a result, Jacob prefers to work long hours, as evinced when Jacob recounts to Laban: "I was there in the day—the parching heat ate me, and ice—in the night and my sleep wandered from my eyes" (31:40) and avoids being home with Leah or her children as he returns home from the field only in the evening, "And Jacob came from the field in the evening" (30:16).

The idea that Jacob's relationship with his children hinge on their maternal origin becomes truly apparent later in the Joseph saga, but Reuben may have sensed a tension between his mother and his Aunt Rachel already at this point. Reuben deliberately gives the *dudaim* to his mother, rather than to his aunt, who is also present. In Reuben's eyes, Rachel is also competing for Jacob's attention. Thus, it is already at this stage that the competition between the sisters begins to seep down to the next generation.

In recognition of the strained relationship between herself and Leah, Rachel neither attempts to coax Reuben to give his Aunt Rachel some *dudaim* nor to tell her where he found them. Rachel understands that Reuben is not the proper respondent for her petition. Instead, she asks her sister—with whom she shared her childhood—to share the *dudaim* with her. She does not request that Leah give them up in her favor, but rather requests to give her "from" her son's *dudaim*—to share.

Rachel, in her request, acknowledges the separateness that has grown between them, coldly referring to Reuben as "your son," rather than by name or as her nephew. Indeed, Reuben's name and many of Leah's other children's names are digs at Rachel and highlight Leah's attempt to win over Jacob's love of Rachel. It is no wonder, then, that Rachel cannot bring herself to mention Reuben by name. The text also records Reuben as being Leah's son in contrast to Rachel not having a son of her own. In Rachel's eyes, her firstborn nephew is a painful reminder of her inability to conceive a son of her own, and his very presence threatens to undermine her relationship with Jacob. Her terminology of "your son" unveils the competitiveness in her request for the *dudaim* and draws out Leah's responding in kind, referring to Reuben as "my son."

Leah's response is quite telling. To a seemingly courteous request on the part of her sister, Leah no less than lambastes her for the mere suggestion. Leah sees Rachel's request for what it really is—a desire for children, which, for Leah, translates into an attempt to win Jacob's love. However, as pointed out above, Rachel is not motivated to have children in order to win Jacob's love. Rachel already sees that mothering children does not have an effect on Jacob, and must sense Jacob's preference for her despite her barrenness. Thus, Leah correctly interprets Rachel's request as an expression of her desire for children but mistakenly assumes that the motive is the same as her own—to procure Jacob's love.

Leah, threatened, retorts: "Do you belittle that you took my husband that you take also my son's *dudaim*?" (30:15) The language employed by Leah equates the taking of the *dudaim* to the taking of her husband ("**kahtekh** *et ishi*" and "**velakahat** *gam et duda-ei beni*" 30:15). In temporal terms, the language also allows both events to have already occurred. This would imply that Rachel, upon seeing the *dudaim*, helps herself to a handful while still asking—a practice commonly seen amongst siblings regarding snack foods. Leah's harsh response seems to describe what has already occurred rather than an offer for negotiations. Rachel possibly cannot give them back even if she wanted to.[204] Rachel then offers Leah a chance at procreating with Jacob and having children in exchange for her opportunity to have children with the help of the *dudaim*. In response, Leah begrudgingly agrees after-the-fact to the suggested trade.[205]

Leah's bitter response reflects the probability that she has been holding a grudge against Rachel since the moment Rachel marries Jacob.[206] Although she technically accepts Rachel's proposal, Leah's earlier verbal

---

204 Perhaps the *dudaim* were eaten or immediately used by Rachel in some other irreversible manner.

205 The unwanted trade is reminiscent of Esau's sale of the birthright to Jacob for food in their youth. The agreed-upon sale reveals elements of a non-consensual, if not coercive, transaction. Esau openly belittles the subject of the sale, the birthright, and in the same vein, by giving up her conjugal rights, Rachel belittles the supposed subject of the sale here, Jacob's love and attention.

206 Her response also shows that Leah is prepared to break from the model of "sameness" by being the one with "more." Otherwise, she would have been willing to "share" Jacob gratis until her sister regained equality and should have volunteered giving the *dudaim* to Rachel.

response—"Do you belittle that you took my husband that you take also my son's *dudaim*?"—is audacious. Leah refers to Jacob as "her" husband as she did in the naming of her children. However, this time Leah does not make her statement anonymously or to Jacob, but rather directly to Rachel.

Revisiting the Conjugal Switch

Leah's comment raises a number of questions: How could Leah utter those words? Does she not feel any indebtedness at all to her sister for her life-altering act of loving kindness, years earlier, when she participated in the conjugal switch? Does she feel no empathy for her sister's barren, and almost suicidal, state? Could she not have graciously given her the *dudaim*?

Even more surprising is Rachel's response. She does not contest Leah's point. Logically, Leah's charge should have been met with Rachel's indignation at this ludicrously audacious claim. However, after Leah charges that Rachel has taken *her* husband, Rachel does not respond substantively to this claim. Moreover, Rachel's response begins with "therefore" (30:15), which essentially is conceding the legitimacy of Leah's claim.

Furthermore, why does Rachel acquiesce to Leah's claim that she took her husband? Was it not Leah who took Jacob away from Rachel on the wedding night? Did not Rachel help Leah become Jacob's wife in the first place by allowing the switch? Did not Rachel risk Jacob's wrath and possible loss of the man who loves her by going along with the plot in order to help Leah? If Leah has justified the switch in accordance with the dictates of local custom, has Rachel convinced herself that Leah's delusions are actually true?

Given the heightened emotional tension between them, one would probably expect an unrestrained physical clash. Instead, however, Rachel seems to do no less than actually legitimize Leah's claim.

In searching for a solution that will shed light on the women's behavior, one needs to recall the Midrashic assertion that in order for the conjugal switch to be successful, the interested parties, Laban, Leah, Rachel, and perhaps the townsmen all need to collaborate. The various levels of participation and the characters' motivations were analyzed at length in the previous chapter. However, there exists a new possibility that Jacob cognitively entertains and which we, as readers, can emotionally identify as the truth of what happened on that fateful night. The elusive solution to all our queries is that *no one aside from Laban has anything to do with the switch at all.*

According to this understanding, Leah and Rachel know *nothing* of the work agreement between their father and Jacob. On the wedding night, both Leah and Rachel think that Leah *is supposed to be the bride*. Laban brings Leah to Jacob and *Leah honestly believes that Jacob expects to see her and not Rachel*. [207]

Jacob's reaction the morning after mirrors that of Leah's. She acts as if everything is as it should be, and Jacob realizes that Leah does not think anything is wrong. Perhaps because of Leah's unconcerned attitude, Jacob decides to take his complaint to Laban rather than rebuke Leah. [208]

Rachel's participation in the plan is *unnecessary* because she *never thinks that she is going to marry Jacob*. Until Jacob married Rachel a week later, Rachel

---

207 See also Rabbi David Zvi Hoffman commenting on 29:23 where he states: "And according to the story line meaning of the text, Leah does not know at all that there is an act of deceit here, and she has no part in this act at all. And indeed Jacob does not claim anything against her." While clearly excising Leah from blame, it is not clear as to why Leah does not feel that this is an act of deceit. Is it because she is unaware of what is going on or because she believes she is acting in accordance with local custom? In adopting the thesis presented in the body of the text, Jacob's not recognizing Leah remains an issue as discussed in Chapter Three and the factors enumerated there also resolve how Jacob could not recognize Leah even if she was acting her Leah self. In addition, one may add that even if Jacob could discern between their voices, perhaps Jacob, similar to his father's experience at the usurping of the blessings, dismisses the voice disparity in preference of other external cues. Both Isaac and Jacob are without the benefit of their sense of sight, a similarity that calls for drawing the comparison that while Jacob, just as Isaac, may have doubted who was before him because of certain external cues, they conducted themselves based on the less troubling possibility.

208 See Akeidat Isaac, Vayetse, answering question 2, who states: "And it was in the morning and behold—she is Leah adorned in the ornaments of the bride as she is betrothed to a man and her maid Zilpah next to her and Rachel was sitting and assisting in the house as an unbetrothed virgin girl and he recognized that he tricked him, etc." Rabbi Arama thus posits the morning revelation as taking place after Jacob awoke in an empty bed and milled about the tent. Jacob could only infer that he was duped by the circumstantial evidence. As such, he may sincerely question when exactly the switch took place, before or after the conjugal act, thereby adding to Jacob's confusion. Nonetheless, R. Arama presents the awry "Twilight Zone" reality to which Jacob awakes. Everybody seems fine with everything going on. Jacob must question his very sanity. His question to Laban: "Did I not work for you on behalf of Rachel?" may even mirror his questioning himself about what the agreement was supposed to be.

has no idea that she is going to marry Jacob and questions if he even loves her at all. If Laban's excuse of local custom mandating that the elder daughter be wed first was pure fabrication, Rachel could not help but conclude that Jacob loved Leah more as Jacob assured his marriage to her first. Once Jacob marries Rachel a week later, Rachel and Leah both wonder what exactly the agreement between Jacob and Laban was. At this juncture, the women are seemingly unaware of the new work arrangement and do not know that Jacob has undertaken another seven years of labor for only room and board. It is only as time progresses and the economic arrangement changes at the end of the second seven-year period that anyone can attempt to retroactively decipher what Jacob and Laban originally agreed.

When they look back, the only thing they know is that Jacob marries Leah and Rachel after seven years of work and works a total of fourteen years for only room and board. As such, they would presume that Jacob's deal is to work fourteen years to marry both of them after year seven.[209] Similarly, in Jacob's later tirade to Laban, he mentions that he worked fourteen years for Laban's two daughters (31:41), thereby implying that this was the perceived original deal.

As a result, Rachel *never* learns of Jacob's true feelings of love for her. She *never* learns that it was Jacob's initiative to offer the high bride price for *her*. She *never* learns that, in reality, Jacob works *all fourteen years* only in order to be able to peacefully wed *her*. She *never* learns that Jacob is not only upset that Leah was wed first but that he is wed to her at all. Rachel will never know that Leah was never intended to be her co-wife.[210] This deep and utter frustration accompanies Jacob throughout his life and adds to his need to show favoritism to Rachel's offspring as a demonstration of his burning love for Rachel. Under this theory, *the two sisters live their entire lives without ever knowing that a switch took place.*

---

209 The possibility of working seven years for each daughter as two separate deals is not a natural conclusion as then Jacob should have received Rachel only after year fourteen.

210 This ignorance also contributes to Rachel's desire for Jacob to prove his love for her by guaranteeing her equality with her sister. As she never understood that Jacob already proved his love for her by working for her father for fourteen years she never feels that Jacob did anything special for her. This, in turn, leads to Jacob's angry retort to her request for children. Jacob knows he already proved his love and is exasperated as it seems it is never enough.

That being the case, the sisters perceive that their marriages to Jacob occurred exactly as they were supposed to. When Leah marries Jacob, she considers herself to be his only wife. A week later, when Rachel also marries Jacob, Leah genuinely believes that Rachel is threatening her matronhood and her relationship with her husband. As Jacob's emotional preference for Rachel intensifies, the Midrashic reading is reversed. It is not Rachel who allows Leah to marry Jacob and acquiesces to her sister sharing her husband, but rather Leah who allows Rachel to do so. Rachel herself shares this opinion and may feel indebted to Leah, or at least sufficiently identifies with Leah's stance. Leah's hostility, and Rachel's acquiescence, over the *dudaim* now make perfect sense.

It will be important to keep in mind that while the *dudaim* episode provides the reader with the key to this startling revelation, Jacob is not necessarily privy to this information. Jacob takes into account that the women may not know anything of the switch, but is never certain. In fact, the presentation made earlier indicates that Jacob's estrangement from Leah, and growing hatred towards her, is a result of his suspicion that Leah masterminded the plot. It is only for us, as readers, that the text allows a glimpse into the true goings-on during that fateful night.

Making Sense of It All

Additional support for this theory, aside from explaining Leah's otherwise ludicrous accusation of Rachel taking "her" husband, abounds.

1. This explanation accounts for Jacob's silence and explains why he fails to confront Leah or Rachel. Jacob realizes that neither Leah nor Rachel has any idea that he expected to find Rachel the morning following the wedding party. Jacob recognizes that the Kafkaesque experience of altered realities only exists in his own mind.[211]

2. When Jacob first asks Laban to send him away at the end of the fourteen years of work, he references the work he did for Laban. He asks that Laban give him his wives and children that he worked for: "You know my labor that I labored for you" (30:29). Why

---

211 Not only is Jacob silent the morning following the switch, but the issue never resurfaces anywhere, at any time, even before the children are born or when the children are not present.

is this even a point worth mentioning when requesting Laban's permission to leave? At this point in their conversation, Laban had not yet offered Jacob to stay and state a wage so Jacob was not mentioning this in order to stress his successful past performance. It is only relevant if Jacob means to imply that the original departure date was supposed to be seven years earlier and that "you know" the work I did for you, in other words, the work that I really should not have needed to perform. He does not mention the deceit explicitly to Laban in order to keep the matter private lest anyone overhear his conversation. He also does not want to unnecessarily agitate Laban at a moment when he may be able to leave for home.

3. When Jacob notifies his wives of his plan to leave Laban's home, he makes specific reference to their father Laban's attempts to cheat him out of his wages yet makes no reference to the conjugal switch as an example of Laban's handiwork.

4. During that same conversation, after explicitly delineating—and fabricating—the deceit of the sheep wages, he adds that God Himself testifies that: "I have seen all that Laban is doing to you." This catchall phrase must refer to some deceit other than the sheep wages that Jacob just specifically mentioned. While we, as readers, know of the conjugal switch, the wives are kept in the dark.[212] Thus, Jacob's word choice and phraseology indicate that keeping the silence is a dire imperative for Jacob in order to avoid humiliation and to avoid an upheaval in his family dynamics.

5. When the wives respond, they seem to speak in unison and mention that Laban sold *them*. The reference to both Rachel and Leah as a unit of sale implies that they understand that Laban had sold them both as a unit for fourteen years of Jacob's work and that he would be entitled to marry both of them after year seven.

   If they had known of the switch and partaken in the plan, their reference to this point seems quite out of place. After all, if they were involved with the switch, why would they mention such a sore point while trying to express their unity of vision with Jacob regarding leaving their father's home? Furthermore, if they had

---

212 Perhaps Jacob gently hints at the switch in this manner in order to get a reaction from his wives and see how much they really know.

wanted to mention the sale to denigrate their father and show Jacob that they empathize with his feeling cheated, they should have mentioned the switch explicitly and taken the opportunity to place all the blame at Laban's doorstep.

6. In addition, naming their father Laban as the "seller" implies that the women misunderstand their marriages to be a result of Laban's initiative. Had Jacob shared with the women the details of the original work agreement that he initiated with Laban, thereby granting them knowledge of Rachel's destined role as Jacob's wife and the subsequent aberration from that plan, they would have chosen wording to indicate the agreement being Jacob's initiative or hint at Laban's responsive role.

In order to bypass all these difficulties, one must surmise that they did not know of the work agreement and hence also did not know of the switch at all.

7. Finally and perhaps most conclusively, is the final scene at Gilead. After Laban accuses Jacob of stealing his gods, Jacob becomes infuriated with Laban. During Jacob's self-righteous tirade, in which he relates the detailed history of his relationship with Laban (31:36–42), he makes no mention of the deceit. Poignantly, when mentioning his work for Leah and Rachel, Jacob simply states that he worked fourteen years for both daughters, without explicitly referring to the deceit.[213]

No point would have better served Jacob at that critical moment, as he stands accused of deceit and stealing, than to expose Laban's hypocrisy and make explicit reference to the switch. However, Jacob leaves Laban to understand on his own the true meaning behind his statement about having worked fourteen years for both daughters. As far as Jacob is concerned, the matter will remain a secret forever.

Jacob's vague statement of working a total of fourteen years for both daughters also alleviates a different stress, as it leads Rachel and Leah to believe that the deal was originally for fourteen years

---

213 Jacob technically lied at that point. Jacob did not work fourteen years for Laban's two daughters as he claimed. As Or Hahayyim comments on 30:15, Jacob worked all fourteen years only for Rachel. It was only to the outsiders' point of view that he worked seven years per daughter or fourteen years for both daughters.

of work for both of them. Jacob does not state that he worked seven years for each of Laban's two daughters. Jacob hopes that the sisters will believe that they had begun on equal footing and thus diffuse the impression that Rachel "took" Jacob away from Leah. Additionally, Jacob wants to show Rachel that even before marrying Leah, Jacob loved her just as much as Leah, as indicated by including Rachel in the original deal and not as an afterthought that only arose after marrying Leah.

Similarly, when Laban strikes a covenant with Jacob at Gilead, he requests that Jacob not abuse his daughters saying, "If you afflict my daughters and if you take women in addition to my daughters, no man is amongst us, see, God is witness between me and you" (31:50). The word used for afflict (a.n.eh.) is the same verb usage for rape.[214] Had the family known of the conjugal switch, Jacob should have responded that if anyone was subject to a non-consensual laying, it was surely him on the wedding night. Jacob's continued silence on this matter indicates that the conjugal switch is sealed in Jacob's heart and never revealed to Rachel or Leah.[215] At the same time, Jacob is never able to confirm the sisters' ignorance or complicity in the switch and he hints at the matter at various junctures in the hopes of revealing new information.

Another Conjugal Switch

> And Jacob came from the field in the evening. And Leah went out towards him and said: "To me you shall come, for I have surely hired you with my son's *dudaim*" and he lay with her on that night. (30:16)

Returning to the *dudaim* narrative, we find that when Jacob arrives, Leah preempts him from visiting any other tent.[216] Leah tells him that he is to come to her for she has hired him as a trade for her son's *dudaim*. The

---

214 See 34:2.

215 I am aware that there exist other logically possible variations of who knew what, however, the above thesis resonates best throughout the remainder of Genesis.

216 The setup of separate tents for Leah, Rachel, and one tent for the two maids is gleaned from 31:33.

language "come to me" serves as a double entendre, as both physical and sexual connotations are included.[217]

When Leah informs Jacob of the trade, the text depicts Jacob returning home from the field "in the evening" (30:16). The last time the text pointed out it was evening was when Leah was switched for Rachel on the wedding night (29:23). This textual prompting calls for a comparison between the original switch and the current one. While Jacob may not be certain about who is to blame for the original switch, the current switch focuses the blame on Leah. Leah, believing that she is endearing herself to Jacob, inaccurately reports that she herself hired him for the night in lieu of her son's *dudaim*. In reality, however, it was Rachel who initiated the trade. Thus, Jacob reinforces his conclusion drawn from the conjugal switch and determines that Leah is the one who desires to control his intimate life.

Had Leah accurately relayed the interchange between herself and Rachel, with Rachel initiating the current trade, Leah may have been able to deflect some blame away from herself and on to Rachel for the original conjugal switch. However, when she attributes the *dudaim* initiative to herself, perhaps in an effort to appear magnanimous and above sibling rivalry, Jacob naturally looks to Leah as the culprit.

In addition, Jacob may further extrapolate that just as the current switch is a willful act of the participants, so, too, was the conjugal switch years ago. He may think that Rachel is now offering her sister in her stead in much the same way that she offered Leah to him on the wedding night or as she offered Bilhah as surrogate. Rachel may be insinuating to Jacob that since he is not concerned with her fertility, and is seemingly only interested in her physically, she has taken matters into her own hands. She will meet his physical desires by arranging his being with Leah or Bilhah. She will attempt to meet her desire to have children by acquiring the *dudaim*. She

---

217 Leah, as did Rachel earlier, refers to Reuben only as "my son," perhaps fearing that mentioning the name of Reuben will only reinforce her sense of rejection that the name encapsulates. It is not clear whether Jacob understands that the "son" Leah refers to is Reuben. However, as Reuben is about four to six years old and his siblings even younger, Reuben is the most likely candidate to find the *dudaim*. Reuben's role as bed switcher, both indirectly here and more directly later with Bilhah (35:22), reenact for Jacob the original switch between Leah and Rachel, and will influence the farewell remarks that Jacob issues to Reuben on his deathbed (49:4).

essentially informs Jacob that being with him physically without being able to have children is meaningless to her, to the extent that she would even allow her competitor/co-wife/sister to sleep with him in her stead for the mere possibility of becoming fertile. [218]

Remembered at Last

God remembers Rachel, listens to her, and she bears Joseph. However, after having Joseph, Rachel must be sorely disappointed in her inability to follow her sister's birthing cycle as Rachel will only bear Benjamin at least seven years later.[219] During those years, Rachel's frustration persists yet is somewhat tempered as Leah ceases to birth more children as well.[220]

At this point, Jacob is prepared to leave Laban's home. The text explicitly times Jacob's request to depart after Rachel's birth to Joseph (30:25), such that the birth of Joseph seems to coincide with the end of the second seven years Jacob needed to work for Rachel. The conclusion of the agreed-

---

218　Throughout the ongoing competition between Rachel and Leah, Jacob's role is mostly passive. His one interaction with Rachel, when she expressed her anguish at her childless state, proved disastrous, and Jacob fails to express his true feelings for Rachel. Jacob is thus discouraged from attempting any further involvement. As pointed out above, he avoids naming the children as their names are associated with the sisters' rivalry. Jacob hopes that his passivity will calm the storm between the sisters as he apparently remains unmoved by their bearing or not bearing children. If he does not react, reasons Jacob, there will be no reason for the contest to continue as he refuses to participate. However, Jacob's passivity only serves to send Leah into a shrieking spiral of intensified efforts. Jacob's tactic fails precisely because the status quo that he maintains of favoring Rachel is exactly what Leah desperately seeks to alter.

219　As a result, Joseph is raised as Rachel's only biologically child and benefits from her undivided love and attention. The other brothers grow up needing to share their mother's love and attention. Later, they will grow jealous and hate Joseph when he also benefits from his father's favoritism. They see him as always receiving undivided love and attention while they must always learn to share and struggle for their parents' love and attention.

220　This point corroborates Alter's assertion that Jacob did not frequent any of the wives' tents and instead spent the nights away from home working with the flocks.

upon labor also provides the impetus for Jacob's initial desire to leave.[221] This is also corroborated by Jacob's later tirade against Laban where he states that he worked twenty years for Laban, fourteen years for his two daughters, and six years for the sheep (31:41). The six years of work for the sheep only follow Jacob's request to leave after Joseph is born and after he and Laban reach a new agreement.[222]

With the later birth of Benjamin, the cast of characters that will embark on their life journey together as Jacob's family is complete. Each child upon birth is unknowingly thrust into the competition between Rachel and Leah. Their very conception is laden with layers of complex family history. As the children begin their early years, Jacob remains engrossed

---

221 However, see Alter, *The Five Books of Moses*. pg. 162 note to 30:26 where he suggests that Jacob worked more than fourteen years until Joseph was born. This allows a smoother birthing cycle for the mothers and a reasonable hiatus from Leah's birthing to allow her to feel the need to give Zilpah to Jacob. However, such a reading will need to attribute a more blurry understanding of Jacob's later statements to Laban at Gilead where he delineates that he worked twenty years by Laban, fourteen for his two daughters and six for his sheep (31:41), as well as a need to explain why Jacob would continue working for Laban for free after fourteen years of exploitation.

222 In order for the time sequence to be possible, the textual recordings of the children's birth cannot be without overlapping. Minimally, the births of the maids' children overlap with Leah's own children. One must also posit that when "Leah realizes that she paused from giving birth" (30:9), she notices this quite quickly as all the other births are very close together. This still requires Leah to have had seven children in seven years including the period where she realizes she has stopped birthing. As a result, Joseph must be about the same age as Dinah. From Rachel's comments in naming Naftali ("In mighty struggles I have struggled with my sister *and I also held my own,*"), it would appear that the two children of Bilhah overlap with the first two children of Leah such that one can construe Rachel's comment seriously. Otherwise, how could Rachel claim to be ahead of the competition in any sense if Leah already has four children and her maid has only two? Therefore, Rachel's jealousy of her sister leading to the giving of Bilhah must have occurred shortly after Reuben or Simeon's births. Benjamin is clearly born last and at least seven years, if not more, after Joseph. The later references and ordering of the tribes throughout the Bible do not follow the sequence of birth according to any reading with each later instance following its own internal logic. The difficulty in accurately determining the ages and ordering of the children lends to the amazement the brothers will later have when the ruler of Egypt will accurately seat them according to age (43:33).

in accumulating wealth and works long hours away from home and his children. As the children grow, they will long to be with their father and will seek the means to obtain his elusive love. Their very existence allows them to remain the currency of jealousy between Rachel and Leah, and they unknowingly serve as pawns in yet another competition between family figures, as will be explored in Chapter Five.

Hidden Agendas

I never want to be alone.

⊱ Young Sherlock Holmes

Jacob's Hidden Agenda

As Jacob contemplates leaving Laban's home, he calls Rachel and Leah to the field, to his flocks, to inform them of the divine decree ordering his exit.[223] As will be seen, Jacob's conversation with Rachel and Leah consists of far more than Jacob simply sharing information with his wives. Rather, Jacob's agenda is to actively maneuver the women into throwing in their lot with him even if it means challenging their father, Laban. Through Jacob's word choice and selected topics of discussion, Jacob seeks to subtly shape their opinion against their father and secure their utter allegiances to him. The text recounts:

> And Jacob sent and called Rachel and Leah out to the field, to his flocks, and he said to them, "I see your father's face, that it is not disposed toward me as in the past, but the God of my father has been with me. And you know that with all my strength I have served your father. But your father has tricked me and has switched my wages

---

223 To recall, Jacob works for Laban for fourteen years in order to marry Rachel and Leah, after which time Jacob enters into a work agreement with Laban in return for sheep and subsequently accumulates much wealth. Six years later, God appears to Jacob and orders him to return to his father's homeland.

ten times over, yet God has not let him do me harm... And God's messenger said to me in the dream,[224] 'Jacob!' and I said, 'Here I am.' And he said, 'Raise your eyes, pray and see...Now, rise, leave this land, and return to the land of your birthplace.'" And Rachel and Leah answered and they said to him, "Do we still have any share in the inheritance of our father's house? Why, we have been counted by him as strangers, for he has sold us, and he has wholly consumed our money. For whatever wealth God has reclaimed from our father is ours and our children's, and so, whatever God has said to you, do." (31:4–7, 11-16)[225]

Jacob seeks to ascertain his wives' current allegiances in the following ways:[226]

1. Jacob refers to Laban as "their father" four times (31:5, 6, 7, 9). This added emphasis seems to imply that Jacob is trying to gauge his wives' reaction when he speaks negatively about "their father." He wants to see where their loyalties lie.[227]

2. Jacob ambiguously alludes to their father's switching his wages ten times (31:7). In reality, though, as far as the text records, no wage switch other than the conjugal switch occurs. Upon reexamining the verse, the term Jacob uses is not that Laban switched his wages ten "*peamim*" times,[228] but ten "*monim*"—tenfold. Jacob is stating that their father played with him by switching his wages tenfold;

---

224 Abravanel's question 3 on chapter 31 suggests that Jacob fabricated having this prophetic dream. The need for this fabrication and its place in the larger scheme of Haran influences is discussed below. Abravanel himself later dismisses this premise when answering the question, but his anomalous justification of Jacob's fabrication while still listing his questions may indicate the true feeling of Abravanel.

225 Alter's translation.

226 See Abravanel (answering question 1 of ch. 31) who comments that Jacob did not have the power to leave without his wives' desire, knowledge, and willingness.

227 In this context, Jacob mentally revisits the role his wives may have played in the conjugal switch. Had Rachel and/or Leah helped orchestrate the conjugal switch, a matter still unresolved in Jacob's mind, Jacob would interpret such participation as representing their willingness to upset their married life in favor of fulfilling their father's wishes.

228 Cf. Numbers 14:22 where the term "*eser peamim*" (ten times) is used.

that is, by substituting Leah for Rachel, Laban gave Jacob what the latter views as only one-tenth of what was due to him.[229] Jacob tempers this loaded statement by stating that God did not let Laban harm him by this.[230] As the women show no indication of understanding Jacob's allusion, probably because, in reality, they know nothing of the switch, he remains uncertain as to their loyalty. Therefore, Jacob continues to fabricate an entirely new switch of wages and a prophetic dream, in order to divert their attention away from his opening remark and minimize the risk of them realizing that he was referring to the conjugal switch.[231] This new switch of wages casts their father in a negative light while helping Jacob achieve his goal of winning over the women's allegiance.

3. Jacob's subsequent formulation also reveals his desired manipulation of his wives' opinions. Jacob begins: "If so will he [Laban] say: 'The spotted ones will be your wages—all the flocks bore spotted ones'; and if so will he say: 'The brindled ones will be your wages—all the flocks bore brindled ones'"(31:8). In reality, it was Jacob, not Laban, who had initiated the choice of owning the spotted and speckled sheep (30:32–33). Laban had merely acquiesced (30:34).[232] Thus, Jacob's suggestion to his wives that Laban was responsible for whimsically alternating his wages is spurious.

---

229 This derogatory allusion to Leah parallels Elkanah's public, verbal acknowledgment of his being better to Hannah than if she had ten sons (1 Samuel 1:8, possibly alluding to Peninah. Cf. 1 Samuel 2:5).

230 Jacob uses the word "*imadi*" twice when speaking with Rachel and Leah (31:5. 7). The same word appears twice by Laban years earlier, both at the initial proposal for Rachel and subsequently seven years later after the conjugal switch (29:19, 27). As Jacob speaks to his wives, those statements bitterly ring in his ears and reverberate in his speech.

231 See *The Jewish Study Bible*, Adele Berlin, Marc Zvi Brettler, Michael Fishbane eds. (Oxford: Oxford University, 2004), pgs. 63–64 note to verses 4–13, which indicates Jacob's dissembling, but fails to appreciate the purposeful presentation Jacob puts forth.

232 To recall, after fourteen years of labor by Laban, Jacob was ready to leave. In response, Laban requests that Jacob state his wage. Jacob subsequently proposes a form of partnership where Laban will give Jacob all the spotted, speckled, and dark colored sheep and spotted and speckled goats (30:25–33).

In addition, contrary to Jacob's presentation, there was never a differentiation between spotted and brindled sheep. Jacob designated both groups as his own from the start.[233] Jacob's fragmenting of the groups here seeks to dissuade the wives of the legitimacy of the claims of Laban's sons, their brothers, who implicitly also question his loyalty to Laban. Reducing his earned wage to any one group of sheep at a time presents him as a person who can be satisfied with less and detracts from Laban's sons' assertions regarding Jacob's avarice in accumulating "all this wealth."[234]

4. For similar reasons, Jacob omits all mention of his manipulation of the rods. To recall, the text (30:37–43) relays how Jacob peeled moist rods and placed the now multi-colored and spotted rods in the water channels when the flocks would go into heat in the belief that this is what caused the sheep to bear brindled, speckled, and spotted young similar to the coloration of the rods.[235] As Jacob now desires to present his current situation as divinely ordained in order to sway the women's loyalties towards his own camp, he omits any mention of his human intervention that may have contributed to his success.[236] Discussion of his deceitful activities with the flocks, even if he could justify them without revealing the conjugal switch, would only be counterproductive and would further validate Laban's sons' claims.

5. Furthermore, Jacob presents divine intervention as alternating between entirely spotted offspring only or entirely brindled offspring only. "If so will he [Laban] say: 'The spotted ones will be your wages—*all the flocks* bore spotted ones'; and if so will he say:

---

233 See 30:32–33, 35.

234 See 31:1. In order for Jacob to succeed, as he does, with his fabrication, one must presume that Jacob does not share with his wives the details of the real work agreement during the past six years. The women seem only to eye the accumulating wealth without regard to the underlying agreement responsible for its production. This would further buttress the idea that Jacob also did not communicate the original work agreement for Rachel to either Rachel or Leah.

235 See Alter, *The Five Books of Moses*, pg. 164 note to verse 38.

236 The attribution to divine intervention here is similar to the way the servant of Abraham presents his discovery of Rebekah as being divinely ordained (24:48). Further parallels between this episode and the episode of Rebekah and the servant will be pointed out in subsequent footnotes.

'The brindled ones will be your wages—*all the flocks* bore brindled ones'"(31:8). In reality, Jacob presumably believes that he has successfully manipulated the birthing of the sheep by the use of the rods, and the offspring were a mix of brindled and spotted animals (see 30:37–41, especially 30:39, "And the flocks went into heat at the rods and the flocks bore *brindled, spotted, and speckled young*").[237] If nature ran its course, there should have been a regular statistical distribution between speckled and brindled groups, as the text in 30:39, quoted above, attests actually occurred. The mixed distribution would be the fair outcome of Jacob's real work agreement with Laban. Why, then, does Jacob fabricate that God provided uniform birthing patterns with God taking affirmative action to *over*compensate him?

Furthermore, Jacob continues: "And God saved your father's flocks and gave them to me" (31:9). From what exactly did God "save" the sheep and how does God giving them to Jacob constitute saving them?

In response to these two inquiries, the underlying assumption that Jacob projects to his wives is that while his agreement with Laban allotted him only one group of sheep at a time, God felt that Jacob deserved to own *all* the sheep. God is therefore saving them from being "stolen" by Laban by assuring uniform birthing patterns, for Jacob's purported benefit.[238] By attributing this extreme stance to God, Jacob at once avoids revealing any of his own avarice while encouraging his wives to place their loyalty in favor of the divinely ordained position of favoring Jacob.

6. Jacob then proceeds to relate the divine dream he claims to have had in which God's angel shows him spotted, speckled, and brindled sheep and declares that God has seen "all that Laban is doing to you" (31:12). In reality, the divine command to return home is not reported as being communicated via a dream, does not include

---

237 Alter's translation. It is irrelevant for this discussion whether the manipulation of the rods worked genetically or not, as it is Jacob's perception or his presentation of the event that is currently in question.

238 This understanding perhaps explains Alter's translation of "saved" as "reclaimed." The narrative seems to side with Jacob as it records that Jacob called Rachel and Leah to the field "near *his* flocks" (31:4).

any mention of sheep, or of the ominous "all that Laban is doing to you." In order to persuade his wives to join forces with him, Jacob presents himself as someone who is privy to divine communication, enjoys divine protection from Laban, and has divine assistance in accumulating wealth.[239]

The Women's Response

Without being asked for their response, the women tell Jacob that "*all* the wealth that God 'salvaged' from our father is 'ours and our children's'" (31:16). The use of the word "ours" by the wives is not definitively inclusive of Jacob,[240] and this ambiguity might indicate that Leah and Rachel's agreement to leave may be motivated more by their not wanting to live with Laban than their desire to be with Jacob. In any case, the sisters follow Jacob's lead and deny Laban's legitimacy as owner of *any* of the flock. Their reference to the way their father treated them (as items of sale and in utilitarian terms) suggests that while in the past their loyalties rested elsewhere, they no longer have any incentive to side with Laban.[241]

In response to Jacob's introduction of God, Leah and Rachel state: "Whatever God said to you—*aseh*—do" (31:16).[242] The grammar of this statement is difficult given its context. The verse would have read easier as,

---

239 The pressure to join the divinely guided Jacob echoes the pressure exerted by the servant of Abraham on the family in order to allow Rebekah to accompany him to Canaan in light of the divinely guided selection of Rebekah.

240 This point plays into the quest for materialism that weaves itself throughout the narrative.

241 See Tsafrira Ben-Barak, *Ha'arot Leparashat Nisuei Leah veRahel leYaakov al Reka Nehagim MiMesopotamia* (Hebrew) [Enlightening Remarks Regarding the Episode of Rachel and Leah Marrying Jacob in the Backdrop of Mesopotamian Customs], in *Teshurot LaAvishur*, 2004, pgs. 119–136, 127, where she points out that according to ancient customs in Mesopotamia as illustrated in the Nuzi documents, the birth of a naturally born son would supplant the status of the daughters as possible heirs. In this case, as Laban bore natural sons after Jacob wed both of Laban's daughters, the status of the daughters as independent heirs lapsed such that while in the past they indeed had a share in their father's estate and a reason to be loyal to him, they no longer do.

242 This responsive recognition of God's role continues the parallelism to the servant of Abraham's visit when Rebekah's family responds: "The matter came from God." See 24:50.

"Whatever God said—*na'aseh*—we will do." The stress on what God told "*you*" and "*you* should do" leaves Jacob with anything but a clear picture of whether the wives view their threesome as one family. Leah and Rachel may be saying that Jacob should go back home now alone and leave them all the wealth. Indeed, even in Jacob's supposed dream, God's instruction to return is relayed only in the singular form. Perhaps, reason the wives, the divine dictate only refers to him and not to the wealth or the family. Furthermore, in Jacob's dream, it is only Jacob who is reminded of his personal vow made years earlier in Bethel. Rachel and Leah may thus infer that the divine calling does not require them to accompany Jacob to Canaan. Rachel and Leah may be tempted to jettison both Jacob and Laban, while retaining the children and wealth as "theirs."

Regardless of these insinuations, Jacob posits that the women are still dependent on either him or Laban for economic survival. Jacob feels confident that the women's stinging comments demonstrate that they have severed the intense emotional ties to Laban that they may have had at the time of the conjugal switch. Jacob therefore sets out together with his family and wealth towards Canaan.[243]

Maintaining Silence

> And Jacob arose and transported his sons and his wives on the camels. And he led all his livestock and all his acquisitions that he had acquired, his purchases in livestock that he had acquired in Paddan-Aram, to come to Isaac his father in the land of Canaan. (31:17–18)

The sequence of the events mentioned in these verses is significant. Jacob is already reported transporting all his family and belongings towards his father's home in Canaan (31:18).[244] Only after pointing this out does the text record that Laban went to shear his sheep followed by Rachel stealing her father's *terafim*. We then read that Jacob stole the heart of Laban by

---

243 When Jacob leaves Laban's home, the text clearly makes a distinction between the family personnel and the wealth accumulated. This distinction is something the characters themselves have failed to make, as the Haran philosophy drives Rachel, Leah, Jacob, and Laban to interchange people and things.

244 It is noteworthy that the divine order made no mention of returning to Isaac's home, but only to the land of his fathers (31:3).

not informing him of his departure (31:19–20). The textual order implies that it is only when Rachel and Jacob discover that Laban goes to shear sheep that Rachel decides to steal the *terafim* that belong to her father and that Jacob decides to "steal" Laban's heart (because he did not wait for his return to inform him of his departure). Only when all of Jacob's camp is ready to travel does Jacob learn of Laban's absence and decides to leave without telling Laban. Initially, Jacob may have intended to inform Laban that they are leaving due to God's command to return to his father's homeland. Indeed, as Jacob has no knowledge of Rachel's theft, he personally has nothing to hide and ostensibly nothing to gain by making a quick exit. If so, why doesn't Jacob wait until Laban returns before leaving?

Another Hidden Agenda

The text records that the sons of Laban were talking of Jacob taking everything of their father's: "And he heard the sons of Laban saying: 'Jacob took all that our father has, and from what our father has he made all this honor'" (31:1). Jacob perhaps fears that Laban's sons discovered his manipulations with the multi-colored rods (30:37–43) and planned to claim back all the sheep. Given the tense relations between Laban's sons and Jacob, Jacob fears that he will need to forego some or all of his wealth in order to leave in peace. It is as Laban leaves to shear his sheep that Jacob seizes the previously unforeseeable opportunity to leave for home unchallenged. Thus, Jacob's silence and quick exit reveal his hidden agenda to silence the claim of Laban's sons.

Yet further along these lines, perhaps Jacob fears that when Laban returns from shearing his sheep, he will realize just how disparate the numbers are between his and Jacob's flocks.[245] Indeed, as there is a three-day distance between Jacob's and Laban's flocks (30:36), and as Laban's sons are herding one group of flocks (30:35), Laban had not yet confirmed first-hand his sons' opinion of Jacob's wealth. Jacob fears that Laban's sons will provoke Laban and perhaps lead to an uncovering of the manipulation of the rods. Jacob, therefore, cannot afford to wait until Laban returns, for he fears that

---

245 Literally, the shearing of sheep is almost a type-scene for deceit. Here, Jacob utilizes the event to exit before Laban discovers his deceit of manipulating the rods. Tamar deceives Judah while en route to shearing his sheep (ch. 38). Abigail deceives Naval while Naval shears his sheep by presenting David and his men with food that Naval had refused to give (1 Samuel 25) and Absalom utilizes the sheep shearing festival to ensnare Amnon and have him killed (II Samuel 13).

somehow the sons of Laban or Laban will now take away the wealth that Jacob believes is his.[246]

In addition, Jacob may be capitalizing on Laban's absence in order to give Laban a taste of his own medicine. Laban had tricked Jacob at the drinking party with the conjugal switch, causing Jacob to wake up the following morning to a radically different reality than he imagined. Jacob's plan is that while Laban is drinking,[247] he will orchestrate a radically different reality for Laban upon his return.[248]

Once again, as with the conjugal switch, Jacob adopts a mode of silence *vis-à-vis* a family member on a major issue by leaving before Laban returns and before clearing any claims the sons' of Laban may have.[249] After twenty years of working for his uncle Laban, marrying his two daughters, and raising twelve of Laban's grandchildren, one can easily understand Laban's indignant claims of Jacob's folly. The affront of leaving unannounced is clear, and such an act in the ancient Near East may have been sufficient cause for violence, as Laban himself later states.

---

246 Indeed, Laban's right to a follow-up inspection of Jacob's integrity (30:33) has not yet occurred and Jacob has grounds to fear that Laban will contest his dominion over the flocks.

247 See sheep shearing episodes in Samuel I and II referred to above where drink is abundant at the sheep shearing festival.

248 See Netziv commenting on 31:20 for a similar idea where he notes that the text mentions that Jacob stole the heart of Laban "the "Aramean" for the reader to infer that Laban was a trickster (either a "*ramai*"—a play on the word "Arami" or "a person from Aram" because Aram is a known source of sourcerers and magicians [for example, see Numbers 23:7]) and even so—Jacob was able to outdo him. However, Netziv cites Laban's trickster nature from 25:20 which is not a reference to the conjugal switch but the idea is similar in that Jacob's exit gave Laban a taste of his own medicine.

249 On Jacob's characteristic "not telling," see Klitsner, *Wrestling with Jacob*, pgs. 139–140. This general description also lends additional credence to the new understanding presented above regarding the conjugal switch. In addition, the Abravanel (chapter 31, answering question 6) suggests that the later textual reference of "Jacob stealing Laban's heart for not telling him that he is running away" alludes to Jacob not having told Laban 20 years earlier that he is running away from Esau. However, this understanding meets with much difficulty from the text. While Abravanel's explanation about "stealing Laban's heart" may be untenable, the idea that Jacob does not inform Laban of his running away from Esau does remain plausible in and of itself. If such were the case, it would represent yet another major familial issue over which Jacob is secretive.

Jacob's departure from Laban's home is dramatic and traumatic. Jacob, as did Abraham before him, uproots himself and his family from their home to travel to a divinely chosen destination. Jacob's difficult move exhibits his ability to adjust to a new reality and reveals his utmost faith in the prophetic divine promise made to him[250] (31:3). Laban, however, displays no ability to let go of the past and does everything in his power to hold on to his nephew's family despite the discomfort Jacob's continued presence would generate for Laban's sons.

Closing In

> And he took his brothers with him and he chased after him a journey of seven days and he caught up to him (lit. "glued") at the mountain of the Gilead. And God came to Laban the Aramean in a nighttime dream and He said to him: "Be wary lest you speak with Jacob from good to evil." And Laban caught Jacob and Jacob pitched his tent in the mountain and Laban pitched his brothers in the mountain of the Gilead. (31:23–25)

Jacob succeeds in crossing the river with all he has, and climbs Mount Gilead. Laban and his "brothers," after hearing of Jacob's exit three days after its occurrence (31:22), close the gap between Jacob and himself in seven days. From this calculation, ten days have passed without seeing one another, and seven days have passed since Laban learned of Jacob's leaving. Thus, it is possible that during this time, Jacob anticipates and plans to respond to certain arguments were Laban to charge him, but he has no knowledge of the stolen *terafim*. Indeed, from the interaction that follows, it seems that Laban's actual arguments come as a surprise to Jacob.

Before Laban closes in on Jacob's camp, Jacob may assume or hope that, similar to his prior experience with Esau, Laban has either failed to trace his trail or has reluctantly abandoned his efforts to track him. However, in reality, during those seven days, Laban manages to anticipate different scenarios and carefully calculates his tactics against Jacob. Thus, Jacob is

---

250 Jacob succeeds in letting go in much the same way as Abraham let go of his father's home. Yet, the analogy perhaps even runs one level deeper. When the shepherds of Abraham and his nephew Lot quarreled over grazing grounds (13:7–9), Abraham initiated a peaceful and probably tearful separation from his nephew. It is the Abrahamic line that succeeds in letting go and moving on.

less prepared to defend himself against Laban's charges, while Laban has the benefit of seven days of planning and the knowledge of the missing *terafim*.

The text informs us that Laban catches up with Jacob—"*vayaseg.*" However, two verses earlier, we read that Laban "glued—*vayadbek*" Jacob to Mount Gilead. Is the text being repetitive? If so, why does the text employ different wording?

Furthermore, the text associates the name of Mount Gilead with Laban but not with Jacob. Laban pitches his brothers in "Mount Gilead," while Jacob pitches his tent in "the mountain." Why does the same verse refer to the same mountain in two different ways?

In response, the earlier textual reference stating that Laban "glued" Jacob seems to indicate that Jacob is "stuck" on the mountain, *as Laban has his men surround Jacob around the hilltop.* Laban then catches up to Jacob himself while Jacob still does not know of the encirclement. To Laban, the mountain itself is the "*gal*" or "pile" of testimony—the place that he hoped would bear witness to his exposure of Jacob as a thief. For this purpose, he "pitches" or stations his brothers on the mountain to bear witness. For Jacob, who does not know that there is a chase afoot at all, it is simply a mountain. Thus, the disparate terminology and ostensible repetition reflect the characters' varying perceptions of the situation, and Jacob's later brazen tirade takes on new proportions as Laban's surrounding forces close in on Jacob's camp.[251]

Laban's Hidden Agenda

Laban opens his communication with Jacob with the following accusation:

> What did you do?[252] And you stole my heart. And you treated my daughters as prisoners of war. Why did you conceal your quick exit

---

251 Laban's vague mention of his ability to do Jacob harm (31:29) can now be understood as referring to these encircling forces which Jacob does not yet see.

252 Ironically, Laban provides Jacob with a throwback to Jacob's question of decency following the discovery of the conjugal switch. "What is this that you have done to me?" (29:25) Jacob's response mirrors that of Abraham and Isaac when they each face Avimelekh. They all begin with "*ki amarti*"—"for I said" (Cf. 20:11, 26:9). This parallel of response indicates a demand to correctly identify one's wife and explain away another claimed relation. By Sarah and Rebekah, the dual identity conferred is that of sister and wife. Here, the dual identity is that of daughter and wife. As with the other forefathers, Jacob must excuse himself for violating basic social norms due to a fear and correctly identify and take responsibility for his

and you stole me. And you did not tell me and I would have sent you with happiness, songs, drums, and harps.[253] And you did not leave/abandon[254] me to kiss my sons and my daughters—now you have done foolishness. I could do harm to you [plural] but your [plural] God warned me yesterday not to speak to Jacob from good to bad. And now you have surely departed because you longingly pined away for your father's home. Why did you steal my gods? (31:26–30)

Jacob quickly reads the situation. While Laban's final accusation of stealing his gods rings in Jacob's ears, Jacob perceives the charge that he has treated Laban's daughters as prisoners of war as the more direct threat. "What have you done? And you stole my heart. And you treated my daughters as prisoners of war…" (31:26).

It is ludicrous that Laban is charging Jacob with taking his daughters captive. Due to the deception of the conjugal switch, Jacob worked for Laban for fourteen years to marry Laban's two daughters, when the original contract involved only seven years for Rachel. Jacob surely worked hard to earn the right to marry them. Why would Laban log such a complaint?

The remainder of Laban's "charge sheet" provides Jacob with a more complete picture. Laban claims: "And you did not leave/abandon me to kiss *my* sons (grandchildren) and *my* daughters (Rachel and Leah)[255]—now you have done foolishness." The traditional understanding of this claim is that Laban wants to kiss his grandchildren and daughters goodbye before their departure, as he does later before he finally departs (32:1). Jacob's crime would then be his violation of proper etiquette and hurting Laban's feelings. However, Laban's word choice indicates a different mindset altogether.

---

wives. Rachel's theft of the *terafim* allows Jacob to sidestep responsibility for his violation of social norms and, on a certain level, deprives the family of a defining moment.

253 Laban's reference to sending Jacob with "happiness and songs with drums and harps" (31:27) surely conjures up for Jacob the specter of the party preceding the conjugal switch and hints at Laban's offer being disingenuous.

254 The use of the word associated with abandonment, as opposed to the more common "*azavtani*"—left me, serves as a parapraxis for Laban's emotional fears.

255 As this term is in the plural, it must refer to Jacob's wives—unless Jacob had a daughter other than Dinah to whom the text makes no reference.

By referring to Jacob's wives and grandchildren as *his* sons and daughters, Laban reveals his devious long-term plan against his nephew and son-in-law. Laban desires to remain the one that his daughters look to for affection. Laban's plan to marginalize Jacob and usurp Jacob's role as father and husband provides additional motivation for Laban to carry out the conjugal switch. He seeks to wed both his daughters to the same man so that he will have a better chance of perpetuating his parenthood and keeping his daughters close by, thereby preventing Jacob from replacing him as the beloved male figure in his daughters' lives. Jacob's later tirade (31:36–42) depicts his incessant workday, possibly purposefully imposed by Laban, and implies Jacob's absence and lack of family involvement.[256] Jacob's role as husband and father are non-existent in Laban's lexicon.

Laban focuses on Jacob's remoteness and claims that Jacob desires to leave in order to see his father. He reinforces the split between Jacob on the one hand and the wives and the children on the other when he pointedly accuses Jacob: "And now *you* have surely departed because *you* longingly pined away for *your* father's home—why have *you* stolen my gods (31:30)?" Thus, the very language of Laban's accusations isolates Jacob from his family. Laban purposefully chooses Jacob's pining for his father's home as Jacob's possible motivation in order to further distance Rachel and Leah from Jacob as he pits father against father. As his daughters have no such longing for Isaac, having never even met him, they have no apparent reason to be leaving their father Laban and should therefore return home to their own father.

Laban is not simply asking for a kiss goodbye, but is rather seeking to win back his daughters and grandchildren as his own. Laban is implying that Jacob should allow him to continue being the one that "kisses his

---

256 As part of Laban's hidden agenda, the conjugal switch served his ends by imbuing Jacob with the sense that his relationship with Leah and Rachel is essentially mechanical. Jacob's failure to notice Leah in Rachel's stead impedes his ability to develop the emotional component of the relationship. The switch has Jacob question the sincerity of his deepest emotions—for how could he not recognize his true love, Rachel, absent from the conjugal bed? In trying to reduce the trauma of the switch, Jacob considers his love to be a response to a physiological need and de facto adopts Laban's mold of husbandry in which siring children is his sole function.

sons and daughters" and that it is "foolishness" for it to be otherwise.[257] In singling out Jacob in his accusations, Laban further exposes his plan for perpetual parenthood.

Laban's deep-seated need to maintain control over his daughters may stem from his early childhood experience. Laban's sister, Rebekah, was whisked away by Abraham's servant to become Isaac's wife, probably when she was between twelve and fourteen years of age. As a result, Laban, her younger brother, grows up without his sister.[258] In response, Laban develops a need to hold on to his daughters in fear of being abandoned by them after they wed, just as Rebekah abandoned him and left her father's home to wed the unnamed Isaac. Indeed, there are numerous literary parallels between the episodes surrounding the final showdown at Gilead and the episode leading to Rebekah's departure from her father's home years earlier. These parallels, noted throughout, alert the reader to Laban's heightened anxiety as he attempts to ward off a déjà-vu. He does not want to be alone again. Laban states: "And *you* did not tell me, and I would have sent *you* with happiness…." The singular form of "you" implies that Laban would have been happy to send Jacob—alone and empty-handed—back home to Isaac.

This line of reasoning elucidates Laban's initial claims of Jacob leading Rachel and Leah as captives of war and Jacob "stealing" Laban by his quick exit. As the women could not possibly share Jacob's longing for his father's home, Laban sincerely believes *that Jacob has forced them to leave against their will*. Laban understands that Jacob's secrecy surrounding his departure implies that he has something to hide and thus, Jacob is "stealing/kidnapping" his daughters by forcing them to leave against their will. Why else would the women leave their childhood home and their beloved father who has provided for them all these years without even saying goodbye? Laban is convinced that had they seen him upon leaving, they would have chosen to stay with their father over going with Jacob.

According to this understanding, Laban's seven-day chase is not aimed at obtaining a goodbye kiss but rather to save his daughters from being kidnapped by Jacob. Laban's encirclement of the mountain (31:23), his claim

---

257 The reading of the verse, therefore, may also be understood as "And you did not leave/abandon me *in order for you* (Jacob) to kiss my sons and daughters."

258 As the record of births for Bethuel set out in 22:23 delineates only Rebekah, Laban apparently was not yet born at that time.

of refraining from inflicting harm on Jacob (31:29), and his later recorded fear of Jacob torturing his daughters (31:50), reflect Laban's genuine concerns that his daughters are not leaving with Jacob out of choice.[259]

The Terafim Trap

Had Laban's charge been limited to such familial issues, Jacob would have difficulty volleying back a winning argument without devastating Laban's emotional existence. Luckily for Jacob, though, Rachel had stolen the *terafim*. Laban's confidence in Jacob's guilt forces him to add one point too many to his list of accusations. From his speech, it is obvious that Laban is certain that Jacob took the *terafim*, as he charges Jacob personally with stealing them. Laban does not entertain other possibilities as to the identity of the thief or believe that someone had mistakenly packed away the *terafim* with the other belongings.

Jacob realizes that the *terafim* charge is serious and that the charge goes beyond the *terafim*. Laban has created a packaged argument. If Jacob had indeed stolen the *terafim*, he is a thief and Jacob will be guilty of stealing Laban's daughters and sheep as well. Laban will then take back everything that he believes is his—including the family and the wealth. Laban does not need to address the claim of Jacob stealing his sheep because the equation that Laban has set up includes them. It is precisely because he is so confident about the *terafim* charge that he bundles that powerful charge with the charge of stealing his daughters. Laban has calculated that he will be able

---

259 See, Ben-Barak, *Ha'arot Leparashat Nisuei Leah veRahel leYaakov al Reka Nehagim. MiMesopotamia* (notes to the episode of the wedding of Leah and Rachel to Jacob on the backdrop of Mesopotamian customs) (Hebrew), where she sets out that Laban's motivation to wed his two daughters to Jacob was the result of Laban's desire to expand his household. Her conclusion is based on the legal and financial norms as illustrated in the Nuzi documents. Local custom provided for the adoption of a son by way of marriage to one's natural daughter and dictated that the children of that union would become the recognized heirs of the woman's father. The adopted son was also usually forbidden to take additional wives to maintain the purity of the father's line. Thus, Ben-Barak's thesis supports the idea of Laban's plan for perpetual parenthood but from a legalistic and dynastic perspective as opposed to the emotional dimension laid out above. For a similar but less detailed understanding of Jacob's status by Laban, see Sarna, *Understanding Genesis: The World of the Bible in the Light of History* (New York: Schocken Books, 1966) (1970 first paperback edition), pgs. 195–196.

to return home not just with the stolen *terafim* but with his progeny (and sheep) as well.

Jacob's Response

> And Jacob responded and said to Laban: "For I was afraid for I said lest you steal your daughters from being with me." (31:31)

Jacob realizes that he must immediately counter Laban's charge of stealing his daughters by reversing the charge of theft against Laban. Jacob's initial response, therefore, is that he was afraid that Laban would steal his daughters away from him. Jacob here reveals that he understands Laban's threat of claiming back Jacob's wives, children, and wealth as real.[260] Jacob depicts his wives as being "with" him (and not like "prisoners of war"), and implies that if Laban takes them, he will be taking/stealing them "from" Jacob.

Jacob's response also addresses why Jacob leaves without telling Laban, for Jacob feared that had Laban been aware of his plans to leave, Laban may have "stolen" his daughters away from him. To recall, initially, this was not the case at all. It is only after Jacob hears Laban's claims that he feels this way. Initially, he was concerned about giving up sheep pursuant to Laban's sons' claims and in compliance with fulfilling God's command to travel towards his homeland.[261] Jacob does not elaborate on his longing for his father's home (if he longed for home at all), or God's talking to him or to Laban. He realizes that acknowledging any longing for his father's home or any divine command directed towards him alone would only be counter-productive, for as they do not involve his wives, these points do not address Laban's claim of leading his daughters away as prisoners of war. Instead, after stating his fear that Laban would steal from him, Jacob addresses the most looming charge of stealing Laban's gods.

---

260 The Septuagint adds that in Jacob's response to Laban in 31:31, he charges that Laban would not just steal his wives, but "everything of mine," thus indicating that Jacob understands the extent of Laban's true threat.

261 As Jacob was concerned about the claim of stolen sheep, he had a ready response for Laban. When Jacob retorts at Laban's unsuccessful search, his detailed reference to his loyalty as shepherd features prominently and may be part of Jacob's rehearsed response prepared prior to Laban catching up with them.

Jacob's sharp reply implies that he aptly perceives the severity of the theft charge. He therefore carefully diverts all possible connection from himself to an unknown third party upon whom he issues the death penalty.[262] Jacob, unreserved, declares: "With whomever you find your gods shall not live (31:32)." Having noticed Laban's stealing theme and foreseeing where it might lead, Jacob tells Laban that he should make his search not only for the *terafim* but for anything that Laban thinks is his—in front of witnesses. The presence of witnesses—"our brothers"—whom Jacob invites to join Laban—assures Jacob that Laban will not plant the *terafim* or any other item and then "find" it.

Laban will have to state his claim as he comes across the items or across the people he believes are his. This method will work to Jacob's advantage, for Laban is seeking to make a sequential claim. Laban seeks to first discover the *terafim* and then claim the sheep, his daughters, and children. Jacob's protocol denies Laban the ability to this sequential claim by demanding Laban make his claims as he happens upon the "stolen" item. Laban, who is focused on discovering the *terafim* first, is compelled to neglect his claim for sheep, daughters, and grandchildren, and is estopped from further raising such claims again later.

Laban's search is thorough. The text describes the process as starting with Jacob's tent, continuing to Leah's, and then the maids' tents, where Laban does not find anything. Only at the end does he search the tent of Rachel. Rachel takes the *terafim,* places them in the camel seat, and sits on them (31:34).[263] Probably sick from the prospect of being found out, and fearing the wrath of Laban as well as the execution of Jacob's pronounced death sentence, Rachel does not look her best. Therefore, her claim that she cannot rise due to the "way of women"—traditionally explained as either being pregnant and having morning sickness or menstruating—would be

---

262 Jacob's ignorance of Rachel's actions further contributes to the general thesis that family members did not necessarily share or communicate vital pieces of information with one another and further supports the new understanding presented above regarding the conjugal switch.

263 Rachel is sitting on the *terafim* while on the removed camel seat. From Rachel's apology to Laban about her inability to "rise" in her father's presence and not her failure to "descend" from the camel, it becomes clear she has dismounted the camel seat. She has removed the soft cushion part of the camel seat to sit on which allows for an unsuspicious puffy look.

quite believable.[264] Taking into account the emotional overload she is experiencing, even a physiological response of menstruation or nausea is not to be ruled out.

As opposed to the search that takes place in the other tents, Laban's search of Rachel's tent is even more thorough as he physically feels out the entire tent and yet does not find anything.[265] After Rachel says she cannot arise in Laban's honor, the text states that Laban makes yet another search that ends in futility. This seeming redundancy reveals that Laban conducts a second search throughout the camp and not just of all the tents.[266] Laban realizes that if he does not find the *terafim*, his entire plan will fail and he will be unable to justify a return of anything, and, more importantly, of anyone, to his home. As he fails to find the *terafim*, Laban's fear of abandonment begins to crystallize.

Upon Laban's failure to locate the *terafim*, Jacob's self-righteousness flares, for Laban has falsely accused him of a serious crime while simultaneously redefining their entire relationship of twenty years. Jacob neither allows the opportunity to pass nor enables Laban to extricate his way out of his predicament. Jacob is enraged and charges Laban:

> What is my iniquity and what is my sin that you chased me? For you have felt all my things—what have you found from all your household things? Place here! (31:36–37)

---

264 However, one may surmise that literarily, Rachel's "way of women" is a euphemism for treachery. The "women" may refer to Sarah and Rebekah who had assumed sister identities or Rebekah who had assisted Jacob in his usurping the blessings and promoting the ruse for Jacob's leaving to Haran.

265 Laban's search of the entire tent parallels the feeling out that Isaac had made years earlier when he felt (whose root in Hebrew is m.sh.sh 27:21-22) the goatskins on Jacob's arms and neck in a failed attempt to recognize who was seeking his blessing. Here too, the act of feeling (again the Hebrew root m.sh.sh 31:34) fails to reveal the identity of the thief. In both situations, it is the sense of touch that fails to gauge the situation. Such parallelism may also explain the failure of Jacob to uncover the conjugal switch through the sense of touch and can possibly attribute Laban's false accusations and confrontation here to divine retribution for Jacob's former misuse of touch when usurping the blessings.

266 In the latter search, the text makes mention of *the terafim* explicitly. In 31:33,34 the text states that Laban conducted a search and "did not find," but in verse 35 when Laban searches again throughout the camp the text reads, "And he searched and he did not find ***the terafim***."

Jacob's claim reduces all of Laban's previous accusations of stealing his daughters to a desire for only physical possessions—"household things." Laban's failed search speaks for itself.

Jacob's tirade continues:

> It is now twenty years that I am with you… I was there in the day—the parching heat ate me, and ice—in the night and my sleep wandered from my eyes. It is now twenty years that I am in your house. I worked fourteen years for your two daughters[267] and six years for your sheep. (31:38–41)

Jacob thus replies to Laban's claims of thievery with an account of his own loyalty and honest work.

Saving Face

Laban, refusing to admit defeat, pathetically responds:

> The daughters are *my* daughters and the sons are *my* sons and *the sheep* are *my* sheep and *everything that you see is mine.* And as for *my* daughters [whom I claim are mine], what can I do to them today or to their children whom they bore? (31:43)

Laban's misguided understanding of his relationship with his grandchildren, his daughters, and with Jacob, lead him to believe that everything is his.[268] His outburst of emotion tips his hand. If until now the issue of the sheep and wealth remained latent, it now bubbles to the surface from the depths of Laban's heart. Laban now explicitly mentions the sheep for the first time since catching up with Jacob. Embarrassed at his exposed greed, Laban seeks to downplay his material goals by quickly diverting attention back to the daughters and grandchildren, adding: "And as for my daughters, what can I do to them….?" (31:43). Laban delicately tries to extricate himself from his former claim that Jacob forced his daughters to accompany

---

267 Jacob leaves Laban to remember why that was the case without further elaboration in order not to be the one to expose the switch to the women.

268 Similar to Jacob's attribution to God, to the wives' response prior to leaving and to the claims of Laban's sons, Laban espouses the all or nothing attitude towards the wealth.

him. Laban now implies that he is powerless against their (poor) decisions: What is he to do to them today?

Laban also tones down his possessive declaration by switching his reference to the grandchildren from "his sons" to his "daughters' children." Yet, even at this point, Laban refers exclusively to his daughters and their children and omits Jacob from the equation, for he will never consider his son-in-law to be a part of his family.

Indeed, Laban's failure to find the *terafim*, coupled with the fact that neither his daughters nor his grandchildren graciously embrace and kiss him upon his arrival, is a clear indication to Laban that the warm relationship he believes he has with his family is just an illusion. Laban needs an elegant escape clause for not taking the sheep back, thus showing that he is gratuitously "giving" the sheep to Jacob as opposed to Jacob having earned them. The solution Laban devises is to enact a covenant between them. While the sheep receive no explicit mention, the covenant serves as witness that Laban claimed nothing back from the camp of Jacob.

As part of the covenant, Jacob takes a rock and erects a *matzevah*—a monument. Afterwards, he instructs his "brothers" to gather stones that they then place in a pile and they eat there.[269] In suit with Jacob and Laban's disagreement over ownership, even the pile of rocks, which is clearly Jacob's initiative but apparently put together by Laban (or his "brothers"), is a subject of dispute: Whose is it? Does it belong to Jacob or to Laban? Later, Laban states that *he* erected the pile of stones *and* the monument (31:51) even though Jacob erected the monument alone (31:45). This ambiguous state of ownership and facts befits the nature of a border in that both sides claim ownership. Similarly, there is competition surrounding the naming of the site as an indication of sovereignty. Each party gives the pile of stones a name in order to show sovereignty. Jacob gives his name based on Laban's utterance (31:48), while Laban names it the equivalent in Aramaic (31:47). As it eventually will serve as a border between the two, it is only fitting that each party should name their side of the border in their national vernacular.

---

269 Jacob may have instructed Laban's "brothers" to assemble a pile of rocks as representative of Laban's gods, while Jacob erects the *matzevah*—the monument of one rock representing Jacob's monotheistic belief.

Honoring Boundaries

> And Laban said: "This pile is witness between me and you today. That is why he called its name Galed (pile of testimony) and the Mitzpah (lookout point) for he said God should look out between me and you for we shall not see each other. If you afflict my daughters and if you take women in addition to my daughters, no man is amongst us, see, God is witness between me and you." And Laban said to Jacob, "Here is this pile and here is the monument that I erected between me and you. This pile shall be witness and this monument witness if I ever cross over to you over this pile and if you ever cross over to me passed this pile and this monument for evil. The God of Abraham, the god of Nahor shall judge between us, the gods of their fathers," and Jacob swore by the fear of his father Isaac. And Jacob offered sacrifice at the mountain and called his brothers to eat bread and they ate bread and slept at the mountain. (31:48–54)

Laban initially wanted the pile to represent something other than just a border, and takes Jacob aside after the formal and public declaration naming the pile of rocks as Gal-ed in order to procure a particular promise from Jacob.[270] Laban continues to worry about his daughters and asks Jacob to enter a covenant in which God will bear witness that Jacob will neither abuse his daughters nor take other women as wives. Laban's statement concerning Jacob not afflicting his daughters harkens back to his initial claim of Jacob taking his daughters away as captives of the sword. Laban insinuates here that he still views his daughters as Jacob's prisoners of war. It is another subtle way in which Laban tries to save face.

However, Jacob does not respond to Laban's proposal. Jacob *has* taken other women as wives. He has married Bilhah and Zilpah at the request of Rachel and Leah, yet *Laban is unaware of this switch of the maids' status.* Laban most likely would have objected to these marriages had he known

---

270 A number of different points can adduce their being alone. Firstly, note how the text separates Laban's public proclamation from his secluded statement to Jacob (contrast 31:48 to 31:51). Secondly, Jacob needs to call his "brothers" to eat with them as recorded in 31:54, implying that they were no longer present. Finally, and most conclusively, Laban states (31:50) that: "no man is amongst us, see, God is witness between me and you" illustrating that he has taken Jacob aside.

his daughters were voluntarily abdicating their monopoly on their matron status to further their sisterly competition.[271]

Laban realizes that something is wrong and suggests a new proposal (31:51). He now transforms the purpose of the pact to the clan-national level as opposed to protecting his daughters. Laban suggests that neither shall pass this point to inflict harm on each other. Laban perhaps fears later reprisal for the conjugal switch, the possible sheep/wage switch, and the current false charges. He refers to his earlier threat of doing harm, which in public he retracted to endear his family to him, but now reiterates to Jacob (31:52): "If I ever cross over to you over this pile and if you ever cross over to me passed this pile and this monument for *evil* [purposes]."[272] At this juncture, Laban acknowledges that Jacob is as capable of inflicting harm as he is. Additionally, Laban had previously only retracted his statement concerning his ability to harm his daughters and grandchildren. This covenant expresses Laban's commitment not to do Jacob harm as well.

Laban further exclaims that the God of Abraham, the god of Nahor, and the god of their fathers (as encapsulated by the pile of rocks) shall be named arbiters regarding their covenant. Jacob swears by the fear of his father Isaac (as represented by the *matzevah*), an option not offered by Laban.[273] Jacob's ability to initiate a new option reflects his newfound power as an independent entity and demonstrates that he no longer needs to seek his uncle's/ father-in-law's approval.

Mentioning his father's fear may reflect Jacob's intention to return to his father's home and serves as a retort to Laban's earlier ridicule of Jacob's longing for his father's home. As Laban pits father against father, Jacob now heralds Isaac as the triumphant father. Jacob now rejoins by opting to have the God of Isaac judge them even though Laban deliberately

---

271 This understanding contributes to the impression of general silence between family members on material matters. It also explains why the text refers to Bilhah only once as Jacob's *pilegesh*—concubine. This occurs when Reuben sleeps with her (35:22). The text is apparently recording Reuben's understanding of her status.

272 Cf. 31:29: "I have the power [lit. God has my hand] to do with you *evil*."

273 It is not clear whether Jacob's reference is to the source of Isaac's fear—God—such that Isaac's God will judge between them or if this refers to the fear Isaac himself lives—the fear of death—such that Jacob swears by fear of death not to violate the pact.

omitted any mention of Isaac as an option in an attempt to delegitimize Isaac's standing. [274]

In his last effort to save face, Laban arises early to make sure no one runs off before he has the chance to kiss his grandchildren and daughters. Laban wants to give the impression that this is all he wanted in the first place. He blesses them,[275] and then, although he had arrived with "his brothers" (31:23,25,32), he returns "to *his* place" alone (32:1). Laban's "lonely" state represents the "empty nest" that Laban sought to avoid and hence he does not return "home" but to "his place."[276]

Jacob can now return to Canaan without feeling pursued by Laban. Jacob has succeeded in taking the "home" from Haran with him. His successful disentanglement from Laban provides Jacob with the hope and confidence to reenact the same outcome with Esau.

---

274 As a closing to the covenant, the text records that Jacob offered an animal sacrifice on the mountain and called his brothers to eat bread (31:54). Such an action is puzzling. If Jacob offered an animal sacrifice, why is he calling on his "brothers" to eat bread rather than partake of the meat sacrifice? Furthermore, the text already stated nine verses earlier that the brothers "ate on the pile of rocks" (31:46). Why is Jacob conducting a second meal—didn't everyone just eat? By offering an animal sacrifice in Laban's presence, Jacob is exerting uncontested dominion over the flock. Similarly, the parties do not eat the meat, as that may imply that Laban has some entitlement to part of the sheep. Jacob's uncontested ownership of the flocks is now celebrated. The eating of bread is also symbolic of Jacob's dominion over the land on his side of the border and not called on for any nutritional value. Thus, the sacrifice and bread serve a ceremonious and symbolic function and not a dietary one. The parties then sleep on the mountain in order to establish that the chase is over and that no one is stealthily leaving.

275 This parallels Laban's blessing of Rebekah years earlier before her departure (24:60). Laban's blessing "them" may or may not include Jacob.

276 The sudden disappearance of Laban's "brothers" can be attributed to their leaving earlier when they finished the feast with only Laban remaining until the next morning, having a hard time saying goodbye, and in order to give a goodbye kiss to the children. The "brothers" may also have been accompanying Laban as military reinforcement and only remained on the scene in the event of Laban fighting Jacob as Laban initially projects. As the fight never occurs they go back to their own homes and do not have any continuing connection to Laban. In that case, the use of the word "*ahim*"—brothers—would thus carry with it the possible meaning of "allies."

Looking back, Jacob's exit from Haran represents more than his freedom from the materialism of the region but also represents an unshackling from Laban's emotional hold over him. Jacob's vigilance in maintaining possession of his sheep and his adherence to the divine command to return home thwart Laban's long-term plans of perpetual parenthood. Jacob's readiness to leave Haran behind, even if it means facing Esau, prevents Laban from usurping Jacob's own identity as father and husband.

Jacob is now ready to reunite with Esau. While still afraid,[277] his experience at Haran and his confrontation with his "brother" Laban provide him with a sense of coming into his own. As Jacob has become his own man of the field, he can finally jettison the vicarious trappings of Esau that he has emotionally carried since usurping the blessings. The fire of Jacob and the straw of Esau must now meet.

---

277 Jacob's newfound freedom and confidence are somewhat stifled as he comes to the realization that he will have to reenter the territory he left in favor of Esau years ago. His latent fears of being pursued by Esau now come to the fore. Emotionally, Jacob picks up where he left off as if no time had intervened. As his inner tension mounts, he encounters messengers of God and Jacob names the place "*machanayim*," meaning "double-camp"—his camp and God's.

CHAPTER SIX

Jacob and Esau: The Final Struggle for Space

*You gain strength, courage, and confidence by every experience
in which you really stop to look fear in the face... The danger lies
in refusing to face the fear, in not daring to come to grips with
it... You must make yourself succeed every time. You must do the
thing you think you cannot do.*

                                  ~ Eleanor Roosevelt

Jacob is not the same man he was when he left his father's home twenty
years earlier. His experience with Laban in Haran has bolstered his sense
of self-worth, and he is now ready to reunite with his estranged brother.
Indeed, after more than twenty years of self-inflicted separation, Jacob
and Esau seem mysteriously drawn to one another like a set of oppositely
charged magnets.

However, Jacob's strong desire to reunite with his brother is not without fears. His greatest concern is that Esau will destroy his entire family
as soon as he encounters them.[278] Jacob recalls all too well Esau's burning
hatred of him when Jacob usurped his father's blessing. He perceives the
imminent meeting as one of potential danger[279] and therefore does not seek
to enter Canaan unnoticed or to surprise Esau and his parents[280] with his
return. Ignoring Esau or going forward unannounced would be a social

---

278 This fear becomes evident from 32:8–13.
279 See Alter, *The Five Books of Moses*, pg. 177, comment on verse 7.
280 At this point, absent the Midrash HaGadol referenced below, there is no indication
that Jacob is aware of his father and/or mother being alive.

and political faux pas, and the inevitable discovery of Jacob's reentry would expose him to danger before having a chance to make amends.[281] Jacob, therefore, decides that he must initiate contact with Esau.[282]

Jacob's Message

With that purpose in mind, Jacob sends messengers to Esau "toward the land of Seir the field of Edom" (32:4).[283] Jacob decides that he should veil his greeting in terms of the material wealth Isaac's blessings conferred. He chooses not to relay any information about his wives and children,[284] as they are not part of their argument over the blessings.[285] The blessings under dispute are those relating to physical plenty and superiority (27:28–29), and not the Abrahamic blessing of being fruitful and inheriting the

---

281 Jacob's experience in Laban's home reinforced his philosophy that "space equals life." Since Esau had not chased him to Laban's home, Jacob internalized that the physical distance from Esau provided him with safety. Thus, Jacob cannot afford to arrive home and collide with Esau without endangering himself and his family.

282 Hence, Jacob is recorded as sending messengers "before him," preemptively, to his brother Esau. Alternatively, Jacob is planning on confronting Esau in Seir and hence sends messengers "before him" heralding forth his arrival (Cf. 1 Kings 1:5). When the brothers reconcile outside of Seir, Jacob no longer has the need to go forward with his travel plans and postpones his intended visit indefinitely.

283 See A. Korman, *HaParasha LeDoroteha*, pg. 162, citing the Midrash HaGadol that posits that the divine messengers Jacob encountered in 32:2 were none other than Rebekah's messengers (ref. 27:45) and fighters sent to assist Jacob against Esau. Korman suggests that they provided Jacob with information about Esau's general whereabouts. However, regardless of whether Rebekah sent them, the text does not delineate the purpose or message of the divine messengers, as would be the norm for the appearance of a divine being in the Bible (informing of an upcoming birth, saving someone, renaming, etc.). This silence allows for speculation as to their divine role and allows for Korman's inference.

284 A different approach will be presented in Chapter Seven.

285 If Jacob were to begin where he and Esau left off twenty years earlier, Jacob would probably offer an apology for usurping the blessings. However, that would display weakness, expose Jacob to Esau's potentially dangerous vengeance, and reveal that this episode is at the forefront of his thoughts.

land (28:3–4).[286] Yet, if Jacob specifies the robust material bounty that God blessed him with at Haran, Esau may again become jealous of Jacob's good fortune, and such specification may rekindle the smoldering coals of Esau's rage. As Esau ostensibly does not yet know of Jacob's wealth, Jacob chooses to mention the types of wealth he possesses in an ambiguous way. In Hebrew, the word used to depict the types of wealth Jacob mentions can refer to a single member or to many members of that group. Given this ambiguity, Esau may take Jacob's message as describing the singular and the description may arouse the pity/sympathy that Jacob seeks to evoke. Jacob's initial message is as follows:

> So said your servant Jacob, "With Laban I sojourned and I have tarried until now. And there was to me an ox and a donkey, a sheep and a slave and a maid and I sent to tell my master in order to find favor in your eyes." (32:5–6)

Aside from the ambiguity about the number of animals and slaves, Jacob introduces another ambiguity when he states that the purpose of sending the messengers with his message is to "find favor" in his eyes. The terminology of "finding favor" in one's eyes carries an expectation that the person who is trying to find favor is going to ask for something in return.[287] When someone wants to ask for something, the usual syntax is written in the past tense: "If I have found favor in your eyes,"[288] if I have found favor in your eyes until now, then please do such and such. However, as opposed to the other biblical instances of this phrase, Jacob's message "to find favor

---

286 Jacob received the Abrahamic blessing from Isaac before leaving Haran without masquerading as Esau. Jacob's omission of his wives and children taken together with his "sojourning" by Laban, leaves Jacob without "land" and without "offspring." Thus, Jacob is also indicating to Esau that even the Abrahamic blessing of being fruitful and inheriting land has not materialized. In addition, the omission of the wives and children may reflect a vestige of the Haran philosophy focusing solely on material possessions.

287 See, for example, Genesis 19:19, 34:11, Exodus 33:13, 33:17, Esther 8:5 and see, *Concordance Even-Shoshan*, pgs. 382–383, where Even-Shoshan cites over twenty such examples.

288 See *Concordance Even-Shoshan*, ibid.

in your eyes" uses the infinitive form and implies that Jacob wants to find favor in Esau's eyes *in the future.*[289]

Jacob, however, has omitted what it is that he wants Esau to do for him, so Esau (and the reader) is left to interpret Jacob's expectations. Esau also must wonder what the nexus is between Jacob listing his possessions and Jacob's desire to find favor in his eyes.

In analyzing Jacob's message, Esau receives two facts and two attitudinal descriptions.

Two facts:

1. Jacob was delayed by Laban, meaning he was "late"[290] until now.
2. He has animals and slaves.

Two attitudinal descriptions:

1. Jacob relays that he is Esau's servant and Esau is his master.
2. He sends the messengers/the message to find favor in Esau's eyes.

Attempting to correlate the facts with the remainder of the message, Esau may consider Jacob's message and his request to find favor in his eyes as a call for assistance. Jacob is now traveling with his animals and slaves and may want his brother's protection in his travels home. This understanding would better explain Esau's later offer that he or his men accompany Jacob's camp (33:12–16). Esau presumes his inference to be correct and journeys northward to rendezvous with Jacob and his camp.

---

289 In the Bible, only Jacob makes use of this conjugation (32:6, 33:8). The only similar ambiguous request to find favor while not explicitly asking for something is seen by Laban: "If I have found favor in your eyes, I have divinated and God has blessed me because of you" (30:27). There, Laban wants Jacob to figure out on his own what he is trying to say without his having to spell it out. Laban cannot yet bring himself to offer Jacob a figurative blank check. When Jacob fails/refuses to play along, Laban needs to expose his utter vulnerability and need of Jacob. The parallel suggests that just as Laban wanted Jacob to fill in the gaps of his request before starting a new era with Jacob, so too Jacob may desire that Esau fill in the gaps of his request before their relationship embarks on a new era.

290 The wordplay on *va'ehar*—"and I tarried"—also contributes to the theme of Esau being first and Jacob being "after"—*aharei* that will be discussed later on.

Space Equals Life: Jacob's Response

Jacob's messengers return and relay the news to Jacob that Esau is coming to greet him and that he has 400 men with him.[291] Jacob is taken aback by Esau's response. Apparently, Jacob's message was not meant to elicit accompaniment and the large number of Esau's entourage troubles him.[292] The text relays that Jacob had mixed emotions: "And Jacob was very frightened and he was distressed—*veyetzer lo*" (32:8). Grammatically, *vayetzer* derives from *tzar*—meaning narrow.[293] In other words, Jacob's fear translates into his feeling enclosed and cramped for space as Esau's men approach.[294]

Dividing the Wealth

The impact of this "cramping" is that Jacob feels the need to become even more expansive horizontally in order to garner the strength needed to meet Esau and overcome his own feeling of narrowness. However, he does not want Esau to feel threatened by this vastness. Similarly, as will be seen when Jacob presents spacious gifts to Esau, he attempts to give the impression that he is presenting Esau with something that will add physical volume to Esau's camp while diminishing his own. In order to achieve both these goals—expanding while appearing non-threatening—Jacob divides his wealth so that Esau would only see one group at any time.[295]

> And Jacob was very frightened and he was distressed. And he split the people with him and the sheep and the cattle and camels into two

---

291 The terminology "*holekh likrat*"—walking towards—appears here and by Isaac meeting Rebekah (24:65) implying a non-military encounter. On the other hand, the fact that Esau comes with 400 fighters presents the possibility of a military encounter. See Sarna, JPS, pg. 224 and Alter, *The Five Books of Moses*, pg. 177 comment on 32:7). Jacob apparently adopts the latter understanding while Esau's intentions are not clear.

292 What Jacob really sought from Esau will only become apparent later, as analyzed in Chapter Seven.

293 See *Concordance Even-Shoshan* relating the word to the root tz.r.r. and meaning "narrow."

294 On another level, such cramping represents a regression to Jacob's childhood tent enclosure. Jacob feared that uniting with Esau might thrust him back to the old family settings with him a recluse and Isaac, if alive, favoring Esau.

295 I offer a different approach to this issue in Chapter Seven.

camps. And he said: "If Esau will come to the one camp and he will strike it, the remaining camp will survive." (32:8–9)

Jacob's Prayer

Jacob also responds to the news of Esau's approach by praying to God for deliverance from his brother Esau. Reading Jacob's prayer will help highlight a number of points:

> And Jacob said: "The Lord of my father Abraham and the Lord of my father Isaac, God who has said to me, 'Return to your land and your birthplace and I will deal with you favorably.' I have been dwarfed by all of the kindness and by all of the loyalty that you have done with your servant. For with my stick I crossed this Jordan, and now I have become two camps. Please, save me from the hand of my brother, from the hand of Esau, because I am afraid of him, that he might come and strike me, mother with sons. And You said, 'I will surely deal favorably with you and I will set your seed like the sand by the sea, so plentiful that they cannot be counted.'"(32:10–13)

Stick and Sand

In his prayer, Jacob refers to his humble beginnings and his current good fortune. He references the value of his possessions but does so in terms of space, "For with my stick I crossed this Jordan and now I have become two camps…And I will set your seed like the sand by the sea" (32:11–13). Jacob mentions his beginnings as a man with a stick compared to the two camps that he now encompasses. The picture that comes to mind is one of Jacob spreading out from a stick figure to one of great volume. This growth is also a factor in the diminution of space between Jacob and Esau. As Jacob grows, the space between him and Esau grows smaller and magnifies the danger of eventual collision.

In addition to the stick figure description that Jacob uses in his prayer, he also refers to God's promise that he would become like the sands of the sea. The grains of sand, in addition to being numerous, highlight the idea of vastness and spreading out over space. The sand medium thus relates a blessing of space to accompany Jacob's new numbers.[296]

Seeking Atonement for the Past

In Jacob's prayer, Jacob asks God to save him from the hands of his brother Esau. One can learn from Jacob's prayer that his fear stems from the episode of the blessings. There, Jacob took Esau's place when he usurped Esau's identity and took his physical space to receive Isaac's blessing. As will be seen, Jacob now feels that he must allow Esau to take some of the "space" he currently occupies in order to make amends for his earlier violation. Jacob's preoccupation with this past episode—and his wish to atone for it—seeps through to his words and actions. For example, in Isaac's declaration preceding the giving of the blessings, Isaac had misidentified Jacob's disguised hands as the hands of Esau, as he states, "And the hands are the hands of Esau" (27:22). Jacob now references this declaration when asking God to save him from "the *hand* of my brother, the *hand* of Esau." He thus prays that God save him from the retribution expected from Esau for the usurping of the blessings and for his former misrepresentation of Esau's hands.[297]

An additional throwback to that episode emerges from other wordplay employed in this section. The text relates that Jacob prepared a *minhah*, a gift offering, for Esau. However, when Jacob later finally meets up with Esau and beseeches Esau to take the gifts, he switches *minhati,* my gift offering, with *birkhati,* my blessing, "And Jacob said, "Please don't, if I have found favor in your eyes, take this tribute (*minhati*) from my hand....Please take my blessing (*birkhati*) that has been brought to you" (33:10-11). Jacob's (intentional?)

---

296 A similar divine emphasis on Jacob's spreading out and an association between dust and space can be seen in God's earlier address to Jacob when fleeing from Esau. 28:14 records: "And your seed shall be like the dust of the earth and you shall burst forth to the west and the east and the north and the south." The need to feel like sand may be Jacob's reaction to feeling cramped and narrow before his meeting with Esau.

297 See *Sefat Emet* on the beginning of Vayishlah who references this point as well. Similarly, Klitsner, *Wrestling with Jacob,* pg. 74 also mentions this parapraxis.

slip of the tongue reveals that he views the gifts offered to Esau as a restoration of the blessings he usurped years earlier.[298]

Similarly, when Jacob later sends more messengers[299] to bring Esau gifts of animals (32:14–21), a guised apology appears in the message. Assuming that Jacob intended that the messengers relay everything he said, the message includes the following statement: "For I said I shall cover over his [angry] face with the gift going before me and afterwards I will see his face, perhaps he will favor my face" (32:21). Regardless of whether this exact statement reaches Esau's ears, it is clear to the reader that Jacob feels that he needs Esau's forgiveness. Thus, after twenty years, Jacob is the one engrossed in the episodes of the past between the brothers, with the need for space driving much of his actions.

Spread Out and Split Up

Jacob tries to get some sleep, but awakes in the middle of the night to send convoys of gifts to Esau in order to soften the moment of impact and create a buffer zone between the camps. The gift convoys represent the belongings of Jacob melding with and transforming into the belongings of Esau. Jacob thus surrenders the space this wealth occupies in favor of Esau. In an additional number of ways, the gifts themselves also take on the theme of space.

Firstly, Jacob sends numerous emissaries instead of one group of messengers. Secondly, he stresses to his messengers to literally "make space" between each flock: "And space make between flock and between flock" (32:17). Thirdly, Jacob anticipates that Esau will query, "Where do you go?" (32:18), in order to ensure that the convoys will not encroach on his territory, which is a spatial concern. Finally, the message each group is to convey to Esau is made in spatial terms—Jacob is "behind" us.

The result of the spacing of these gifts is a magnification of the space Jacob's camp occupies. The purpose of this magnification is to send a dual message to Esau. On the one hand, the gifts will enlarge Esau's camp by adding volume to Esau horizontally. By doing so, Jacob is voluntarily

---

298 See Michael Fishbane, *Text and Texture* (New York: Schocken Books, 1979) pg. 52; Alter, *The Five Books of Moses*, pg. 185 note on verse 11 and Klitsner, *Wrestling with Jacob*, pg. 73 for a similar idea.

299 These messengers are a second round of messengers. The first round had already returned with the message of Esau's imminent approach with 400 men (32:7).

diminishing his own space while simultaneously enlarging Esau's. On the other hand, it also demonstrates to Esau how voluminous Jacob has become and reveals that he no longer is the limited tent dweller that he was in his youth.

In assessing Jacob's preparations for meeting Esau, it is important to keep track of the order of Jacob's actions. To review, after Jacob first sends messengers and hears back that Esau is approaching, Jacob splits his camp into two in the hopes of saving one camp. Afterwards, Jacob prays to God to save him from imminent doom (32:1–13). When he tries to sleep, he awakens to prepare and send the gifts for Esau (32:14–21). He later tries to go back to sleep but again wakes up (32:22). This time, Jacob fears the worst. He is disquieted by the thought that Esau may attack him and his family during the night and obliterate the camp. As Esau's twin, Jacob may sense his brother's approaching presence. As a result, in what seems like a sudden panic, he crosses the Jabbok ford in the middle of the night with his entire family and belongings (32:22–24).[300]

The Jabbok tributary creates a division and a splitting between the two masses of land on the sides of the stream. The very name Jabbok has the "bak" sound in it as in: "*vaybaka atzei olah*" (22:3)—he split the wood for the offering; "*vayibaku hamayim*" (Exodus 14:21)—and the waters split. This splitting and dividing result in further separation and allow the same items to occupy more space. Yet, the Jabbok does not just separate physically, but rather serves as a figurative demarcation point in Jacob's life as well. As will be shown below, when Jacob crosses over the Jabbok, the various elements of his life also separate from their pre-crossing history.

Once Jacob crosses his family over to the southern side of the Jabbok, he remains alone on the northern side.[301] Jacob becomes vulnerable once he is alone. Alone, he has no volume. Alone, he is but a man with a stick—a stick figure. He thus returns in time to the same position and volume he assumed immediately after the blessings episode.[302] Jacob relives his doubts. For years, he has wondered what would have happened had he confronted

---

300   Jacob's movements will be studied further in Chapter Seven.
301   This puzzling move will be more thoroughly analyzed in Chapter Seven.
302   See also, *The Jewish Study Bible,* Berlin, Brettner, and Fishbane, eds., pg. 67 note to verses 23–25, where this point is also mentioned.

Esau instead of escaping to Laban's home. To recall, even after usurping the blessings, Jacob did not plan to leave home. Jacob, ostensibly, was ready to deal with his angry brother. It is only after Rebekah requests that Jacob leave, and orchestrates Isaac's commissioning of Jacob to find himself a non-Hittite wife, that Jacob leaves to Haran. As we fast-forward twenty years ahead, the imminent meeting with Esau will unavoidably present Jacob with a belated answer to his quandaries about remaining at home and confronting Esau.

Momentous Struggle

Still on the northern side of the Jabbok, Jacob begins to wrestle, literally "to kick up dirt," with a mysterious foe. While the text indicates that the mysterious man initiated the physical wrestling, the text does not indicate *why* the two are struggling or how the struggle began.

Again, the need for space unlocks the mystery of the episode. The word choice employed by the text for their struggle is "*vayeavek,*" to kick up dirt, yet it can also mean that they are fighting over the dirt itself. Therefore, the two are fighting to literally "gain ground" from one another. The theme of sand, mentioned earlier in Jacob's prayer, implies that the fight is also over who will succeed in being voluminous like the dust.[303] For Jacob, it is the ultimate battle over occupying space, claiming space, and letting go.

The Midrash[304] relates an opinion that the mysterious man is the heavenly guardian of Esau. Along these lines, and as pointed out by traditional commentaries,[305] the struggle can be symbolic of Jacob's struggle with Esau, personally or nationally.

On a personal level, Jacob's struggle with his foe symbolizes the outcome of the struggle which Jacob desires with Esau.[306] In support of this idea, one

---

303 This understanding imparts the word *vayeavek* with the added layer of each party "becoming like *avak*—dust"—and not simply struggling.

304 Genesis Rabbah 78:3.

305 Rashi, Rashbam, Radak, and Rabbi Levi Ben Gershon (hereinafter: Ralbag) all commenting on Genesis 32:25.

306 On a national level, the sending of messengers to Edom, Esau's approach towards Jacob with 400 men, and Jacob backing off, parallels the description of Moses sending emissaries to Edom, Edom rejecting the peace proposal and responding by amassing forces to the Edomite border and Israel backing away, as relayed in Numbers 20:14–21.

may reference Rabbi Moses Ben Maimon (hereinafter: Maimonides)[307] and Ralbag[308] who opine that the struggle occurred in Jacob's prophetic dream. This dream, as Ralbag further states, is the result of the thoughts occupying Jacob's mind regarding Esau.[309] The struggle with the man results with Jacob emerging injured but undefeated. Jacob is now profoundly aware that Rebekah's concern of losing both Jacob and Esau on the same day (27:45) need not materialize. Both can leave the struggle alive before the fire-straw dynamic takes hold. However, the meeting must be limited in time and injury may still occur, as in Jacob's brief entanglement with the mysterious man.

Prior to disengaging from the struggle, Jacob insists that the mysterious man bless him.[310] The blessing granted is in the form of changing Jacob's name to "Israel," a symbolic transformation in which Jacob succeeds in shedding his past identity as the one who usurped the blessings from Isaac. Indeed, when Esau discovered that Jacob had usurped the blessings, he cried out referring to Jacob's name as implying trickery. In contrast, the name "Israel" reverses the charge as it implies being "*yashar*," straight, as well as being an officer—"*sar*"—someone in a superior position. Thus, as stated above, the crossing of the Jabbok not only separates Jacob from his family physically but also symbolizes a relational split within Jacob's own identity.

---

307 Moreh Nevukhim, Chapter 43, Part One.

308 Commenting on Genesis 32:25.

309 See also Talmud B., *Berakhot* 55b: "Rabbi Shemuel Bar Nahmani said in the name of Rabbi Jonathan: 'They do not show to a person [a dream] other than from the inner workings of his heart.'"

310 Perhaps this reference also recalls the specter of Jacob's fears prior to masquerading as Esau. There, he also was concerned that Isaac would curse him rather than bless him. This would imply that the mysterious foe does not only symbolize Esau but Isaac as well. The renaming that later takes place is thus carried out by the father figure who originally named him (ref. 25:26) and would represent Jacob's desire that his father would have named him and raised him differently. The name Jacob, representing being behind or crooked, leaves Jacob with feelings of rejection and secondary importance to Isaac whose love was not forthcoming. Jacob wishes that Isaac bless him as being Israel, straight (y. s. r.) and important, recognizing his intrinsic value. The mysterious man's request to be released would symbolize Isaac telling Jacob to cease his quest for his father's elusive love and accept things the way they are. Jacob refuses, and in his persistence succeeds in forcing a new reality where his feelings are legitimized, recognized, and maybe even reciprocated. A yet different approach will be presented in Chapter Seven.

Finally Letting Go

The struggle with the mysterious man ends without a clear victor. Dawn breaks and the mysterious man asks to be freed. The dawn represents a new beginning. Jacob realizes that he can endure a meeting with Esau without meeting destruction. He realizes that he is entitled to occupy his own space and volume without living in the shadow of the usurped blessings where he needed to occupy someone else's space. Thus, in order to emerge from Esau's shadow, symbolized by the night, and allow the new beginning to commence, the brothers' clash for space must end by separation.

The need for separation from the mysterious foe mirrors the wrestling between Jacob and Esau in the womb. The birthing of Jacob and Esau heralded a new dawn when they emerged from the darkness of the womb and entered into the light of the world. That exit also called for their physical separation. Just as in birth, Jacob would not let go of Esau, so, too, in the current wrestling, Jacob would not let go of the mysterious man. Now, Jacob will only release the struggle for space if blessed. Such a blessing would serve as atonement for his usurping the blessings when Jacob took Esau's "space" before his father years earlier. In addition, Jacob's leg injury is his atonement for attempting to reverse the natural order at birth by holding on to Esau's heel. By receiving the blessing from the man and then releasing him, Jacob is enacting his desired script for his meeting with Esau. Jacob hopes that Esau will leave to make space for him while blessing the current space that he occupies. Jacob is determined to finally let go of Esau's heel and accept his own space and his own blessing.[311]

Jacob's stamina in his struggle with the mysterious foe can be attributed to his enhanced self-worth following his interaction with Laban. He now feels strong enough to let go of being Esau and to go on being Jacob. Jacob demonstrates that when we relinquish that which we think defines us, we discover our true self.

---

311   See Klitsner, *Wrestling with Jacob*, pgs. 123–143 for a close reading of this passage. Klitsner notes that Jacob's wrestling is an internal struggle and that Jacob's affirming his name as Jacob when asked by the man for his current name serves as a reversal of Jacob's denial of his identity as Jacob and the usurping of Esau's identity by the blessings episode. A different approach will be presented in chapter Seven.

Face to Face

Soon after Jacob completes his wrestling match, he rejoins his family and sees Esau and his men approaching. Jacob's thoughts shift to red alert. In possible preparation for flight, and in an effort to increase his camp's "space," Jacob splits the family into groups, but does not separate them from himself. Again, Jacob magnifies his household by creating groups, and again, the text relates the matter in terms of space and spatial relations: "And he placed the maids and their children *first* and Leah and her children *next* [literally, 'last'] and Rachel and Joseph *next* [literally, 'last']. And he passed *before* them" (33:1–3).

As opposed to only splitting the wealth into camps, as occurred prior to the crossing (32:8), now that all have crossed the Jabbok, Jacob also splits his family into camps (33:1). The physical divisions that take place after they cross the Jabbok reflect a relational split within the family as well: Jacob groups the children respectively with their mothers, with Rachel and Joseph getting preferential treatment by being last both in their initial set-up and in the order of their bowing before Esau.[312] Jacob's favoritism certainly does not go unnoticed.

In describing Esau's running, embracing, and kissing Jacob, the text parallels the beginning of the struggle between the mysterious man and Jacob. Esau, like the mysterious man, initiates the physical connection. Yet, his behavior also hints that Esau has another issue woven into the struggle. For Esau, the struggle is not only for space but also for precedence—who is first? Esau was born first, married first, and bore children first. Later, he will obtain political power and establish a dynasty first. At birth, Jacob held Esau's heel and impinged on Esau being clearly "first." Jacob's success in usurping the blessings was due to Esau's failure to arrive first in front of his father. Jacob not only usurped the blessings but also usurped Esau's "first" status before his father. Indeed, upon discovering Jacob's deception with the birthright, Esau did not only cry because he felt cheated anew by the blessings, but because throughout his life, Jacob had perpetually usurped him of his "first" status. Just as the mysterious man was first to initiate the wrestling, Esau wants to be the first to hug, to kiss, and to forgive.[313]

---

312 Cf. Rashi commenting on 33:2: "The very last is the most liked."

313 In his earlier message to Esau, Jacob shows awareness of, and sensitivity to, Esau's desire to be first by ordering his messengers to inform Esau that Jacob is behind them. By doing so, Jacob promotes Esau's "first" status, as Esau is always "ahead" of Jacob (32:19).

With all players in their proper space, Jacob bows towards the quickly approaching Esau, shortening the distance between them. His approach is a cautious one, as the moment of imminent impact is fraught with the possibility of danger.[314]

Esau invades Jacob's space when he hugs him. Tellingly, the text does not record Jacob as returning Esau's hug. The text then records that Esau kisses Jacob. Again, Jacob does not reciprocate, "And Esau *ran* towards him and he *hugged* him and he *fell* on his necks and he *kissed* him and they *cried*" (33:4). The masoretic tradition records that there are a series of dots over the word *vayishakehu*—"and he kissed him." In trying to explain the need for the dots, the Midrash presents differing opinions as to whether Esau's kiss is a sincere one or an attempt to bite Jacob's neck and kill him.[315] This disagreement and Jacob's non-mutuality embodies the very essence of the moment of impact. At that moment, it is difficult for the brothers to maintain the emotional stability necessary to sustain a sincere kiss in face of the constant fire-straw dynamic. As Esau locks Jacob in an embrace, the fire of the house of Jacob begins to overtake Esau and transforms the warm reunion into a conflagration, the sincere kiss into a deadly bite.

The only verb the text assigns to both brothers is that of crying—the result of a mixed outpouring of emotion. On the one hand, the brothers are relieved to be reunited after so many years of separation. On the other hand, both Jacob and Esau are forced now to relinquish their personal space during this intense brotherly reunion, and acknowledge in anguish that their brotherly union cannot endure without strife because of the fire-straw dichotomy in which they are both gripped.

---

314 Esau's actions also mirror a previous interaction between the twins—Esau's succinct actions at the sale of the birthright. Five successive actions: "And Esau *ran* towards him and he *hugged* him and he *fell* on his necks and he *kissed* him and they *cried*" parallels: "And he *ate* and he *drank* and *arose* and he *went* and Esau *despised* the birthright." This parallel, as well as Jacob allowing Esau his place as "first," indicate that the reconciliation occurring is meant not just to atone for the usurping of the blessings but for all the possibly negative Jacob-Esau interactions.

315 Genesis Rabbah 78:9.

Maintaining Space

> "Who to you is all this camp that I met?" And he said, "To find favor in the eyes of my lord." And Esau said, "I have a lot, my brother, be for you what you have." And Jacob said, "Please don't, if I have found favor in your eyes, take this tribute from my hand, for because of this I have greeted your face as one might greet God's face, and you will accept me. Please take my blessing that has been brought to you, for God has favored me and I have everything." And he insisted, and he took it. And he said, "Let us travel and go, and I shall walk before you." And he said, "My lord knows that the children are tender and the nursing sheep and cattle are my burden, and if they are pressed onward one day, all the sheep will die. Let my lord now pass on before his servant, and I will meander along at my own slow pace, at the heels of the animals before me and at the heels of the children, until I will come to my lord in Seir." (33:8–14)

After their embrace and Jacob's introduction of his family, Esau asks Jacob about the gift convoy that Esau identifies as a "camp": "Who to you is all this camp that I met?"(33:8). Since Esau's question is "who," Jacob's answer should then be that they are "x." Jacob should have replied that they are a gift to Esau from his possessions and wealth. Instead, Jacob seemingly answers the question that Esau did not ask. He answers "why" he sent the gifts—"in order to find favor in the eyes of my lord." Why does Jacob choose to answer Esau in this manner? The spatial theme explored above helps decipher this puzzling interaction.

Esau's query of "who to you is all this camp" is to be understood in terms of space. Esau keenly observed the dual message the camps embodied. From one perspective, Jacob is now a voluminous force and thus the "gifts" are a veiled threat. From another perspective, the gifts enlarge Esau's camp while diminishing that of Jacob. This latter aspect shows subservience to Esau. Esau wants to know which of these Jacob intended—veiled threat or subservience.[316] Jacob responds that his intention is to find favor in Esau's

---

316 See also Alter, *The Five Books of Moses*, pg. 184, where he translates and explains, "who to you" as "what do you mean by all this camp," thus carrying a similar understanding to the query as explained above.

eyes; in other words, the gifts are not a veiled threat. Nonetheless, the repeated desire to find favor in Esau's eyes, as with the initial message relayed by the messengers, still leaves Esau (and the reader) wondering what Jacob will ask as a favor.[317]

Jacob and Esau are together for mere moments before Esau suggests walking and traveling in tandem. Note that Esau does not suggest traveling *together*. Esau knows that this is not possible. Rather, Esau desires to return to the dynamic of their youth where the amount of space between the two could be minimal. Esau's language is revealing: "*ve'elkha lenegdekha*"—"and I shall walk before you"—thus preserving Esau's "first" status.[318] However, for Jacob, such travel restrictions are not an option. The danger of constant collision is too great, and Jacob refuses Esau's offer.

Jacob reinforces Esau's "first" status further by justifying his refusal with the following excuse: "I will meander along at my own slow pace, at the heels of the animals *before me* and at the heels of the children, until I will come to my lord in Seir " (33:14). Given his current position, face to face with Esau, the addition of the animals being "before me" may be one way of Jacob reinforcing the idea that he does not desire to be first, even when it involves his own camp.

Another understanding of Jacob walking behind his flocks, despite their being slow and his gathering them together and tending to them, may be that Jacob is referring to the other half of his wealth that he sent ahead of him previously ("the animals *before me*") and of which only he, Jacob, is aware. Jacob thus also refuses Esau's offer to walk in tandem because he realizes that were he to accept Esau's offer, Jacob would eventually meet up with the other half of his wealth while Esau or his men would be present.[319] Esau would realize that Jacob yet again tricked him into forgiving him and relinquishing his claim on the blessings by aggrandizing the gift he gave Esau. By presenting only half his wealth, Jacob made the gift seem twice as big in relation to the rest of his presented net worth. This may ignite matters

---

317 This quandary will be addressed in the next chapter.

318 The use of the word "*negdekha*" meaning "in front of" is common in the Bible with the *Concordance Even-Shushan* listing ten such occurrences.

319 See Abrabanel, Chapter 32, answering question 7 where he mentions that after Esau went on his way Jacob reunited with the second camp.

with Esau even more. Jacob therefore opts to place time and space between his entire wealth and Esau by refusing the accompaniment.

Another reason behind Jacob's refusal is that Jacob no longer needs Esau. He has received Esau's absolution for the usurped blessings and other past wrongs. Esau's suggestion that Jacob remain with the offered gift/blessing made to him, as well as his comment, "My *brother*—be for you what you have," evinces such exoneration. Esau's comment also acknowledges their brotherhood and fills the void that Jacob sought to satisfy with Laban during his stay in Haran.

As Jacob insists that Esau accept the gifts, he parallels his insistence of a blessing from the mysterious man. Esau's acceptance of the gifts is his way of blessing Jacob and further demonstrates his forgiveness of Jacob's usurping of the blessings years earlier. Jacob thus not only receives Esau's forgiveness but also his blessing.

Esau proceeds on his path to Seir (33:16) where he later establishes political power. By encountering Esau, achieving reconciliation with him, and emerging relatively unscathed,[320] Jacob successfully reenacts his struggle with the mysterious man. At this point, Jacob travels to Sukkot[321] and builds a home for his family and shelter for his flocks (33:17). After being away from his parents' home for over twenty years and a mere sojourner by Laban (32:4), Jacob is now finally able to occupy his own space and establish a home of his own.

---

320 While Jacob is not physically harmed when meeting Esau, his need to relinquish the space and wealth of the gift convoys to Esau represent a type of damage to Jacob.

321 It is textually unclear whether Sukkot is on the Eastern or Western side of the Jordan. If located on the Eastern side, it would indicate that Jacob did not yet fulfill the divine command to return to his homeland.

CHAPTER SEVEN
The Crumbling of a Master Plan

When the solution is simple, God is answering.

੩ Albert Einstein

Jacob's Strategy

One has to wonder whether Jacob, at least initially, has a plan in mind in anticipation of his reunion with Esau. Jacob is recorded as initiating contact and sending messengers to Esau which would seem to indicate that Jacob indeed has a plan. However, once the initial group of messengers returns with news of Esau's 400-men entourage, Jacob is distressed and seemingly makes new arrangements in response. If Jacob does have a plan, it seems that he is adjusting it or changing it in light of the new development.

Reexamining Jacob's movements will help determine if Jacob is being proactive or reactive. For example, in what seems to be a defensive ploy, Jacob divides his camp. Is this merely reactionary on Jacob's part or is this part of a larger plan that he has in mind? Ostensibly, one would presume that such division serves as a reactionary military tactic. However, as Abravanel[322] correctly points out, Jacob only divides the wealth—not the family members. If Jacob were employing a battle tactic of trying to diminish the risk of fatalities by dividing the camp, he should have divided the family

---

322 Commenting on Vayishlah, on the section beginning commentary on verse 8—in the middle of the second column. See also Alter, *The Five Books of Moses*, pg. 177, commenting on verse 32:8.

as well. It seems, therefore, that there is more than meets the eye to Jacob's puzzling behavior.

Furthermore, while Jacob states that his motivation for the division is to save one camp, Jacob does not delineate his reasoning. He does not explain *why* the other camp will be spared if Esau destroys the "one" camp. He does not state that the division will allow the second camp time to flee or provide any other reason. Indeed, there would be no guarantee that if Esau strikes one camp, he would not proceed to strike the other.

Since Jacob does not divide his wealth out of a desire to reduce risk by use of statistics, why would Jacob be interested in saving the second wealth-only camp? The fire-straw dynamic may assure that "space equals life," but what guarantee did Jacob have that Esau would specifically strike the family-free camp? Should Esau destroy the family-filled camp, Jacob would have no successor. In fact, as his brother, Esau may even be the next in kin to legally inherit Jacob's estate.[323] This seemingly illogical move may imply that Jacob has a well-planned and undisclosed subterfuge afoot.

Perhaps the most striking unanswered quandary is why, after his family crosses to the southern side of the Jabbok, does Jacob backtrack and remain alone on the northern side? Under the assumption that Esau is approaching from the South,[324] crossing the Jabbok places Jacob's family *closer* to the dangerously approaching Esau. Jacob thus seemingly demonstrates cowardice by placing his camps ahead of him to deal with matters on their own, leaving them to act as his "human shield."[325]

---

323 Cf. Numbers 27:9.

324 See Sarna, JPS, pg. 226–227, where he suggests that Jacob is intentionally bringing his family's camp closer to Esau by crossing the Jabbok. See also, Alter, *The Five Books of Moses*, pg. 179 on verse 23 who also opines that Jacob's camp is moving *towards* Esau.

325 See Nahmanides 32:4 and see also Rashbam commenting on 32:23, 24 who states that Jacob was intending to run away from Esau and thus moves in the *opposite* direction of Esau. Abravanel, Chapter 32, answering question 7 adopts a middle position stating that Jacob entertained the possibility that Esau could arrive from either side of the Jabbok and tried to hedge his bets by splitting the camps. However, Abravanel's approach is difficult in that the geography seems to indicate that Esau could only approach from the South of the Jabbok unless he outflanked Jacob's camps, somehow learned of this fact, and then backtracked from the northern side of the Jabbok southward.

To elaborate, as illustrated by the map below, the Jordan River runs from north to south of today's State of Israel and flows into the Dead Sea in the south. The Jabbok tributary runs from east to west, starting in the Gilead

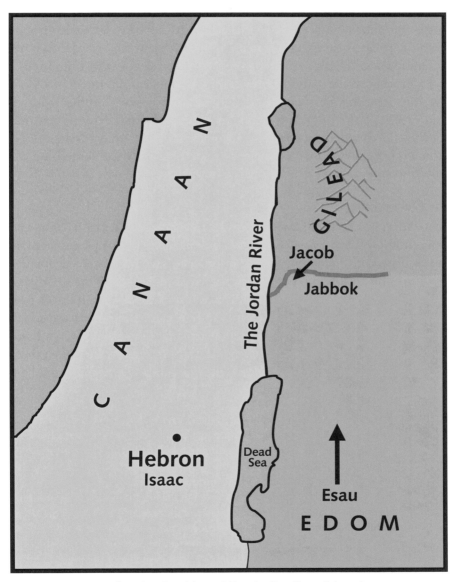

Map 1: Area map showing Jacob's and Esau's direction of travel

region, in what today is the State of Jordan, and flowing into the Jordan River. The Jabbok tributary is thus perpendicular to the Jordan River. Jacob is traveling towards Canaan southwest from the Gilead region where he had his showdown with Laban. Esau is traveling north from Seir/Edom located southeast of the Dead Sea towards Jacob. The Jabbok tributary is between them. As Jacob crosses the Jabbok, he is removing this natural barrier between his camp and his brother's. If Esau's camp represented a military threat, why was Jacob moving his family *towards* Esau by crossing the Jabbok instead of *away* from him?[326]

Can this be the same Jacob who, just hours earlier, prayed to God to save him from his brothers' hands lest he destroy him "mother with children"? (32:12) Not only does Jacob's movements exhibit extreme cowardice, but they fail to reflect Jacob's general concern for his family's welfare.[327] This anomalous behavior further suggests that there must be something more profound stirring beneath the surface of the text.

The Decoy Camp

Jacob's irrational behavior leads the reader to conclude that Jacob has a plan all along. In this instance, *Jacob has created a decoy camp*. Jacob's plan is to sacrifice half of his wealth (including slaves) in order to save his family. Jacob's initial splitting of his wealth into two camps as relayed in 32:8 describes this division: "And Jacob was very frightened and he was distressed. And he split the people with him[328] and the sheep and the cattle and the camels into two camps." Jacob then sends this decoy, wealth-only camp towards Esau. Jacob wants Esau to discover and possibly destroy that camp. If Esau's intentions are violent then he will strike the camp: "If Esau comes to the one camp—*vehikahu*—and he will strike it, the remaining camp will survive" (32:9).[329]

---

326   In this regard, the Midrash (Tanhuma Yashan, Vayishlah 6, also cited by Rashi commenting on 32:9) posits that Jacob prepared himself for battle with Esau. However, this could not have been alluding to Jacob preparing for a full scale military battle for Jacob does not arm his men or have any line of defense when he actually meets up (by surprise?) with his brother Esau.

327   Similarly, can this be the same Jacob, who, even in the heights of his self-absorption, as he rebuked Simeon and Levi for their massacre of the people in the City of Shekhem, still ends his rebuke with: "And I will be destroyed, *me and my household*" (34:30)?

328   This includes only non-family personnel as the text later records that Jacob crosses his wives and eleven children over the Jabbok in the middle of the night (32:22).

329   The word *vehikahu* can also carry the meaning of—"then let him strike it"—as if it was Jacob's wish for that to happen.

Jacob can be certain that Esau will not destroy the family-filled camp because Esau will never know of its existence. Looking back, Jacob's ploy is already obvious when he sends the initial group of messengers to Seir. In the message they were to convey to Esau, "So said your servant Jacob, 'With Laban I sojourned and I have tarried until now. And there was to me an ox and a donkey, a sheep and a slave and a maid and I sent to tell my master to find favor in your eyes'" (32:5–6), Jacob omits to mention his wife and children in his initial laundry list of acquired belongings while at Laban (32:5–6). Rather than their omission being a cloaked reference to the lack of fulfillment of the Abrahamic blessing, or his being a materialistically absorbed boor, uneducated in social custom, Jacob reveals himself to be a master strategist. Since Esau is unaware of any details about Jacob's life since Jacob left Beersheba over twenty years ago, Jacob realizes that Esau will only know that which he tells him. By actively omitting the women and children, Esau may infer that Jacob has none.

Jacob sends his family-free decoy camp ahead of him towards Esau in the hope that the "other" camp with his family will survive. It is Jacob's hope that after Esau encounters the decoy camp he will think that he killed all of Jacob's camp before even seeing Jacob. Jacob then plans to face Esau alone after Esau already encountered the decoy camp. Indeed, Jacob had instructed his servants to inform Esau that "*he*"—in the singular and "your servant Jacob"—again the singular—is alone behind the decoy camp (32:19, 21). Jacob leads Esau to believe that the only person Esau will see after encountering and possibly destroying the first camp is Jacob. The first camp is not in hiding or off to the sides. We can conclusively posit that Jacob parades it forth as the desired target and sends it directly towards Esau.[330] Jacob's loyalty and love for his family, expressed here in the most basic desire for survival, brings him to employ his cunning wit to devise a tactical master plan for meeting Esau.

---

330 Abravanel, chapter 32, answering question 7, mentions a similar idea: "For he thought that if Esau will come to the one camp that is more ready, and that is the one without the women and children, that Esau will be busy with the people there that will fight him to save the flocks and he [Esau] will steal all the wealth that is there *and perhaps will think that that was all his wealth and that he has nothing else.* And with this—time will pass so that the camp with the women and children will survive because they will have time to make a quick getaway or that Esau will not pay attention to them and they were the main part of the household—not the wealth." Unfortunately, Abravanel does not develop this point further.

Given the reality of the plan, the reader can even pinpoint its very inception as the text relays Jacob's encounter with the messengers of God as recorded in 32:2–3. To recall, Jacob parts ways with Laban and meets up with messengers of God. Earlier it was suggested that Jacob called the place "double-camp" as representing his camp and the camp of God. However, Jacob's naming of "double-camp" may embody the "double-camp" plan— of transforming his one camp into two. This cunning plan may have actually been the content of the message that the messengers of God deliver to Jacob or the workings of Jacob's mind as he transposes the idea of the "double-camp" he sees onto his own camp.[331]

With a firm and possibly divine plan in place, the reader still encounters staunch difficulties. Jacob's mysteriously moving his family-filled camp *toward* Esau (by crossing the Jabbok) seemingly contradicts the idea of Jacob tactically using a decoy camp. For if Jacob's strategy was to fool Esau with the decoy camp, Jacob should have moved the other, family-filled, camp *away* from Esau to improve the odds of their remaining undiscovered. By crossing toward Esau, Jacob's family risks being discovered by Esau before Jacob meets him. This negates the inference made above that Esau would think that only Jacob—in the singular—would be seen. Why then, would he have them cross the Jabbok, only to get *closer* to Esau?

A discerning look at Jacob's prayer will lead us in the right direction. The text records: "*And he said*, 'If Esau will come to the one camp and he will strike it, the remaining camp will survive.' *And Jacob said*: 'The Lord of my father Abraham and the Lord of my father Isaac, God who has said to me, "Return to your land and your birthplace and I will deal with you favorably." I have been dwarfed by all of the kindness and by all of the loyalty that you have done with your servant. For with my stick I crossed this Jordan, and now I have become two camps.'" (32:9–11). The text opens Jacob's initial statement with, "And he said" (32:9) and then again begins Jacob's prayer with an independent opening remark of, "And Jacob said" (32:10). The introduction of Jacob's prayer with its own "And Jacob said" indicates that Jacob's prayer was said later in the evening, and not as a continuous statement of his prior remark about one camp surviving that was uttered earlier during the day.

---

331 See also *The Jewish Study Bible*, Berlin, Brettner, and Fishbane, eds., pg. 66, where the idea of "two camps" is seen as prospective of Jacob's splitting of his camp. The idea of the camp serving as a decoy is not mentioned.

Chronologically, therefore, Jacob's prayer should be seen as concomitant with the verse that *follows* it (32:14): "And he slept there on that night and he took from what came into his hand[332] a tribute to his brother Esau." As opposed to the prayer that takes place at night, the decoy camp was sent out earlier during the day before "this Jordan" (32:11) came into eye's purview.[333]

Integrating the area map with the above timeline yields the following: After hearing that Esau is approaching with his men, Jacob organizes and deploys the decoy camp ("the one camp" that Esau will smite as in 32:8–9) in a southerly direction towards Esau during the daylight hours. After sending out the decoy camp, his own camp continues southwest to try to cross the Jordan in hopes of escaping to Canaan. By nightfall, the stress of knowing that Esau is advancing with 400 men and the gnawing knowledge that Jacob personally will need to face[334] Esau, causes Jacob to enter a state of alarm. Jacob's evening prayer reflects this angst, and he loses his orientation to the dark and to the unfamiliar territory.

Lost Compass

Jacob's pre-sleep prayer documents his lost compass: "I am unworthy of all the kindness that you have steadfastly done for your servant. For with my stick I crossed *this Jordan*, and now I have become two camps" (32:11). However, before sleeping, the camp did not reach the Jordan River but rather the Jabbok tributary.[335] Jacob thinks he has reached the Jordan River

---

332 This again serves as a throwback to Jacob's desire to atone for disguising his hands as Esau's. He is now symbolically returning Esau's "hands" through the tribute.

333 The foot of the Gilead mountain region, where Jacob would reach after leaving Laban via the Gilead mountains (see 31:22–25), is approximately fifteen kilometers east of the Jordan River and approximately five kilometers north of the Jabbok tributary.

334 Referencing Reggio's understanding that Jacob and Esau are identical twins (commenting on 25:23), Jacob's traumatic fear is heightened as seeing Esau's "face" or coming "face to face" with Esau may symbolize Jacob's fear of seeing a disturbing permutation of himself. The theme word "face" is prevalent throughout this episode as noted by Klitsner, *Wrestling with Jacob*, pgs. 119–120. Indeed, the "face-to-face" aspect is explicitly referred to by Jacob in naming the place of Peniel (32:31).

335 The text identifies the body of water near Jacob and over which he crosses his family as the Jabbok in 32:23.

but he is really at the foot of the Jabbok tributary.[336] Varying widths and crossing depths of the Jordan River and the Jabbok tributary, as well as their close proximity to Jacob's location, easily accounts for Jacob's confusion, even for an experienced hiker. One needs to bear in mind that Jacob has not traveled this terrain in over twenty years, if at all.[337] The following photos also reveal a similar topography to the region and help the reader readily identify with Jacob's confusion even in the light of day. In the middle of the night,[338] without proper sleep, and under tremendous, life-threatening stress, who could tell the difference?

After Jacob's nighttime prayer, he lays to sleep but awakes to arrange and send the tribute to Esau. The people accompanying the tribute are to relate that Jacob, only, is behind them (32:14–21). Jacob tries to go back to sleep, but once again awakes (32:22–23). He is afraid that if Esau meets up with the decoy camp, and destroys it, the decoy camp and the tribute groups may not sufficiently impede Esau's progress. He may continue onwards to find Jacob still during the night. Fearing that Esau is closing in on his position, Jacob realizes that his continued presence with his family will jeopardize their safety. Jacob's fear moves him to attempt a daring nighttime crossing of what he thinks is the Jordan River. Referencing our second

---

336 Many classical commentators ignore the switch between what should be the Jabbok tributary and the Jordan River. In a recent scholarly article by Jeremy M. Hutton entitled: "Mahanaim, Penuel, and Transhumance Routes—Observations on Genesis 32-33 and Judges 8," the author notes: "It should strike the reader as odd that...the river named is the Jordan, not the Jabbok: Jacob states, 'with only my staff I crossed this Jordan (*'et-hayyarden hazzeh*)' (32:11). Has the author or redactor (or copyist?) miswritten the name of the river, or was 'Jordan' a generic term for any perennial river?...Presumably, Jacob means the Jabbok River, here, using 'Jordan' as a general noun rather than the specific geographic name." *Journal of Near Eastern Studies*, Vol. 65, no. 3, July 2006, pg. 167 ftn. 25. While the author was keen enough to hone in on the problem, his solution is far from adequate. As will be shown, Jacob's use of the Jordan is certainly deliberate and the supposed error in transmission reveals itself as the integral key that will unravel the intricacies of the episode.

337 It is not absolutely certain that he ever passed through this particular region of the Gilead.

338 Jacob's nighttime failure to discern between the Jabbok tributary and Jordan River recalls Jacob's failure to discern between Leah and Rachel on the night of the conjugal switch and further serves as a throwback to Jacob deceiving the blind Isaac, who lives in perpetual darkness, years earlier in the usurping of the blessings.

The Jordan River; photo courtesy of Gal Forenberg.

The Jabbok Tributary, photo courtesy of Stefan Meierhofer.

map, Jacob thinks he is placing them on the western side of the Jordan River (in Canaan) out of harm's way. In reality, though, they are moving across the Jabbok ford further south, in the direction of Esau's projected path.

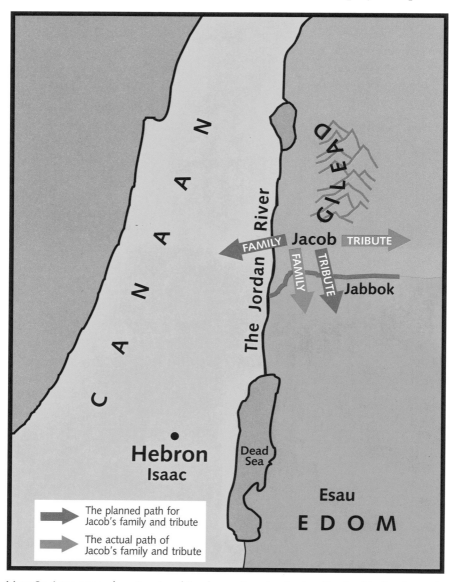

Map 2: Area map showing Jacob's planned and actual paths for his family and for his tribute to Esau

Jacob then backtracks, to what he thinks is the Eastern side of the Jordan, in order to face Esau alone should Esau attack during the night after striking the decoy camp. In reality, though, Jacob had backtracked over the Jabbok ford northward, farther away from Esau's path. Jacob remains alone and vulnerable, and courageously waits to be attacked. As the night progresses, Jacob is indeed attacked, not by Esau, but by the mysterious man.

Throughout the dark night, Jacob's continued lost compass is excusable, but when dawn breaks, the direction of the imminent sunrise in the east threatens to expose Jacob's nighttime debacle. Directed to the breaking dawn by the mysterious man[339] (32:27), Jacob realizes his terrible mistake—he has sent his family due south directly in Esau's projected path. Jacob is terrified. Should Esau chance upon his family-filled camp without Jacob being present he may annihilate everyone Jacob holds dear—including Rachel and Joseph. Jacob can no longer engage the mysterious man. Jacob pleads with the mysterious man to be released.[340] The mysterious man refuses, demanding a blessing from Jacob, but realizes that Jacob may consider the granting of a blessing to be a sign of defeat. The mysterious man therefore opens the dialogue again and asks Jacob for his name and blesses Jacob, renaming him Israel. Once the mysterious man blesses Jacob, Jacob asks the mysterious man for his name so that he can reciprocate. The man enigmatically responds by questioning why Jacob needs to know his name, and Jacob

---

339 A. Korman, *HaAvot veHashevatim*, pgs. 166–175 suggests that the mysterious man was Esau's prize warrior sent in advance to defeat Jacob. If such were the case, Jacob's fear of being spotted with his family and their night crossing of the Jabbok is further justified. Korman's thesis would also provide Jacob with the battle he anticipated and deshrouds much of the mystery that surrounds the episode.

340 The verse reads, "And he said, 'Let me go for dawn is breaking'" (32:27). The current understanding could allow for the reading to be, "And he said, 'Let me go!' for dawn was breaking" shifting the predicate to the narrator as opposed to the speaker. Jacob's pleading tone is attested to by the prophet Hosea, "And he [Jacob] strove with an angel and was able, *he [Jacob] cried and pleaded to him*" (12:5). Explaining this verse in Hosea otherwise, that Jacob caused the angel to cry, does not correspond with God's "punishing Jacob for his conduct, requiting him for his deeds" that the prophet opens with (Hosea 12:3). This latter explanation, positing that the angel cries, would also require grammatically shifting subject mid-sentence. Furthermore, one may opine that Jacob's crying, as described by the prophet, might be attributable to his injury but only the explanation offered in the body of the text above can properly deal with Jacob's accompanying "pleading."

blesses "him" there. As their wrestling reached a stalemate they each bless each other before parting ways. Jacob no longer waits for Esau at his current location because he realizes he has sent his family into danger while he has inadvertently remained behind.[341]

"And the sun rose for him when he passed Penuel and he is limping on his thigh" (32:32). Valiantly limping, and probably in tortuous pain, Jacob musters the strength to try to catch up with his family who may unknowingly begin traveling onwards towards Esau at sun-up. Jacob needs and wants desperately to get to his family before Esau, but his injury impedes his speed. Jacob's mind races as he envisions the worst. What will be of his family? What will happen to Rachel and Joseph? Jacob hobbled from dawn to sunrise, including his second crossing of the Jabbok ford, to meet up with his family in time.[342] No sooner does he arrive at his family's camp than Esau and his men come within sight. Jacob does not want Esau to see his wives and children, but now it is too late. While Jacob desires to keep the family-filled camp a secret, they are now face-to-face with Esau. Hence, Jacob acts surprised upon seeing Esau because Jacob is caught off-guard with his family and his master plan begins to crumble.

In a last-ditch effort to buffer his loved ones from Esau, he arranges his wives and children. Arranging them at all is actually unnecessary—they could have all been standing in one group. Yet, in that traumatic moment, after having thought of the worst as he limps towards his camp before sun-up, Jacob's preferential love for Rachel and Joseph peers through as he places

---

341 Abravanel (chapter 32, answering question 15 and 16) interprets the request to be released as the mysterious man's and comments: "And when it took so long that dawn broke, he told Jacob, 'Release me, for the dawn has broke'; that is to say, and you need to be on your way for Esau is coming quickly. Therefore, for your own benefit and for your own good I would advise you to release me and be on your way."

342 It is precisely because of Jacob's valiant efforts to save his entire family, the progenitors of the entire nation, that the national memorialization of the event is recorded. It is only here, and not when the text informs us of Jacob's injury to his hip-socket during his struggle, that: "Therefore, the children of Israel do not eat the sinew of the thigh which is by the hip-socket to this day, for he had touched Jacob's hip-socket at the sinew of the thigh" (32:33) (Alter's translation). Having saved his family from Esau at that critical moment despite his painful injury obliges his offspring to commemorate his bravery and courage.

Rachel and Joseph last.[343] Undoubtedly, this blatant act of favoritism does not go unnoticed and will be internalized in the psyches of the other family members. It is the first public indication to all of the sons of Leah that Jacob prefers Rachel and Joseph.

When Esau meets and finishes crying with Jacob, he is surprised to see Jacob's wives and children.[344] Based on Jacob's initial message and list of acquisitions, Esau did not expect to see wives or children. Esau finds it puzzling that Jacob would omit this integral piece of personal information and asks: "Who are these to you?" (33:5). Jacob admits that they are the children that God graced him with—leaving out any reference to the women.[345]

After the family bows, Esau asks, "Who to you is all this camp that I met?"[346] (33:8). Esau's question is surprising. Why does he group together the three gift convoys as one camp? Did not Jacob explicitly instruct the groups to remain three separate and distinct gift parties and "to make space between flock and flock"? (32:17–20)

Similarly, why is Esau asking about the identity of these convoys altogether? Did not Jacob instruct his slaves to tell Esau that these flocks were his gifts? (32:19) Did not Jacob insist that his servants use those words verbatim: "And you shall you say"? (32:19)

---

343   Being last represents being the most guarded and hence, most beloved, and adds new meaning to the adage cited by Rashi (33:2): "The very last is the most beloved." See also Ibn Ezra 33:2.

344   33:5. Esau is reported as "lifting his eyes and seeing" just as Jacob had when seeing Esau approach. Both indicate that they are seeing something they did not expect to see. The word "*hineh*"—behold, is also used there. See also Zornberg, *The Beginning of Desire*, pg. 214, and Adele Berlin, *Poetics and Interpretation of Biblical Narrative* (Indiana: Eisenbrauns, 1994) pgs. 62–63, 91–95, for the functions the word "*hineh*" serve.

345   Jacob feels that mentioning his wives may be a sore point as it reminds Esau of why he left and of Esau's old perception of falling out of grace with Isaac and Rebekah because of his own Hittite wives. Esau may not want to allow Jacob to return home to garner more parental love as the obedient son who married the non-Hittite wives.

346   The previous chapter analyzed Esau's interrogatory word of "who" and discussed the logic of Jacob's answer responding to "why" he sent them. At this juncture, one notes that Jacob sent Esau three gift convoys as a "*minha*"—a tribute. However, Esau mistakenly calls them a "*mahaneh*"—a camp.

According to the above reading regarding the decoy camp, the scenario is quite different. Esau is not referring to the three groups of gifts that Jacob sent to Esau during the night. When Jacob awakes during the night, he is still unaware of his navigational error. Referencing again our second map,[347] Jacob, during the night, sends the gift envoys due east (his left), thinking it is south. Had Jacob been facing the Jordan River, as he thought, sending the convoys to his left would have indeed been south towards Esau. These convoys are supposed to convey the message to Esau that they are gift convoys and that Jacob—only—is behind them. However, due to Jacob's lost sense of direction, these spacious gift convoys never reach their intended destination. Instead, they journey onwards further east of the Jordan River, and Esau never receives the messages. Those groups never met Esau. Had they met Esau, the messengers would have conveyed Jacob's message, informing Esau that they are Esau's gifts.

Rather, Esau's reference to the "camp" is referring *to the decoy camp* itself that Jacob sent out earlier during the day. Jacob sees the decoy camp amongst Esau's party and does not see the gift envoys. Jacob realizes that due to his geographical error, the gifts never made it to Esau. Jacob understands that if he claims ownership of the decoy camp, he will need to explain why he divided the camp and admit that he tried to outsmart Esau yet again. By claiming ownership of the decoy camp, Jacob would also de-facto be meeting Esau empty-handed despite his plenty, as Esau is unaware of Jacob's attempted tribute. Esau will read such a gesture as an insult and as a declaration by Jacob that he rightfully deserves the usurped blessings of physical plenty. Esau will see that Jacob did not change and continues to make a mockery of him. With 400 men in Esau's shadow, who may have been promised a share of the booty to be extracted from Jacob's remains, and having been ready to sacrifice the decoy half of his camp earlier, Jacob deftly converts the decoy camp into the gift convoy and tells Esau that the "camp" that he encountered is intended "to find favor in the eyes of my lord" (33:8).

Jacob is no longer offering Esau a sampling of the bounty that God has awarded him during his stay with Laban, which the gift convoys would have provided, but offers instead to give Esau half of everything he has. The

---

347 See page 160. The second map highlights the intended versus actual paths of the family and the tribute.

underlying message that Jacob sends is that although he had usurped the blessings years earlier he is willing to make Esau full partner in everything he has acquired. Jacob is not seeking to be Esau's superior as in Isaac's blessings but rather an equal.[348] Esau realizes that the camp is a significant portion of Jacob's net worth and repeatedly refuses as would be proper etiquette. Esau also hesitates because he understands that Jacob is not simply offering him a tribute but is seeking to find favor in his eyes. If this large gift is to find favor in his eyes, Jacob's request of him can be expected to be equally as large. However, upon Jacob's insistence, Esau accepts the magnanimous gift. Jacob's reconciliation with his brother is now complete.

The Favor

> And Esau said, "Let me station with you from the people that are with me." And he said, "Why is this I will find favor in my master's eyes? And Esau returned that day on his path to Seir." (33:15–16)

Esau's refusal to accept Jacob's significant gift indicates that he understands the deep underpinnings of Jacob's offer. Esau is hesitant to wipe the slate clean at this point and is reluctant to be granting Jacob any favors. In Jacob's initial message to Esau, Esau remained unclear what Jacob was after when he sent messengers "in order to find favor in his eyes" (32:6). Amongst the possibilities, Esau presumably chooses to view Jacob's request to find favor in his eyes as a request to provide Jacob's camp with secure passage.[349]

When Esau extends such an offer, Jacob refuses, using the pace of his children and flocks as his excuse, while alluding to some later visit to Esau in Seir.[350] Esau, still trying to figure out what favor Jacob is asking from him, offers to station some of his men with Jacob at his own slow place. If this is the favor that Jacob was seeking, then Jacob should accept. Yet, having

---

348 It is Jacob's implicit call for equality that elicits Esau's suggestion that they travel in tandem.

349 This would explain why Esau comes to greet Jacob with 400 men. They were to serve as a friendly military escort for Jacob's camp.

350 Jacob must also be concerned that the gift convoys will soon also learn of their directional error and backtrack towards Jacob. If they arrive while Esau is there Jacob will again have a lot of explaining to do.

already reconciled with Esau, Jacob seeks to disengage from Esau's presence and responds enigmatically: "Why is this I will find favor in my master's eyes?" (33:15). Jacob's innuendo questions why Esau is deeming an entourage as the favor that Jacob seeks. In his enigmatic statement, Jacob implies that Esau should rethink his basic premise. At this point, the text obliquely records that Esau simply returns to his path to Seir (33:16). The text records no further interaction between Jacob and Esau other than burying Isaac (35:29). Reaching what ostensibly represents a point of heightened tensions, the text simply shuts down midstream. What happened? Does Jacob forfeit the significant favor he was seeking? What does Esau make of Jacob's enigmatic statement that ends the conversation? Before drawing a conclusion, another textual reference requires attention, as will be set out below.

After reaching the end of the exhaustive detail recorded in chapter 33:1–17 regarding the brothers' actual meeting and parting of ways, it is startling to learn what seems to be contradictory information when reading chapter 36:6–7. There the text reads:

> And Esau took his wives, children, cattle, animals and all his possessions which he acquired in the land of Canaan and went to a land from the face of Jacob his brother; for their wealth was too great to dwell together and the land of their dwelling could not support them because of their herds.

The text in chapter 33, analyzed in detail above, does not report that the brothers dwelled together in Canaan for any time nor did it ascribe the reason for their not staying together as being a result of their great wealth and herds. How could the text in chapter 36 introduce their parting based on the two brothers living together in Canaan when the text in chapter 33 indicates that this never occurred?

Based on the above analysis, this puzzling contradiction can be reconciled. Each of the brothers accumulates great wealth during their twenty-year separation. Indeed, the text in chapter 36 stresses that the reason Esau and Jacob separate is specifically due to the great amount of cattle each possess. The meeting of these vast camps presents an intolerable situation.

Jacob's first set of messengers succeed in relaying Jacob's greeting as Jacob intended. Esau is not certain of Jacob's intent and presumes that Jacob is asking for Esau's assistance in finding his way peacefully back home. Since

Jacob refused his offer for such protection, Esau entertains other possibilities that may have already crossed his mind earlier.

Jacob's initial message relayed that he owned animals, slaves, and maids. The singular/plural ambiguity allows Jacob's "ox," "donkey," and "sheep" to consist of many herds and his "slave" and "maid" to consist of numerous individuals. Esau now sees that this is indeed the case. Esau realizes that Jacob's message may have been more a concern for logistics than a description dictated by social etiquette. As their parents are older, if not already dead, Esau will be in charge of the household. Jacob, therefore, needs to inform his prospective host to make the proper arrangements for his return home. Esau now realizes that the only way to accommodate for Jacob and his vast possessions is if he leaves home and voluntarily allows Jacob to take his place. Jacob would surely need Esau's favor to uproot his family and belongings and to allow Jacob to take his place at home—a staunch reenactment of the usurping of the blessings.

Esau now understands that he has misread the entire situation. Jacob offers a response about his slow pace as a polite refusal. However, the actual reason why Jacob rejects the offer is because of his awareness that they would be unable to sustain the necessary separation of the "herds" that comprise their camps, and hints at his need to have his own space for himself and for his camp.[351]

Having just achieved reconciliation with Esau, Jacob does not have the temerity to ask Esau for such a favor directly. Instead, Jacob drops a heavy hint which can be found at the end of his statement: "Until I come to my master *to Seir*." Esau picks up the hint. He now understands that the favor Jacob is requesting is that he will always be able to find Esau in Seir and not elsewhere.[352] *Esau now understands that Jacob is asking him to leave home permanently to make "space" for him.* Esau responds in actions rather

---

351 The added factor of Jacob now having his own camp also shapes Jacob's decision to go on alone without Esau. As opposed to his youth where Jacob's need for space could be satisfied in limited tents, Jacob's current need for space required a vast area.

352 In doing so, Jacob is replaying his covenant with Laban and setting a border in order that each of the parties keeps a safe distance between the camps.

than words: "And Esau returned on that day to his path to *Seir*" (33:16).[353] This is then followed by Esau moving away from home permanently, as described in chapter 36: "And Esau took his wives, children, cattle, animals and all his possessions which he acquired in the land of Canaan and went to a land from the *face* of Jacob his brother; for their wealth was too great to dwell together and the land of their dwelling could not support them because of their herds."

Jacob does not immediately return home but curiously sojourns at Sukkot and later, Shechem. As Esau does not respond orally to Jacob, Jacob is not clear whether Esau acquiesced to his subtle request, rejected it or even understood it. By delaying his return home, he hopes to allow Esau time to establish his permanent home in Seir and gather his family and belongings from Canaan without further dealings with Esau.[354]

Separation Out of Choice

Some might dismiss the above explanation because it ascribes Esau with a quite generous attitude towards Jacob. Would Esau unilaterally move his entire existence from Canaan to Seir to provide Jacob and his family their needed space? Abravanel already suggests such magnanimity on the part of Esau as follows:

> And since their cattle was great and the land could not sustain them, *Esau, in his love for Jacob, left him in Canaan knowing that Jacob wanted it (the land of Canaan) and was destined to inherit it*[355] *and he (Esau) and his children and his cattle left to move permanently to Seir* and this

---

353 A possible objection to this line of thought is that Jacob had already sent messengers to Seir towards Esau in his initial parley. If so, it seems that Esau was already living in Seir and could not now be asked to now move there for the first time by Jacob. However, as posited by Radak (commenting on 32:4 and 33:14) as well as Abravanel (beginning commentary to ch. 36), this interaction may have occurred when Esau may have set up temporary residence or hunting grounds in Seir before his ultimate conquest and inhabitance of the region.

354 This also explains why it is only after Esau's interaction with Jacob that the text can relate the annals of the house of Edom *in Seir* (36:9). It is only at this later stage that Esau established himself in Seir in a permanent manner.

355 Abravanel apparently posits that Esau heard Isaac bless Jacob with the Abrahamic blessing before leaving to Paddan-Aram. (28:4, 6)

is what is mentioned here regarding his traveling with his wives and children and cattle.[356]

Abravanel thus adopts the idea that Esau unilaterally uprooted his existence to accommodate Jacob's need for space. For Esau, the detailed meeting as recorded in 33:1–17 serves as a confirmation that they will logistically be unable to remain together in their father's home in Canaan without invading each other's space. Esau's initiated move, as recorded in 36:6–7, is thus justified. When Jacob rejects Esau's final attempt to join forces, Esau understands that, perhaps tragically, they cannot coexist peacefully around their parents. Thus, the separation of the brothers occurs immediately after they meet as related in the text in 33:1–17 and because of the reason recorded in 36:6–7.

In addition, Esau realizes that he chose to accept Jacob's gift without knowing the favor that would be asked of him. Esau accepting Jacob's proposal to be equal partners binds him to afford Jacob equal time at home. As Esau enjoyed over twenty years of time alone with his parents, it is now Jacob's turn, as equal partner, to try to enjoy the same.

Jacob's brotherhood with Esau reveals itself to be fraught with difficulties and deceptions. Jacob's brotherhood with Laban was similarly beleaguered with friction and trickery, as illustrated by the conjugal switch and Jacob's manipulation of the rods. In both cases, this led to the need for the "brothers" to separate. The model of brotherhood that Jacob's children have to draw from unfortunately leads to a perpetuation of these complications and machinations. For example, the brothers' relationship with Joseph will also be fraught with deceit and will lead to a separation between him and his brothers as well.

---

356 Abravanel, beginning commentary on Genesis 36. I have rejected the precise time line set out by the Abravanel as he fails to explain why the death of Isaac precipitates the change and the sudden realization that the two cannot be sustained on the same land. He also fails to explain how they lived together in Canaan when the description of the same events in ch. 33 indicates otherwise.

However, Jacob's reunion and tepid[357] reconciliation with Esau provide hope for healing the family's fractured fraternity. Years later, Joseph and the brothers will unwittingly reenact key elements of this brotherly reunion witnessed in their youth.[358] Yet, Jacob's family dynamic is still in formation and several pivotal moments will transpire before their arrival in Isaac's home—the first of which is the rape of Dinah.

---

357 Esau is more emotionally effusive and Jacob more formal. Picturing the scene creates an awkward imbalance between the characters and detracts from the flow of the reunion. One senses a similar imbalance at the Jacob-Joseph reunion which will be addressed in a later volume of this work. Such imbalance implies that the more formal party is not really comfortable with the reunion itself or the way that it takes place.

358 A full discussion of this parallel will be found in a future volume of this work.

Chapter Eight

Dinah's Brothers and Their Father

We must distinguish between speaking to deceive and being silent to be reserved.

                                   ✎ *Voltaire*

Jacob journeys to the city of Shechem[359] where he encamps outside the city, and buys the grounds from Shechem's family. While encamping outside the city, Jacob's daughter Dinah is raped by Shechem.

> And Jacob came in peace[360] to the town of Shechem, which is in the land of Canaan, when he came from Paddan-Aram, and he camped before the town. And he bought the parcel of land where he had pitched his tent from the sons of Hamor, father of Shechem, for a hundred *kesitahs*. And he set up an altar there and called it El–Elohei-Israel.
>
> And Dinah, Leah's daughter, whom she had borne to Jacob, went out to go seeing among the daughters of the land. And Shechem the son of Hamor the Hivite, prince of the land, saw her and took her and lay her and abused her. (33:18–20, 34:1–2)[361]

---

359 Although Alter uses "kh" to represent the Hebrew letter *khaf*, he uses a "ch" in the word Shechem. Despite the apparent inconsistency, I have adhered to Alter's spelling.

360 Jacob's peaceful intentions are to be contrasted with the ultimate violence that ensues from Shechem and from Simeon and Levi.

361 Alter's translation.

After some discussions, the sons of Jacob presumably agree that should all the inhabitants of the city undergo circumcision, they will allow for the union of Shechem and Dinah. Three days after the inhabitants are cajoled into performing the circumcision, Simeon and Levi enter the city and massacre the entire male population. The other brothers loot the city and take captives. Jacob rebukes Simeon and Levi, fearing reprisal from the surrounding nations.

The three brief introductory verses, above, leading to the rape of Dinah, usually do not receive adequate attention. Perhaps most noteworthy is the fact that the text identifies those who sold the land to Jacob as the sons of Hamor, father of Shechem. The text leaves out whether Shechem himself is included in the group of "the sons of Hamor," but clearly, Shechem's brothers are involved. The consequence of this fact is that when Shechem rapes Dinah, Jacob's dilemmas are compounded by having to confront not only the rulers of the land, but also the father of his past business associates.

In addition, this set of relations adds an additional layer of brotherhood and fatherhood to that of Jacob and Dinah's brothers and further serves as a foil to their dynamics. It is through these verses that we know that Shechem has brothers. Shechem's brothers do not play a role in the rape episode and its aftermath whether as proponents or opponents of Shechem's actions and requests. Shechem's father, however, plays a dominant role in accompanying and presenting Shechem's wishes *vis-à-vis* Jacob and the brothers. The resulting equation from the dual foil is that there exists an inverse relationship between the degrees of activity of brothers and fathers. Dinah's father, Jacob, is passive, while the brothers of Dinah are active in dealing with the situation. Shechem's father, Hamor, is fairly active on his son Shechem's behalf, while Shechem's brothers are so passive that they receive no mention beyond the verse regarding the purchase of the parcel of land. The resulting family dynamics in the respective households are similarly inversed. *When support and security are available from the parent, the siblings do not need to develop the cohesive and active group nature that they do when it is absent.*

Another important point these introductory verses provide is the designation of the sellers as the "sons of Hamor" instead of as "Shechem's brothers." This seems to imply that Hamor is the central figure in the family. In this vein, one may suggest that it is Hamor, not Shechem, who is prince of the land—thus further enhancing Hamor's central position in the household.[362] Once one realizes that it is Hamor who is prince, his interaction with Jacob is no longer simply a confrontation between two sets of fathers and sons on an equal footing, but between the local ruler and prince and the sojourners and newcomers.

So Why Is Jacob Passive and Silent?

> And Dinah, *Leah's daughter*, whom she had borne to Jacob, went out to go seeing among the daughters of the land. (34:1)

Dinah, the Daughter of Leah

The text opens the episode referring to Dinah as the daughter of Leah and suggests that it is *because* Dinah is *Leah's* daughter that Jacob does not later respond. As pointed out earlier, Jacob directs his resentment of the conjugal switch towards Leah and her children. This general emotional estrangement to Leah and her offspring predisposes Jacob to be silent regarding avenging her honor. Furthermore, beyond the general estrangement, Jacob feels that when Leah took Rachel's place on his wedding night, Leah in essence tricked him into sleeping with her non-consensually. Jacob may feel that Dinah was also involved in a non-consensual laying.[363] From Jacob's

---

362 This understanding can also be deduced from the second verse of chapter 34, which states that "Shechem, the son of Hamor, the Hivite, prince of the land, saw her." The description, "prince of the land," could just as easily refer to Hamor as it could to Shechem. In fact, attributing the title of prince to Hamor and defining Shechem only as the "most respected of his father's home" would explain Shechem's need to involve Hamor when later addressing the Hivites. If Hamor holds no official title, his presence would not add anything to Shechem's request of the Hivites. However, if Hamor is prince, Shechem needs Hamor's presence to legitimize and legalize his request that all men circumcise themselves, and transform that request into binding law and an acceptable local practice.

363 As Rashi (commenting on 34:1) and the Midrash (Genesis Rabbah 80:1) point out, Dinah was associated with her mother to specifically link her behavior to the behavior of her mother. Leah was "*yatsanit*" — outgoing—in the pejorative sense, and so, too, her daughter. Yet, the sages did not stop at making this derogatory parallel. Rather they also stated that the common known proverb of "like mother like daughter" is based on Dinah's behavior in comparison to Leah's—just as Leah had "gone out" to meet Jacob after trading the *dudaim* with Rachel, so, too, Dinah had "gone out" to see the daughters of the land. Just as Leah went out to Jacob in order to invite him to sexual relations, so, too, did Dinah issue an invitation

perspective, the rape perhaps served as Leah's measure-for-measure punishment for her earlier behavior or as a behavioral parallel of being party to non-consensual relations whether as perpetrator or as victim. Jacob may also feel that just as his non-consensual laying led to his marriage to Leah, her daughter Dinah's non-consensual laying should lead to her marrying Shechem—"like mother like daughter."[364]

Blaming Dinah

As part of the social norms of the time,[365] Jacob's non-response may stem from his attributing blame to Dinah for the rape. The Midrash[366] expounds that the rape occurred because Dinah was promiscuous and exposed her shoulder (in Hebrew, "*Shekhem*"[367]) and thus attracted undesirable elements (Mr. Shechem). Similarly, the Midrash[368] goes even further and notes the similar language employed by Leah when going out to meet Jacob and Dinah's going out to see the daughters of the land. "And Leah went out (*vatetse*) towards him and said: 'To me you shall come, for I have surely hired you with my son's *dudaim*'" (30:16) and Dinah's going out mentioned here, "And Dinah, Leah's daughter, whom she had borne to Jacob, went out (*vatetse*) to go seeing among the daughters of the land" (34:1). The Midrash equates the *yatsanit* (outgoing) aspects of Leah and Dinah as meaning they each went out adorned as prostitutes. If this is the case, Jacob's non-response

---

to have sexual relations. Yet, the additional emphasis of the Midrash connecting Leah and Dinah beyond their being *yatsaniot* "outgoing" and establishing the "like mother like daughter" principle allows for drawing the parallel between their behavioral patterns and helps explain why Jacob does not respond to Dinah's rape as one might expect.

364 Later Torah law would also opt for Shechem marrying Dinah as part of his punishment/rehabilitation. (See Deuteronomy 22:28–29.)

365 Also see Deuteronomy 22:23–24.

366 Genesis Rabbah 80:5.

367 The word "Shekhem" is spelled with a "kh" here, because it is not referring to Mr. Shechem, or the place Shechem, but to the Hebrew word for "shoulder."

368 Genesis Rabbah 80:1.

may be indicative of a certain callousness to the situation as he blames what happened, at least partially, if not wholly, on Dinah's behavior.[369]

Furthermore, Jacob may blame Dinah for using poor judgment in going out to see the daughters of the land altogether. Jacob's parental perspective is that there is nothing to see,[370] and that no good can come from his daughter mingling with those girls. Jacob feels this way because the very reason for his leaving his parents' home years ago was to find a non-Hittite wife in Paddan-Aram. Esau's Hittite wives had been a cause of great grief to Rebekah and Isaac. However, Rebekah's dramatic declaration to Isaac expanded the circle of undesirable women beyond the Hittites: "If Jacob takes a woman from the daughters of Het like these, from the *b'not ha'arets*—the daughters of the land—what good to me is life?" Any member of the *b'not ha'arets*—from the daughters of the land—is to be avoided. The only other textual reference in the Bible to this group of women is when Dinah goes out to see the *b'not ha'arets*—the daughters of the land (34:1). This social categorization further colors Jacob's negative perspective on the exchange of the daughters, since he would be wary of merging with the Hivites, who are also *b'not ha'arets*.[371] Jacob must later be mortified after the pillaging when his sons now have multiple "daughters of the land." Jacob

---

369 In contrast, Rabbi Meir Leibush (hereinafter: Malbim), commenting on 34:1, opines that Dinah's behavior is exceptionally modest and Dinah is *not* to blame for what happened. In support of this view, one notes that Shechem was the most respected of his father's household and prince of the land. Dinah knew that he was also brother to her father's business associates and she was perhaps previously in Shechem's family home with her father on a previous occasion. Given this background, it is unthinkable to Dinah that Shechem would perpetrate such a crime. The textual description of the crime also supports the idea that Dinah was not in any way to blame for the rape. Shechem saw her, took her, "slept her," and raped her. Dinah is referred to as a passive object being acted upon while her goal was to interact specifically with the local *girls*.

370 See Kass, *The Beginning of Wisdom*, pg. 478 where he notes the Samaritan addition of Dinah's desire not only to see but "to be seen" apparently playing on the Hebrew *lir'ot* as *le'raot*.

371 It is not suggested here that Jacob is aware of the textual reference of the Hivites as *"b'not ha'arets"* but rather that he recognizes that these are the same social/ethnic class of women that Rebekah opposed him marrying.

is further concerned that it will seem like a slap in the face to Isaac and, if still alive, Rebekah as well.[372]

Daddy's Little Girl

As Jacob fathered eleven boys and only one girl, Jacob was perhaps initially overprotective of his "little girl." Maybe in his desire to see her as his "little" girl, he failed to realize that she had grown into a sexually attractive young woman. Jacob's overprotective nature is illustrated by Radak, who cites the Midrash[373] declaring that had Jacob not hid Dinah from Esau when the two reunited, she would have married Esau and not "fornicated." Radak, therefore, implies that Dinah's activities were that of a prostitute that may have been averted had she been "exposed" earlier to more of the outside, Esau-like, world while under her father's auspices. Had she been exposed in a controlled manner by her father she may not have desired to "go out" and "see" the daughters of the land of Shechem. Jacob shelters Dinah and this sparks Dinah's curiosity to see what is "out there." As a result of his failed efforts in protecting her, Jacob loses the confidence to be proactive now and reverts to his passive and silent role.

Jacob's Fear for His Sons (and Property)

> And Jacob heard that he defiled Dinah his daughter, and his sons were with his livestock in the field, and Jacob remained silent until they arrived. (34:5)

The text records Jacob's deafening silence at the same time as it relates that Jacob's sons were with his livestock in the field. Such juxtaposition

---

372 Perhaps Isaac and Rebekah are the "dwellers in the land" in whose eyes Jacob feels he has now become putrid (34:30).

373 Genesis Rabbah, 76:9 who cites Rav Huna in the name of Rabbi Aba Cohen Bar Dalia. The Midrash describes Jacob hiding Dinah in a container to keep her out of Esau's sight for fear that he may want to take her as a wife. The idea of protecting Dinah by keeping her in an equivalent of his own youthful enclosed tent represents Jacob's overprotective nature. This would imply that Jacob *was* aware of his daughter's attractiveness but failed to provide her with a controlled exposure to the outside world.

suggests a causal relationship between the two. Namely, Jacob does not know what has happened to his sons and therefore remains silent. As readers of the text, we know that they are in the field with his flocks. Jacob, though, is not sure where they are. Perhaps they have been harmed in trying to prevent the rape or in avenging the rape before Hamor's arrival. Jacob realizes that any harsh reaction against Hamor, such as killing him, would spark a family feud between Shechem and Jacob's sons. Jacob may have been concerned that any action on his part would elicit blood avenging by Shechem or his allies and jeopardize his sons who might be caught off guard while in the field. Linguistically, the text sets up "his daughter" versus "his sons," "And Jacob heard that he defiled Dinah his *daughter,* and *his sons* were with his livestock," to inform us that Jacob's dilemma is to balance his concern of the one—his daughter—with his concern for the many others—his sons. Hence, Jacob's initial non-response (as opposed to the prolonged non-response throughout the episode) may be attributed to his desire to await their arrival. Only then could he properly assess the gravity of the situation.

In addition, the text not only mentions the sons as being in the field but also mentions his flocks being with them. This textual cue hints that Jacob desires to properly assess the damage to his livestock as well. Are his sheep stolen or damaged? Was the rape a crime perpetrated against him (and possibly his sons and/or flocks) as an immigrant group or was it a crime against Dinah, as an individual female?[374]

Jacob may be concerned about his hard-earned wealth being in jeopardy should he react harshly. Jacob just recently invested a hundred *kesitah* to acquire the land owned by the rapist's family. Should the affair force Jacob to relocate, he may lose his investment. In Shechem's later proposal to

---

374 Hamor's proposal, which appealed to the national level of union, leaves Jacob to ponder the nature of the crime even after the sons and sheep return. The reader, however, is privy to a response to this query as the text's description of Dinah being the daughter of Leah and the description of the rape informs the reader that the rape had no national "anti-Jacob" tint to it, but rather was a criminal act against a "daughter of Leah" and a result of Shechem's uncontrolled lust. Jacob, again, did not benefit from such textual cueing and maintains his silence in the hopes of ascertaining answers to these questions.

Jacob, he makes reference to Jacob obtaining an "*ahuzah*"—a family estate—status regarding the land. Shechem may have been hinting at the converse as well; that if Jacob would not agree, Shechem may order that the land revert to the Shechem clan by eminent domain or by a forcible taking.[375] Jacob, therefore, wanted every person and every thing to be safe and accounted for so that he could properly assess the situation before reacting. Consequently, this protective stance helps explain Jacob's initial non-responsiveness.[376]

Mitigating Damages

Jacob's silence may also develop out of practical considerations. Jacob may reason to himself that the rape is already a *fait accompli*. There is nothing that can reverse the damage that has been wrought,[377] and Jacob explores the idea that perhaps something good can even come of it.

Jacob also considers that if Dinah marries Shechem, her economic security would be assured, as Shechem is the prince of the land or at least son of the prince. Emotionally, the text attests to Shechem's love for Dinah after the rape and Hamor conveys to Jacob Shechem's passion for Dinah. Jacob can doubt the authenticity of this statement, as he doesn't have the textual confirmation that we, as readers, are privy to, but it does give reason for Jacob to pause and think. As awful as it may sound, the text hints that Shechem may yet have become a loving husband.

Perhaps, reasons Jacob, Hamor's after-the-fact proposal may be the best alternative under the circumstances. After all, as Shechem is willing

---

375 Jacob may reason that if Shechem is ready to take a woman by force then he may also be ready to acquire his possessions by force as well.

376 All the above assumes that the field, the sheep, and the sons were some distance off from Jacob's tent. However, the text records Jacob's purchase of the land from Hamor as the purchase of the field where he pitched tent. As such, the fields may have been in eye's view and his sons in shouting distance. If such is the case, the above analysis would truncate Jacob's concerns to his possible concern for his sons' readiness to ward off immediate attack and fear of losing his investment in the field.

377 See Malbim commenting on 34:5–6.

to marry Dinah, Jacob will not be forced to contend with marrying off a non-virgin rape victim who, possibly, may already be pregnant.[378]

In thinking over his position, Jacob finds himself in the same quandary he experienced the morning he realized that he slept with Leah and not Rachel. Jacob must choose between what is instinctually correct and what is pragmatically beneficial. Undoubtedly, Jacob's life experiences to date leave Jacob giving deference to practical considerations over emotional impulse.[379]

Fulfilling One's Destiny

In addition, Jacob remains silent because Hamor offers Jacob the right to do business in the land and to seize the land as an *ahuzah*. The *ahuzah* offer is appealing in two ways. The *ahuzah* status will bring economic prosperity and stability to Jacob's nomad existence to date. The additional business incentive must also tug ever so slightly at Jacob who, after having left Laban's home, may be looking for new avenues of economic growth.

In addition, on some level, it represents God's fulfillment of His promise that Jacob and his children will be given the land. By agreeing to Hamor's proposal, Jacob would be able to obtain the land for his children without a war, while fulfilling God's will and his personal divine destiny. In this case,

---

378 Indeed, the Midrash (Genesis Rabbah, end Parsha 80) relays the concern of Dinah's eligibility by describing Dinah as being forcibly dragged out of Shechem's house by Simeon and Levi. As they do so, Dinah is weeping and wondering about where she will be able to take her disgrace. (See also the same statement made by Tamar to Absalom, II Samuel 13:13.) The Midrash relates that it is only after Simeon promises to take care of her that she leaves Shechem's house. This Midrash interestingly adds a dimension of Dinah's victim paralysis by revealing that she may have been convinced that she should *willingly* stay in Shechem's house. This may have been part of Shechem's persuasion tactics in speaking "to the young woman's heart" (34:3).

379 As other examples of Jacob's preference for practicalities, one can point to his cunning when he swapped the birthright for the bowl of stew to Esau, his willingness to usurp the blessings once assured that Rebekah will assume the downside risk of any curse, his flight from his parent's home, his dealings with Laban for wages, his behavior concerning the conjugal switch, his running from Laban's home, and his offering of tributes to appease Esau.

the land would be devoid of other nations by agreement as the two nations would merge and become one new nation.[380]

Physical Constraints

One practical, physical, reason why Jacob does not retaliate is because he is outnumbered. In addition, he hurt his leg in wrestling the mysterious figure in the night. Some commentators[381] opine that his leg is already healed when entering, or by the time he enters, the city of Shechem. Indeed, the injury was sustained prior to his building his house and shelter for his flocks in Sukkot which preceded his entry to Shechem and thus afforded ample time for healing. Others[382] opine that he was permanently lamed in his encounter with the mysterious man. Nonetheless, perhaps Jacob fears actively entering into battle when physically unable to cope with the situation or fearing that his leg may be prone to injury.

Keeping it Quiet

Finally, Hamor and Shechem do not allude to the rape in their proposal to Jacob and his sons. This leads Jacob to believe that the matter may still not be public knowledge and that the reports received by Jacob were limited in circulation. Having Dinah wed Shechem—local royalty—would help keep the matter private and eliminate any questions and public embarrassment for his family.

---

380 However, the proposed national merger and *ahuzah* status presents an additional difficulty for Jacob. The text mentions Shechem's nationality as being Hivite. As such, it adds a new dimension to the rape. It represents not only a personal tragedy that triggers moral outrage but also one that runs across national lines. As the Hivites are destined to be expelled from the land (as a descendant of Canaan, see 10:17, 15:21) while Jacob's children are destined to inherit the land (28:13), the union of two such groups cannot seemingly coexist according to the divine plan. The rape represents not only the personal forcing of Shechem unto Dinah but the Hivites forcing themselves upon the offspring of Jacob. In weighing the practical cost benefit analysis, Jacob is left with the confusing choice of accepting the proposed union and possibly fulfilling God's plan or of rejecting the union and ostensibly passing up on the opportunity to fulfill God's will by acquiring the land without a war. In such a case, the merging of peoples and their circumcision may allow them to be identified as non-Hivite.

381 Genesis Rabbah 78:5, 79:5, Rashi and Radak on 33:18.

382 Alter, *The Five Books of Moses*, pg. 180, note to verse 27.

Identifying with the Villain

During the episode of the conjugal switch, Jacob is forced to accept the switch and uphold the societal norms. His powerlessness costs him seven years of additional labor. Undoubtedly, Jacob is embittered that he had to comply with an external source of control. Jacob knows how hard it was for him not to act on impulse when seeing Leah in the morning.

Undoubtedly, in this situation, the locus of moral disgust is reversed, as here it is the villain who breaks with societal norm, but perhaps on some subconscious level Jacob finds himself understanding someone who disregards societal norms and acts on impulse. In Jacob's eyes, denying Dinah to Shechem because Shechem violated the societal norm of marriage would be the equivalent of denying Jacob's claim of deceit against Laban based on the local custom of marrying the elder before the younger. Jacob may subconsciously want Shechem to succeed in retaining Dinah as his wife, in much the same way that he would have wanted to succeed in marrying Rachel immediately after discovering the conjugal switch.

Purpose of Punishment

Jacob's non-responsiveness is acutely felt by the reader because the reader feels that punishment is in order. In a practical world, there are four main reasons behind administering punishment on an individual or on a societal level. They can be summarized as follows:[383]

1. Punishment can serve as a means of revenge against the perpetrator.
2. Punishment serves as a specific deterrence to prevent the perpetrator from repeating the crime.
3. Punishment serves as a general deterrence for anyone in society from committing a similar crime in fear of punishment.
4. Finally, punishment can serve as a means to rehabilitate the criminal into becoming a different kind of person who would not commit the crime.

According to Hamor's proposal, Shechem will be rehabilitating himself by marrying Dinah legally. It will also serve as a specific deterrence as

---

383 The list is compiled from memory from the course on Criminal Law taught by Professor Harry Subin at the NYU School of Law, 1991.

once the marriage takes place there would be no fear of a future rape by Shechem.[384] Their union would also serve as a general deterrence as anyone who knew what happened would realize that they cannot rape someone, especially a member of Jacob's family, without further repercussions. With three out of four motivations for punishment achieved by accepting the proposal, Jacob may be leaning in favor of acceptance and hence Jacob's silence. The only motivation that the proposal did not address is that of revenge. It is this motivation that moves Simeon and Levi to massacre the city, for in their view, this factor outweighs all the rest.[385]

Dinah is Being Held Hostage

As pointed out by Meir Sternberg in *The Poetics of Biblical Narrative*,[386] a major factor that is left concealed by the text until after the massacre is that Dinah is being held in Shechem's home. Jacob hears of the rape, and is concerned that they may further harm her. Jacob cannot even be sure where Shechem is holding her.[387] It is only when the sons of Jacob take Dinah out of Shechem's home that the text reveals that she had never left. This point

---

384 Along the lines of the Talmudic adage, "You cannot compare one who has bread in his basket to one who does not have bread in his basket" (B. Talmud, Yoma 74b).

385 Interestingly, Malbim (commenting on 34:31) does not see Jacob arguing with Simeon and Levi only about the proper value to attribute to avenging the crime but also as to which course of action better serves as a general deterrent against possible future attacks from the surrounding nations. Jacob's view is that a vengeful massacre would cause the surrounding nations to view them as a threat that requires elimination. Simeon and Levi, on the other hand, contend that the massacre is a display of strength that sends the message that anyone who inflicts harm to Jacob or his family will meet with a severe reckoning. For Simeon and Levi, the display of strength is the best deterrent of all. Yet, as Jacob believes that the disadvantages of meting out punishment would far outweigh the advantages, he prefers to remain silent throughout the episode.

386 Pg. 467.

387 Ralbag, 34:25, Beiur HaParasha proposes that Simeon and Levi infiltrated the city under pretense of visiting and trying to tend to the men recovering from their circumcision. When alone with the men, they would kill them and close the door behind them while informing the women and children not to enter so as to allow them to rest. This ploy would allow them time and opportunity to kill the men of the city undetected as well as search for Dinah within the city.

retrospectively sheds a new light on the entire affair. Jacob finds himself in a terrifying hostage situation where he must deal face-to-face with the kidnapper and rapist. In this situation, there is no ransom demand. If Jacob agrees to the marriage, he will still not get Dinah back. However, not agreeing to the marriage may result in dire consequences for Dinah. Jacob is therefore brought to the point of paralysis and silence.

Fear of Being Destroyed

Another veiled factor in explaining Jacob's silence, and one that is only revealed after the massacre, is Jacob's fear of obliteration at the hands of the surrounding nations. "For you have sullied me, to make me stink amongst the inhabitants of the land and I am few in number and they will gather and destroy me and I will be destroyed—I and my household" (34:30).

Jacob's fear is comprised of various elements of which three were already listed: Firstly, he will lose favor in the eyes of the public. Secondly, he is small in number. Thirdly, the nations shall unite and destroy him. Lastly, they will destroy his household.[388]

Circumstantial Evidence

Unless the news received about the rape assumes some form of a confirmed communiqué from Dinah, Jacob is uncertain of what actually happened. Similarly, this point sharpens the criticism against Simeon and Levi, who acted without any substantial evidence and at Dinah's peril. It is only once they locate and extricate Dinah from Shechem's home that they could possibly hear her first-hand account for the first time and ensure her safety. By then, the text records that they had already killed all the males of the city. For Jacob, acting harshly without hard evidence is an unacceptable response and he therefore adopts the position of silence and passivity.

Having better understood the difficulties that Jacob faced, his inaction and silence become but a reasonable response to an unreasonable situation.

---

388 Jacob's self-centered focus is not only embedded in the linguistics of his statement, as he employs the singular possessive form whenever referring to his household camp, but is also reflected in the very argument that the surrounding nations will stop whatever they are doing in order to gather and destroy Jacob and his household.

Hamor's Proposal

As pointed out above, while Jacob is silent on Dinah's behalf, Hamor speaks on behalf of Shechem:

> And Hamor spoke with them, saying, "My son, Shechem, his soul strongly desires your daughter. Please give her to him as wife. And you will intermarry with us—your daughters give to us and our daughters take for yourselves. And you will dwell with us, and the land will be before you: settle and trade in it and make a family estate in it." (34:8–10)

As Jacob remains silent, the brothers assume the paternal role and deal with Hamor. Indeed, when speaking with Jacob's *sons*, Hamor refers to Dinah as "your daughter" (34:8). In turn, the brothers allow themselves to refer to Dinah as "our daughter" (34:17).[389]

As pointed out above, Hamor makes no reference to the brutal rape of Dinah, nor does he allude to the fact that Dinah is in Shechem's home. In fact, Hamor's proposal is that Dinah be wed to Shechem as the beginning of a national merger between the groups, independent of past events.[390] Hamor and Shechem also provide Jacob economical incentives in general terms of conducting business in the land in order to procure his consent. Their proposal fulfills the desires for a homeland and possibly the fulfillment of the divine promise as Hamor offers the family an "*ahuzah*"—a family estate. Jacob and the brothers are not quick to accept. Shechem then adds:

> And Shechem said to her father and to her brothers, "Let me find favor in your eyes, and whatever you say to me, I will give. Name me however much bride-price and clan-gift, I will give what you say to me, and give me the young woman as wife."[391] (34:11–12)

---

389 See Ibn Ezra commenting on 34:17.

390 Abravanel (Vayishlah, question 4, ch. 34) explains that Hamor thought that the brothers were unaware of what had occurred. However, the mere proposal by Hamor of a national merger as opposed to a one to one marriage proposal suggests that Hamor understands that more is at stake than a usual union of marriage between two people.

391 Alter's translation.

Shechem's offer of dowry and gifts is magnanimous.[392] Shechem, similar to Laban's granting Jacob a "blank check" and requesting that Jacob set his price, twice offers to give them whatever they tell him to in order to obtain their consent to marry Dinah.[393]

The "sons of Jacob" answer by stating that they cannot allow any such union with an uncircumcised man:

> And the sons of Jacob answered Shechem and Hamor his father deceitfully, and they spoke as they did because he had defiled Dinah their sister, and they said to them, "We cannot do this thing, to give our sister to a man who has a foreskin, as that is a disgrace for us." (34:13–14)[394]

The text emphasizes that the sons of Jacob speak "as they do" because they are addressing the person who raped *their sister*. The brothers are now acting and reacting as Dinah's brothers on behalf of their "sister" rather than in lieu of Jacob on behalf of their "daughter."

It is clear from the text that the brothers respond deceitfully, but it is not clear at this point how they are being deceptive. From the later actions of Simeon and Levi, one might contend that the plot to massacre the town was already hatched at the time of the proposal to circumcise the men. If that were the case, the brothers are being deceitful in that they anticipate that the townsmen will comply with their demand, but have no intention of honoring their stipulation, and plan to kill them all on the third day.[395]

However, if the massacre is the plan from the start, why does Jacob pick to rebuke only Simeon and Levi after the massacre and does not rebuke all the deceitful sons?[396] Also, if the deceit is clear from the moment

---

392 As Sternberg points out, the word for gifts is "*matan*," which also carries with it the connotation of harlot's pay, thus serving as its own parapraxis.

393 See 34:11,12.

394 Alter's translation.

395 See Ralbag commenting on 34:13–17, Beiur Haparasha, second of three explanations

396 34:30, 49:5–7. While some contend that 49:5–7 may be referring to Joseph, and not Shechem, see Targum Onkelos on 49:6 where the words "In their group my soul shall not come" (future tense) "*Besodam al tavo nafshi*" are rendered as "In their secret my soul was not" in the past tense, thereby explicitly excluding Jacob from the plot of the massacre of Shechem. See also Nahmanides commenting on 34:13.

it is uttered, why does Jacob wait to rebuke Simeon and Levi until *after* the massacre? Didn't he know they were being deceitful earlier on? Furthermore, even if Jacob did *not* know of the deceit,[397] why didn't the other brothers participate in the massacre? Were they not all part of the deceitful plot to massacre the town? Given all of these difficulties, it is unlikely that the deceit described in the text is referring to the upcoming massacre.[398]

Others[399] suggest that the brothers acted deceitfully because when they put forth their proposal, they never thought that it would come to pass as they anticipate that the townsmen would never agree to be circumcised. As will be seen, the incentives that Shechem will need to offer the townspeople to cajole them to undertake the circumcision substantiate the premise that the brothers never dreamed that Shechem would be able to succeed. They are certain that Shechem and Hamor will fail and they will then take Dinah from Shechem as per their agreement, or, if Dinah is not returned amicably, they will then be justified in the eyes of the world to use physical force to extricate her. However, this explanation robs the word *bemirmah*—deceitfully—of its full force. According to this explanation, they do not lie and their speech is not deceitful but rather they make a bona fide offer feeling confident of the outcome in advance.

As it is difficult to attribute the deceit to the intent to carry out the massacre or their proposal, the more plausible suggestion is that the brothers lie in the very statement they make to Shechem. The brothers claim that it is an embarrassment for them to give their sister to an uncircumcised man. It is *this* statement that is deceitful. The real reason and the real disgrace in allowing Shechem to marry Dinah is because he raped her and not because he is uncircumcised.[400]

---

397 See Abravanel (Vayishlah, ch. 34, answering question 10).

398 It seems far-fetched to presume, therefore, that their collective deceit as outlined in this verse anticipated Shechem's success in having all the males circumcise themselves, waiting for the third day, and then having only Simeon and Levi kill them all.

399 See Ralbag, 34:13–17, first explanation, Nahmanides commenting on 34:13, first explanation.

400 See Malbim's commentary on 34:13. This reading also explains the odd textual formulation in verse 13 ending with "that defiled Dinah their sister." As opposed to the regular (mis)reading, the end of the verse, "that defiled Dinah their sister," should not be explained as saying that the brothers are about to lie to the person "who defiled Dinah their sister," but "*because* he defiled Dinah their sister." In

The Counterproposal

In their response, the brothers reject Shechem's personal request for he is uncircumcised, "We cannot do this thing, to give our sister to a man who has a foreskin, as that is a disgrace for us"[401] (34:14). Shechem's private offer of dowry and marriage is not to be entertained. The brothers reject dealing with the rapist, but understand that dealing with the rapist's father is necessary for disentanglement from the delicate web of circumstances presented to them. The only avenue available for negotiations is on the national level offered by Hamor. The brothers propose that the national merger take place while omitting any reference of economic incentives, which they view as demeaning.

The brothers' daring counterproposal further reinforces the idea that they never agree to Shechem's personal plea to marry Dinah, but only to the nationalistic goal of becoming one nation. The brothers say that:

> We cannot do this thing—to give our *sister* to a man who has a foreskin—as that is a disgrace for us. [Full stop and end of subject.] However [in regards to the national offer], with this [condition] we will agree to you ["*lakhem*"—plural—nationally] if you are to be like us to circumcise for yourselves *all* males. And [then] we will give our *daughters* [in the plural and not including Dinah who was referred to above as their sister] to you, and your daugthers we will take for ourselves and we will dwell with you and [if all the conditions are met] *we will become one nation*. And if you will not obey us to circumcise we will take our *daughter* [in the singular and purposefully ambiguated to refer to Dinah] and go. (34:14–17)

In addition, even if Shechem would succeed in fulfilling the circumcision clause, the brothers only speak about giving, consensually, *their* daughters—not Jacob's—to the Hivites. They essentially reject outright Shechem's plea requesting Dinah as his wife even were he personally to become circumcised.

---

this verse, the word "asher," "that," should really be translated as "because." See a similar use in Genesis 30:18. *Concordance Even-Shoshan* also records the use here as meaning "because." Similarly, this phrase is translated by Alter as "and they spoke as they did *because* he had defiled Dinah their sister."

401 Alter's translation.

In addition, the plural form of the negative formulation employed by the brothers of: "if you [plural] will not obey" makes clear that the offer for marrying any "daughter" is only valid if circumcision is carried out by all the people in the city. Were the brothers prepared to allow Shechem to marry Dinah once he became circumcised, and were the uncircumcised status of Shechem the true basis for their initial denial, the terms should have allowed for his marrying Dinah even if the rest of the townsmen refused to follow through. By their stipulating the need for full town compliance, they reinforce their initial refusal of Dinah to Shechem personally because he is the rapist, whether circumcised or not.[402]

Identity Crisis

The text records that Hamor and Shechem, the son of Hamor, like what they hear:

> And their words seemed good in the eyes of Hamor and in the eyes of Shechem son of Hamor. And the lad lost no time in doing the thing, for he wanted Jacob's daughter, and he was most highly regarded of all his father's house." (34:18–19)[403]

The brothers artfully convince Hamor and Shechem that the only obstacle standing in the way of the marriage proposal is the fact that Shechem is uncircumcised.[404] This allows Shechem to misinterpret the ambiguity in the brothers' reference of allowing marriage to "their daughters" in his favor

---

402 The brothers' negative formulation of their counter-proposal: "And if you will not obey us to circumcise—then we will take our daughter and go" (34:17) seems redundant. However, being that at the end of the narrative we learn in retrospect that at this point Dinah was in Shechem's home, this statement, looking back, transforms from describing the natural consequences of not concluding the deal to a threat to forcibly take Dinah out. See Sternberg, *The Poetics of Biblical Narrative*, pg. 458 and see pgs. 445–475 for an in-depth reading of the entire episode.

403 Alter's translation.

404 As Alter points out, their demand for circumcision is not only a physical sign of their collective identity, but mandates "the infliction of pain on what is in this case the offending organ." Alter, *The Five Books of Moses*, pg. 191, note to verse 14; see also Sternberg, *The Poetics of Biblical Narrative*, pg. 471, pointing out the poetic justice of choosing circumcision as punishment for the rape.

to include Dinah. Shechem implies that if he fulfills the circumcision clause that he will be able to marry Dinah personally. For Shechem and Hamor, this provides a difficult solution to a complicated situation.

As analyzed above, the response of the brothers to Hamor and Shechem constitutes a counterproposal to Hamor's offer. To recap, Shechem and Hamor suggested that Jacob and his camp dwell in the land together with them (the Hivites) and that the land will be open for trade before them. They stated that Jacob could dwell and do business in the land and gain an *ahuzah*—a family estate—in the land. Shechem then offered dowry and gifts and undertook to give whatever they would say. The brothers' response references the national offer made by Hamor, but rejects Shechem's plea for Dinah on the false grounds of his being uncircumcised. Similarly, any mention of the economic incentives is omitted even when addressing the national level lest Hamor or Shechem think that their predicament can be resolved by money. The brothers further add that they want the two peoples to become "one nation." This would imply that, on the economic level, they do not want a right of free trade but rather equal standing as Hivites. This was something that Hamor's offer did not include. Thus, of Hamor and Shechem's original proposal, the brothers amend all material terms and all that remains is the idea of becoming one people and the daughter exchange.

Not Even Close

Just as the brothers' response *seems* to mirror, in part, what Hamor offers while substantively changing almost every term, so too when Shechem and Hamor relate the offer to the townsmen are the terms substantively changed. It *seems* that they are repeating the brothers' new offer. However, a close reading will reveal that not much of the brothers' offer remains.

> And Hamor, with Shechem his son, came to the gate of their town, and they spoke to their townsmen, saying, "These people are at peace with us and they will dwell in the land and will do business here, and the land is vast before them. We shall take their daughters as wives and we shall give our daughters to them. However, it is with this [condition] that the people will agree to dwell with us to become one nation: when we circumcise all our males as they are circumcised." (34:20–22)

189

Hamor and Shechem begin by telling the townsmen that "these people" are at peace with us.[405] This choice of reference to Jacob and his camp is not coincidental. By referring to them as "these people," they avoid anyone identifying them as Dinah's family or as a family at all. Therefore, if anyone did know about the rape, they would not now make any connection between Shechem's crime and the proposition brought before them. In the entire request, as in Hamor and Shechem's proposal, Dinah's name is not mentioned even once, and the history of the rape is never alluded to. In addition, Shechem further throws off any suspicion by stating that these people are already at peace with them. As they are already at peace with them, any thought that Shechem is trying to gain something personally from the union and trying to avert a feud would be dismissed. The deadly aftermath reveals Shechem's statement to be far from the truth.

Shechem and Hamor then state that these people will "inhabit the land and do business here." In the original offer made to the brothers, they were also offered an *ahuzah*. As the brothers did not take up Hamor's offer for gaining an *ahuzah* in the land, Shechem now leaves that out as well as it suits his needs. However, the brothers also left out their doing business in the land while Shechem recounts that they *would* do business in the land when speaking to the townsmen in order to entice the townspeople through economic incentive.

Also, Hamor told Jacob that Jacob and his camp would live "with them" in the land. The brothers echoed that term, subject to circumcision, in their offer. Yet, when speaking with the townsmen, Shechem states that these people are peaceful "with them" and they will live "in the land." The impression is that the aspect of being "with them" thereby shifts from living together to being at peace together. This formulation allows the townspeople to presume that Jacob's living in the land can be accomplished by giving them any part of the land to inhabit even if inferior or isolated, as opposed to the equal status the brothers understood and intended.

Shechem and Hamor state that the land is very spacious. This, too, especially at this point in his sentence, leads one to understand the opposite of what was offered to Jacob. As opposed to the idea of living with

---

405 For the reader, this reference to Jacob being at peace with the town is meant to recall that this was indeed his original intention as set out in 33:18.

them, Shechem now implies that the newcomers will have plenty of space to choose from so they need not live with or overcrowd the Hivites.[406]

This statement also contrasts the existing markets with the wide open spaces. One presumes from this formulation that Jacob's family will be expected to start new markets somewhere out in the open spaces, rather than compete with the current markets in town.

Shechem and Hamor then state that the Hivites will take their daughters as wives and in return, they will give their daughters to them. This is the reverse order of what was offered to Jacob and echoed by the brothers.[407] When speaking to Jacob, Hamor and Shechem promised that Jacob's family will do the giving and taking of daughters, implying that they have the power to choose which daughters will be taken and given. Abravanel[408] goes even further and explains that Hamor was saying that Jacob and the brothers would be able to take their daughters by force just as Shechem raped Dinah.[409]

When approaching the townsmen, however, Shechem states the reverse. Shechem promises that the townsmen will do the giving and taking of daughters and, according to Abravanel's understanding, even by force.[410]

The only condition for their living in the land and becoming one nation, continues Shechem, is that they circumcise themselves. For obvious reasons, the reference of being uncircumcised constituting a disgrace to Jacob's family and the brothers' threat of forcibly taking Dinah are completely omitted.

---

406 See Abravanel, Vayishlah ch. 34, answering questions 7,8, and 9.

407 See Rashi's commentary to 34:16 and Malbim's commentary to 34:21.

408 Vayishlah answering questions 4 and five on chapter 34 (and contradicting his previous opinion that Shechem and Hamor opine that the brothers and Jacob are unaware of the rape).

409 This also sheds new light on the brothers' proposal. Even if they deem Dinah as one of "their" daughters, if they could choose which daughter would go to whom, if at all, then they would be able to veto Shechem marrying Dinah. Similarly, they can choose never to give anyone to the townsmen at all and/or never to ask for any women from Shechem. Thus, even after all the townsmen comply with the order of circumcision, the brothers would not be obliged to give Dinah or anyone to Shechem or to the Hivites as wives. Dinah would be returned and no further national repercussion need be felt.

410 Vayishlah ch. 34, answering questions 7,8, and 9. The aspect of forcible taking is learned from the identical word choice for "taking" at the outset of the chapter referring to the rape and the "taking" to be done under the terms of the agreement.

In stating the condition in that way, the relationship between the families of Jacob and the people of Shechem is reversed. In their counterproposal, the brothers demanded that the circumcision be performed before they would agree to partake in the daughter exchange, and thus creates a causal connection between the two events. As it is stated (34:15–16): "However, it is with this [condition] that we will agree to you: *If* you are to be like us to circumcise all males. [*Then*] we will give our *daughters* to you and your *daughters* we will take for ourselves and we will dwell with you and we will [then] *become one nation*." In stark contrast, when Shechem relates the matter to the townspeople, the daughter exchange precedes the condition of the circumcision, and the only event causally linked to the circumcision is that of becoming one nation.[411] As it states (34:21–22): "These people *are* at peace with us and they *will dwell* in the land and *will* do business here, and the land is vast before them. We *shall* take their *daughters* as wives and we *shall* give our *daughters* to them. However, it is with this [condition] that the people will agree to *dwell* with us to *become one nation*: *when* we circumcise all our males as they are circumcised." As noted, the dwelling in the land and the becoming of one nation are thus subject to the condition precedent of circumcision, but the exchange of daughters is not.

This plea, despite adding the economic incentive of doing business in the land, apparently was not as appealing to the townspeople as Hamor had envisaged. Although there is no formal paragraph break or other blatant linguistic indication, there seems to be a pause in the announcement. At this point, no one is recorded as agreeing to be circumcised. The next sentence proposed to the townsmen is completely new and is added only in order to close the deal with the townsmen. "Their cattle and herds and all their animals—are they not ours? We just need to find favor in their eyes and have them live with us." Shechem unveils a new plot to expropriate all of Jacob's wealth once they come to live with the Hivites. It is as if Shechem is saying that once these people come to live with us, all their belongings will become communal property. Here, Shechem even changes the terms

---

411 While becoming one nation would imply the ability to intermarry, it might simply refer to a natural process of assimilation. In contrast, the rights that the sons of Jacob and Shechem seek go beyond permission to marry and set up an expectation of a formal daughter exchange. Similarly, Shechem's opening remark distinguishes between their dwelling in the land to do business and his later remark regarding their dwelling in the land to become one nation.

he mentioned just moments before. He refers to them as living "with" the Hivites (34:22,23) as opposed to his earlier description of their living "in the land" (34:21). He does this because in order to actualize the new plot to expropriate all the wealth as communal property, they would need to grant them the right to live "with" them and not merely in a secluded or inferior area. As mentioned above, especially in Shechem's formulation, the only way to live "with them" is to comply with the terms of circumcision. Thus, in order to gain all the wealth, circumcision becomes a must.

Suddenly, everyone is recorded as carrying out the request:

> And all who sallied forth from the gate of his town listened to Hamor, and to Shechem his son, and every male was circumcised, all who sallied forth from the gate of his town.[412] (34:24)

The added economic feature, which clinched the deal, was not merely omitted when speaking to Jacob, but Jacob was explicitly told the opposite: Jacob could do business and have an *ahuzah* in the land. The textual recording of this last distortion by Shechem adds justification, for the reader, for the sons' looting after the massacre as a measure-for-measure punishment for the intentions of the townspeople.[413]

Brotherly Love

When Simeon and Levi take up the charge of avenging their sister's honor, they are described as "Dinah's brothers" (34:25):

> And it happened on the third day, while they were hurting, that Jacob's two sons, Simeon and Levi, Dinah's brothers, took each his sword, and came upon the city unopposed, and they killed every male. And Hamor and Shechem his son they killed by the edge of the sword, and they took Dinah from the house of Shechem and went out. Jacob's sons came upon the slain and looted the town, that/because they had defiled their sister. Their sheep and their cattle and their donkeys, what was in the

---

412 Alter's translation.

413 See Abravanel answering questions 7, 8, and 9 in ch. 34 who extends this justification to the pillaging sons themselves. It should be noted, however, that it is highly unlikely that Jacob's sons were aware of Shechem's reformulation.

town and in the field, they took, and all their wealth, and all their young ones and their wives they took captive, and they looted everything in their houses.[414] (34:25–29)

Simeon and Levi kill all the males, Shechem and Hamor, and take Dinah from Shechem's house. The recording of the killing of Shechem and Hamor being joined together implies that they are both in Shechem's house with Dinah at the time. This, in turn, implies that Hamor knows or has learned of Dinah's presence in his son's home and does nothing to return her to her family, thereby adding to his criminal complicity.

The description of Simeon and Levi as "Dinah's brothers" is to be contrasted with "Jacob's sons" who came upon the dead and pillaged the city after the massacre "that/because they defiled their sister" (verse 27). "Jacob's sons" are the ones who were recorded earlier as answering Shechem in deceit (verse 13): "that/because he defiled Dinah their sister." This linguistic parallel between verses 27 and 13, the epithet of the "sons of Jacob" and the ambiguous "that/because," leads to an interesting insight. As Sternberg points out,[415] drawing attention to the Aramaic rendition of Jonathan Ben Uziel on verse 27, the "sons of Jacob" who pillage the town are identified as the group of brothers to the exclusion of Simeon and Levi who are recorded as exiting the city in verse 26 along with Dinah and uniquely described as the "brothers of Dinah."[416] By paying attention to the epithets the narrative chooses for its characters, the reader is rewarded with precise information.

Therefore, the reference to the "sons of Jacob" in verse 13, where the brothers lie to Shechem, must also *exclude* Simeon and Levi. Thus, Simeon and Levi are never party to the proposal to allow the daughter exchange whether including Dinah or not. All along, Simeon and Levi planned to avenge their sister's defilement. When they heard the other brothers' proposal, they waited to see its outcome. Should the people fail

---

414 Alter's translation.
415 Pgs. 469-470 and pg. 537 note 11.
416 The "exit" of the brothers in verse 26 frames the episode as it began with Dinah "exiting" to see the girls of the land (Sternberg, *The Poetics of Biblical Narrative*, pg. 470). Hamor's "exiting" (verse 6) may reflect an innocence on his part just as Dinah's "exit" was innocent. This would imply that he had no knowledge of Shechem's crime. On the other hand, his "exit" could be paralleled to the "exit" of the brothers, implying guilt and culpability.

to be circumcised they would attack Shechem to release Dinah. If the people performed the circumcision, they would attack on the third day when it is traditionally believed that the pain from the procedure is at its height. Thus, while they kill the townsmen, they do not actively partake in the brothers' proposal. The fact that the perpetrators of the massacre, "the brothers of Dinah," did not partake in the proposal of "the sons of Jacob," as recorded in verse 13, serves as further proof that the deceit recorded there in the name of the other brothers cannot refer to the plot of killing the townsmen.[417]

Noble Avengers or Greedy Manipulators?

Simeon and Levi kill all the males due to practical concerns—in order to eliminate any possible risk of a messenger calling for help from a nearby ally and to avoid any blood-avenging feud that may result from their actions. Additionally, as Shechem is the most respected of his father's household and has brothers, Simeon and Levi have reason to anticipate city-wide resistance in freeing Dinah and avenging the rape.

Having understood Simeon and Levi's possible motivation in killing all the townsmen, to what end does the pillaging serve?

The text records that: "Jacob's sons came upon the slain and looted the town, because/that they had defiled their sister. Their sheep and their cattle and their donkeys, what was in the town and in the field, they took, and all their wealth, and all their young ones and all their wives they took captive, and they looted everything in their houses" (34:27–29).[418] From a practical standpoint, the human captives further ensure that no communication reaches any of Shechem's allies. They also might double as hostages in case the sons of Jacob encounter hostilities.

---

417 Jumping ahead to Jacob's departure from Shechem to Beit-El, the text reports that Jacob's camp travels towards Beit-El and a fear of God overtakes the surrounding cities and they did not chase the sons of Jacob (35:5). The text does not record that the nations did not chase "the brothers of Dinah," but rather that they did not chase "the sons of Jacob." As delineated above, the reference to the "sons of Jacob" excludes Simeon and Levi who are referred to as the "brothers of Dinah." The inference is that the surrounding nations were able to reconcile the massacre with the crime but not the pillaging. According to this reading, Jacob's anger with Simeon and Levi over the pillaging (49:5–7) is misplaced and should have been directed at the other sons.

418 Alter's translation.

In addition, the textual description of the pillaging corresponds to the proposal stated by Shechem to the townspeople: "Their cattle and herds and all their animals—are they not ours? We just need to find favor in their eyes and have them live with us" (34:23) corresponds with "Their sheep and their cattle and their donkeys, what was in the town and in the field, they took, and all their wealth" (34:28), and the captives taken, "And all their young ones and all their wives they took captive" corresponds with the idea that Shechem took their daughter and sister, Dinah, captive. These parallels couple with the reference of taking "all that was in *the* house," referring to Shechem's home, and which played a central role in holding Dinah hostage and concealing the crime. Thus, each aspect of the pillaging gains a dimension of measure-for-measure punishment as it involves the very characters, items, and locations involved in the crimes perpetrated and planned against Jacob and his family.

Similarly, it is interesting to note that the people the sons of Jacob take captive are none other than the same "*b'not ha'arets*" that Dinah went to see in the first place, which began the entire affair. These are also the same daughters from whom the family was going to be able to choose to wed, according to the deal with Hamor. Their capture thus serves as an additional measure-for-measure punishment exacted against the townspeople for their attempt to control the daughter exchange. Thus, on some level, the pillaging served as measure-for-measure punishments for the key players and their motivations in the story.[419]

However, on another level, the pillaging may be a manifestation of the lessons the sons learned from watching their father's obsession with money.[420] As they observe Jacob's dealings, the older siblings desire to accumulate wealth of their own and the pillaging satisfies that desire.

Similarly, by acquiring wealth, they hope to win their father's approval and love. The sons had interpreted Jacob's readiness to execute the deal with Hamor as resulting from the economic incentives of doing business in the

---

419 As pointed out earlier, these last points are accessible to the reader but were not readily available to the sons of Jacob.

420 This manifestation was documented above in Chapter Two.

land and gaining an "*ahuzah*."[421] The pillaging thus serves to counter any disappointment Jacob may feel as a result of not being able to consummate the deal.

However, as when he confronted Esau, Jacob's obsession with money comes second when faced with a question of survival. Jacob is not concerned about money if the result of the pillaging is possible destruction—as Jacob feels is the danger here. Instead of gaining paternal love and approval, the pillaging only further alienates the sons from their father.[422]

Jacob's Response

Jacob's reaction to Simeon and Levi was analyzed earlier.[423] To further expound on his response, Jacob's focus is not on the actual act itself, but rather on the ramifications of the action in the international arena:

> For you have sullied me, to make me stink amongst the inhabitants of the land and I am few in number and they will gather and destroy me and I will be destroyed—I and my household. And they said, "Is he to make our sister into a harlot?" (34:30–31)

Jacob feels that the massacre and the pillaging will make him putrid[424] in the eyes of the nations. On the one hand, Jacob believes that his relations with the nations had been good until Simeon and Levi spoiled it. Until now, Jacob and his family were seen as sojourners who bought what

---

421 This is alluded to in their stinging response to Jacob's rebuke after the massacre where they imply that Jacob's course of inaction rendered their sister like a harlot. After the massacre, a new reality is created where gaining an *ahuza* and doing business in the land have become impossible to achieve as Jacob needs to now move on and is unable to dwell and establish an *ahuzah*. However, later textual reference (37:13) implies that the family retained control of the area even after the massacre.

422 Their alienation becomes fully expressed upon Jacob's deathbed when cursing Simeon and Levi's anger and indicating that it was their desire, and not his, that uprooted the ox (49:5–7).

423 See section above, "Fear of Being Destroyed."

424 The verb "b.a.sh" that Jacob uses (34:30) usually refers to something which was fresh and then became spoiled. (See Exodus 8:10 and 16:20.)

they needed. They did not pose a threat to anyone. If anything, they only presented the locals with opportunities to make money. After the massacre, however, they are viewed as a physical threat and as untrustworthy men. Jacob will need to be alone and isolated from the local inhabitants who will no longer believe his word and this will negatively impact his ability to conduct future business with the locals.

On the other hand, Jacob may feel somewhat jealous of Simeon and Levi who have acted out of emotional outpouring and not practical considerations. They struck out in violence as Jacob may wish he had done against Esau instead of capitulating with gifts. Jacob's demonstration of weakness by Esau may even have been the formative event for spearheading Simeon and Levi's militant and vengeful philosophy.

Jacob's outrage with Simeon and Levi is countered with a short and deliberate response of "is he to make our sister into a harlot?" (34:31). The reference to harlotry fits in with the subtlety of the word "*matan,*" referring to a harlot's pay used in Shechem's address (30:12) coupled with the idea of his paying whatever they ask in order to be given the *na'ara* as a wife—insinuating that money could resolve the sexual offense.[425] Simeon and Levi's response also implicate that it is not only Shechem who is seeking to make her into a harlot but that it is also Jacob's choice of inaction that allows Dinah to be treated as a harlot. Jacob once more does not respond.[426]

The children of Leah view Jacob's inaction as inexcusable. When Simeon and Levi successfully kill all the townsmen, Jacob does not even acknowledge the justice of killing Shechem, and even berates them for their

---

425 Sternberg, *The Poetics of Biblical Narrative*, pg. 474. The formulation of the response employing the word *ya'aseh*—will make—in third person allows their remark to refer either to Shechem or, if said when not in his presence, to Jacob as the one who is making their sister into the harlot.

426 Based on the missing "And they said *to him,*" my friend and colleague Rabbi Ya'akov Beasley posits that Simeon and Levi's stinging comment was uttered after they left Jacob's presence. He continues that this is the ill report that Joseph brought to his father (37:2), who in turn remained silent on the matter until his deathbed rebuke. According to this reading, the mounting internal tensions were not only Jacob's, but Simeon's and Levi's as well.

actions.[427] The children of Leah witnessed how Jacob, the master negotiator and tactician, remained silent when faced with Hamor's proposal. Jacob's silence allowed them to infer that although his daughter was raped, Hamor's proposal to do business in the land and gain an *ahuzah* could heal Jacob's wounds. In their mind, Jacob allowed money and practical considerations to take precedence over the honor of their sister, Leah's daughter.

This chain of events creates an experiential shift in the family dynamics emotionally and economically and also serves as the backdrop for the chapters dealing with Joseph. The entire episode presents a tension between the father-daughter versus brother-sister bond. Ultimately, the fraternal bond, as expressed through the massacre, surpasses and quashes the paternal one. Indeed, the last word of this episode and the last reference to Dinah is that of her being a sister.

In response to their sister's rape, the brothers had started out by saying "for an outrage was committed with Israel to sleep with the daughter of Jacob and such shall not be done" (34:7), relying on Dinah's being Jacob's daughter to suffice as the basis for meting out punishment. The brothers began as "Jacob's sons" and had no need to step into their role as brothers. Shechem's request reveals a shift and ascribes Dinah as their daughter, not sister. The brothers are asked to act in the capacity of father as if Jacob is absent. Initially, the brothers reject the association as guardian *ad litem*. They begin with a definitive statement: "We cannot do such a thing to give our *sister* to a man who has a foreskin"(34:14). When Jacob remains silent throughout their proposal they realize that they have no recourse but to assume the parental role. The brothers lay out their ultimatum and state that if their terms are not met, they will (forcibly) "take" their "daughter" and leave.[428]

---

427 In attempting to ascertain the narrator's stance on Simeon's and Levi's actions, one notes an interesting parallel between the verse describing the massacre here (34:25–26), the verses describing the death of Aaron's sons (Leviticus 10:1–2), and the Korah rebellion (Numbers 16:18,19,35). In each case, the protagonists defiantly "take" their offending instrument, prepare and execute their crime, resulting in death and in a recorded "exiting." This would imply that the narrative views Simeon's and Levi's actions as a capital crime.

428 Sternberg, *The Poetics of Biblical Narrative*, pg. 458.

However, instead of assuming the parental role indefinitely, the brothers don their brother hoods and bond through this event. It is at this point that they begin to strengthen their brotherly ties. They stand united against Shechem and Hamor and clearly forge a bond that will not be easily shaken.

The family also experiences an economic shift as a result of the crisis. Economically, the massacre leaves the pillaging brothers with much wealth. Their quick riches stand in stark contrast to the wealth Jacob amassed so painstakingly over the years. This, too, serves to upset the familial status quo that existed until that time and only serves to further alienate the sons from their father as they grow more independent of him. Jacob silently acquiesces to the new family order in the name of family tranquility and continues to repress his deep-seated hostile emotions for the children of Leah.[429] Following the massacre, Jacob resumes his paternal leadership role to guide the family via divine command, but is more than aware that things will never be the same again.

---

429 The crisis accentuates the difference between the children of Leah and the children of Rachel and despite Joseph presumably partaking in the deception and pillaging, the episode deepens the emotional rift both for Jacob and for the children of Leah. They have already had opportunity to see Joseph as favorite when meeting up with their feared uncle Esau. The current discrimination against a daughter of Leah catapults Joseph out of favor with the sons of Leah. As will be recorded later, even before Joseph begins his grandiose dreams, the text records his association only with the sons of Bilhah and Zilpah. The sons of Leah had already alienated him. The rape of Dinah serves as the natural break-off point for such alienation. The dreams will later serve to alienate even the sons of Bilhah and Zilpah and further reinforce the distance between Joseph and the sons of Leah.

CHAPTER NINE

Homecoming

Much unhappiness has come into the world because of
bewilderment and things left unsaid.

         ~ Fyodor Dostoevsky

Avoidance

After having cleared the air with his estranged brother, Esau, one would have expected Jacob to immediately visit his father, Isaac,[430] whom he has not seen in over twenty years. However, the reality is that Jacob does not show any intention of returning home to his father. It is only after the massacre of the city of Shechem, when God instructs Jacob to: "Rise, go up to Bethel and dwell there and make an altar there to the God Who appeared to you when you fled from Esau your brother," (35:1)[431] that Jacob begins a path back home.[432] Why didn't Jacob return sooner?[433]

---

430 Absent the Midrash HaGadol quoted earlier indicating that Rebekah sent the initial messengers to Jacob to infom him of Esau's whereabouts, there is no evidence that Rebekah is still alive at this point. All future references to Jacob's home only mention Isaac.

431 Alter's translation.

432 The divine command clearly states that the purpose of such travel is not to flee the nations or to specifically see Isaac, but to repay the vows he made earlier.

433 Some may wish to contend that Jacob's return home occurred earlier, but was recorded later in the text, akin to the principle of "there is no early or late in the Torah." However, technically, the visit to Isaac must have happened after the rape of Dinah as the text records Jacob's arrival to Kiriath-Arba (35:**27**) immediately after recording the progeny of Jacob in the same textual paragraph. The list there

In the complex reality of life, it is highly conceivable that after over twenty years of not seeing someone, even a beloved parent, there is an apprehension of actually going back home. One must keep in mind that nothing is the same as it was when Jacob left. We have no report of Rebekah's death; perhaps she has already passed away at this point.[434] Jacob realizes that the longing he may have had or still has for his father's home has little to do with missing his father's physical presence. Rather, he longs for the pristine innocence of his youth—when he sat in the tents without fear of being cheated or killed. He fondly remembers the days when he didn't have to worry about his family's wealth, welfare, and future, or the trials and tribulations of raising thirteen children and dealing with four wives. This is the "home" that Jacob maintains as his psychological safe place. Therefore, to return home and realize that those times and feelings can never be recaptured is a serious threat to his emotional stability. Jacob, being risk-averse and playing it safe, purposely delays returning home.

In addition, another emotional danger for Jacob is that he may fall back into or be forced back into the same family dynamic that existed prior to his leaving where Isaac loved and preferred Esau. Jacob has been absent for a long time, giving Esau the opportunity to interact with his parents unhindered. To find Esau holding center stage of his parent'/s' love[435] would be a severe blow to Jacob's psyche. After having received his father's blessings, Jacob left his parents' home feeling loved by both his mother and father. Why would he risk losing that feeling which had remained with him all these years only to discover that Esau resumed his role as favorite?

Not only does one not need to explain why Jacob tarries on his way home, but it becomes self-evident that avoidance is the natural course of

---

(35:24) includes Benjamin who was only born after Jacob left Bethel and arrived at Bethlehem and prior to his arriving at Kiriath-Arba. Thus, Jacob could not have visited Isaac prior to the rape episode, as Benjamin was not yet born.

434   Rashi (35:8), citing the Midrash, and the Abravanel answering question 12 on chapter 34 commenting on the name Alon Bakhut given by Jacob to the place where Rebekah's nurse died, indicate that Rebekah died at about the same time her nurse died.

435   As pointed out earlier, Jacob may also be waiting for Esau to voluntarily move his family out in favor of Jacob's. Thus, even though Esau would not be there physically, the emotional configuration would already be in place.

action and perhaps even a desirable one.[436] Preserving his childhood memories without tarnishing them with the scars of his life experiences allows those memories to serve as a reference point for future accomplishments and as a gauge of his success or failure to realize his original goals and dreams.

Coming Full Circle

In instructing Jacob to return to Canaan, God brings Jacob full circle. Upon leaving his childhood home, Jacob prayed to return in peace to his father's home (28:21). Although Jacob might not be driven by this goal in the same way that he was when he left his father's home twenty years earlier, God nonetheless grants Jacob the opportunity to take stock of his path and his life and measure himself up to his earlier aspiration. Jacob must return to his home and return to the God that appeared to him when he first ran from Esau (35:1). God does not remind Jacob to build an altar for the God that recently saved him from Esau, Laban, or the nations, but rather for the God that appeared to him when first fleeing Esau. He must remember and rediscover the person who made that promise.

Jacob heeds God's command, and announces that he will ascend to Bethel and make an altar to the God that answered him in his time of sorrow (35:3). Jacob is not yet ready to fully identify with his earlier self and cannot yet identify God as the God who appeared to him when fleeing Esau. Instead, Jacob relates to God as the God who accompanied him through his life journey, his times of sorrow. However, when Jacob renames Bethel as El Beth-El (35:7), when he stands at the very place where it all began, he succeeds to reconnect with his former self and describes it as the place where God appeared to him when fleeing from Esau.

---

436   At this point, absent the Midrash HaGadol referenced above, it is not clear if Jacob has any information about his father and/or mother. Furthermore, Jacob's return to Canaan would be sufficient to fulfill the divine command of returning to his birthplace without seeing his parents. Even if one were to argue that the divine command to return to his "birthplace" meant to the city where he was born, it would ostensibly refer to Beersheba, not Hebron. Thus, Jacob could fulfill the divine command by returning to Beersheba without seeing his parent/s now living in Hebron. Also, see Zornberg, *The Beginning of Desire,* pg. 219, who also discusses Jacob's delay in returning home.

Making Good

Jacob building an altar and renaming Beth-El serves as a partial fulfillment of his vow made over twenty years earlier. Jacob had vowed that if God will be with him and protect him on his journey, give him bread to eat and clothes to wear, then when he returns to his father's home in peace, God will be his God, the rock which Jacob erected will mark the house of God, and Jacob will tithe everything to God (28:20–22). Jacob's description of God as being with him on his path and answering him in time of sorrow parallels his original vow of God being with him and protecting him on his journey.[437] As will be seen, he commands the people with him to change clothes in preparation of his ascent to Bethel which testifies that God has provided clothing. His erection of the altar is a rededication and demarcation of the place where he had formerly erected the rock as the house of God. He later rededicates a rock and pours oil upon it as he did when leaving his parent's home and taking his vow (28:18, 22 and 35:14, 15). Similarly, the text references the location of Bethel as "the place" three times (35:13,14,15), clearly echoing the six references to "the place" mentioned when Jacob leaves home and makes his vow (28:11,16,17,19).[438] Aside from tithing, another unfulfilled term of Jacob's vow at this point is his returning in peace to his father's home (28:21). The text leaves the reader in suspense towards the fulfillment of this penultimate term as Jacob still needs more time to muster the courage to return to his father's home.

---

437 God's most recent protection is also still tangible as the nations do not chase Jacob's sons when ascending to Bethel.

438 The text, however, makes no mention of Jacob tithing everything to God. While the reader will recall that Jacob attributed all his wealth as coming from God (31:7, 42), we also observed how the materialistic influence of Haran distorted Jacob's ideas of ownership and elevated the accumulation of wealth to paramount importance. This theme was fully explored earlier. For example, see Genesis 30:30 where Jacob foregoes returning home to fulfill his vow in order to make more money. Having left the confines of Haran, Jacob gains perspective and is able to part with some of his wealth. However, the text, which so painstakingly recorded the acts of Jacob and his camp as paralleling the vow, makes no mention of such tithing. Perhaps Jacob considers his substantial gift to Esau as adequate "atonement" (cf. 32:21), or perhaps Jacob feels that the removal of foreign gods, which may have included animals or precious stones and metals, fulfills his tithing requirement.

Deadly Deceit

In preparation for his visit to Bethel, and in an attempt to recreate his pristine youth, Jacob instructs "*beito*"—his household—and all those who are with him to remove all foreign gods, to purify themselves, and change their clothes.[439] All acquiesce and give the foreign gods in their possession to Jacob and he hides them under the tree by Shechem.[440]

An overlooked point in understanding this sequence of events is that until now, the text never records Rachel as discarding the *terafim* she stole from her father. Jacob's command to remove the foreign gods now serves as the perfect opportunity for Rachel. When we consider the Talmudic definition of "*beito zo ishto*"[441]—that his "household" refers to his wife—the textual innuendo indicating that Rachel discarded them at this point becomes even more focused. As Jacob's household relinquishes the foreign gods in their possession (literally, in their hands) and the earrings in their ears,[442]

---

439 The presence of foreign gods can also be explained when one remembers that the Hivite women of Shechem recently joined the camp and the need to be purified—when one recalls the dead of the city of Shechem. However, Jacob's request of "his household" seems to also include a request of the family members to remove foreign gods from their midst.

440 Aside from recreating his pristine youth, the hiding of the gods may have served an additional purpose as well. The news of the massacre had reached the surrounding nations. However, the text records that the nations were gripped by trepidation of God, which deterred them from chasing after the sons of Jacob. After Jacob leaves, the surrounding nations will enter the city and try to understand what occurred. They will see the dead of Shechem and understand that there is nothing of value left. When they come to bury the dead (they may have had a custom to bury the dead under a tree as Jacob buried Rebekah's nurse), they would then reveal the foreign gods which Jacob buried. The revelation could lead to a number of responses on the part of the nations. The foreign gods could have been made of precious metals or stones and lead to a "gold rush" in an attempt to discover more buried treasures. The language of the verse supports this reading as it does not state that Jacob "buried" the gods but rather that he "hid" them. In the meantime, Jacob and his family could successfully flee from the scene. Another response could be that the nations interpret the discovery to mean that an overwhelming force defeated the foreign gods and thus instill the trepidation of God into the nations as recorded by the text.

441 B. Talmud, *Yoma* 2a and *Shabbat* 118b.

442 This is reminiscent of the later recorded events at the Golden Calf (Exodus 32:2–3) and furthers the theme of Rachel's betrayal.

Rachel hands over the *terafim* to Jacob for burial. At that moment, Jacob discovers the truth about the stolen *terafim,* and realizes that his self-righteousness with Laban was based on a lie. He must question his own integrity and wonder which of Laban's other accusations rang true. Additionally, Jacob must feel further estranged from his true love, his wife, Rachel, who could not confide in him and withheld this secret from him until now. His estrangement must be tinged with feelings of belittlement and anger. How could she do this to him? Did she not believe in the God of his fathers? By stealing the *terafim,* she placed him at risk of losing everything and everyone, including herself, to Laban, not to mention placing him at risk of extreme embarrassment, had her plan failed. Did she not value their relationship? Did she not care about him? The cold distancing that took place following Jacob's marriage to Bilhah grows chillingly colder. Fifteen verses later, as a fulfillment of Jacob's curse when arguing with Laban[443] (31:32), Rachel tragically dies during childbirth.

Rachel had excused herself from rising for Laban during his search for the *terafim* stating, "For I have a woman's way" (31:35). The "way" Rachel refers to can be interpreted as either menstruation or pregnancy. As the text does not mention Rachel's becoming pregnant with Benjamin, as it did when dealing with the pregnancies of the wives with the other twelve children, Rachel's "way" may indeed refer to her pregnancy with Benjamin. Her death would thus serve as poetic justice; since she utilized her pregnancy to conceal her crime, her birthing will bring about her death. As further support for this idea, the word employed for Rachel's "way" is "*derekh*" (31:35) and, as a measure-for-measure punishment, Rachel dies and is buried on the "*derekh*" (35:19; 48:7).

Naming Benjamin

Ironically, Rachel's death is not only a fulfillment of Jacob's curse but also that of her own as well. Rachel had voiced that if she does not have children she will die. (30:1) As Rachel is not destined to have any more children after Benjamin, her own words come back to haunt her as she dies immediately after birthing her last child.

---

443 Additionally, looking back, Jacob's curse was worded to take effect only upon the culprit being found with the *terafim.* "With whom the *terafim are found*—shall not live (31:32)." Until now, Rachel had not been discovered and hence the delay in meting out her punishment is textually grounded.

At the moment of the birth, the text adds that the midwife assures her not to fear "for this too is for you a boy" (35:17). The midwife addresses two concerns: the sex of the child and the attribution of the child to Rachel. Apparently, Rachel had voiced concern over the prospect that she would have a girl. It is only after she hears the news of having a boy that she allows herself to die, and not before she names him Ben-Oni.

However, before she dies, Jacob, significantly referred to here as "his father," names the child Benjamin. The commentators discuss the significance of the names given by Rachel and Jacob. Malbim attributes the name given by Rachel, Ben-*Oni*, as referring to her strength, as in 49:3: "My power and the first of "*oni*"—my strength." Thus, Rachel names the child "Ben-Oni" as the child that came into being by taking her life's strength. Jacob, in turn, echoes the sentiment and calls him *bin-yamin*, the son of might.

Rashi attributes the name "*Binyamin*" to mean, "while going southward." Indeed, grammatically, the word "*bin*" does not always mean the same thing as "*ben*." "*Bin*" can mean "son" as in Numbers 13:8, "*Hoshea Bin-Nun*," Hoshea, the son of Nun. However, it also means "while" or "during" as in Deuteronomy 25:2: "And if "*bin*"—during—the flogging of the wicked."[444] According to Rashi, Jacob names Benjamin based on his direction of travel.

In attempting to elucidate the meaning of the names, it is pivotal to appreciate the moment at which the naming occurs. Jacob and Rachel realize that she is about to die as she has lost too much blood during the birth.[445] In her dying words, Rachel names her child. It is an emotionally powerful moment and a dramatic statement. What would motivate Jacob to "one-up" his only true love, in her last moment of life? Is it fathomable that in such a moment Jacob would rename the child based on compass readings? The approach suggested by Rashi is very difficult to accept under the circumstances. The approach suggested by Malbim has Jacob restating Rachel's choice of words. Could it be that Jacob strips Rachel of her dying act of naming their joint child by providing synonyms? This, too, seems inappropriate given the situation.

---

444   Thus, the correct English version of the name should be B*i*njamin, not B*e*njamin.

445   Rachel's cause of death as a loss of blood is gleaned from other verses in the Bible: "For the *nefesh* of all flesh is the blood" (Leviticus 17:14), and the text here states (35:18): "And it was when her *nefesh* left her for she died."

Nahmanides[446] and Abravanel[447] provide an alternative suggestion that alleviates the emotional stress. Rachel calls the child "*Ben-Oni*," meaning the son of my pain and bereavement. The word "*oni*" is thus associated with the language of bereavement as used in Deuteronomy 26:14: "I did not eat of it [the second tithe] in my '*oni*,' bereavement."[448] Jacob does not want Rachel to die in pain and sorrow. As he witnesses his true love fade from existence, he imparts to her his feelings of love for her and her offspring. He will not allow Rachel's death to envelop the living. Her children will always hold an especially dear place in his heart and her memory will live on through them. Jacob focuses the wellsprings of his emotions and infuses the renaming of the child with great impact. The child will be Benjamin, the son of strength, for he was born from Rachel's strength and the love for him will always be strong.

In appreciating the moment, the text states that "his father" named him Benjamin. Thus, the naming of Benjamin must contain something essential which expresses Jacob's fatherhood. With the possible exception of Levi, Jacob did not name any of the other children. By naming this child, he expresses a personal and special fatherly connection with him. His active role in granting his name shows that Jacob is determined to be active in fathering this child as opposed to his inaction during the recent episode with Dinah, which Rachel witnessed. Thus, the naming of Benjamin proves to be yet another pivotal event shaping Jacob's favoritism towards the sons of Rachel.

Despite the effusion of emotion at the naming of Benjamin, the text does not record that Jacob mourns, eulogizes or weeps for Rachel, but only that he erects a *matzebah*.[449] By the death of Sarah, the text explicitly records Abraham's eulogizing and crying. Jacob is also recorded as crying on

---

446 Commenting on 35:17.

447 Answering question 17 in Vayishlah.

448 Indeed, Ibn Ezra in Deuteronomy explicitly explains Rachel's calling her son *ben-oni* as a parallel usage of the word *oni* there.

449 The erection of a *matzebah* parallels Jacob's erecting a *matzebah* to mark his pact with Laban after Laban failed to find the *terafim*. Only now, at Rachel's death, when the deceit against Laban is rectified, does Jacob find it appropriate to reenact the erection of the *matzebah* that was the result of her misdeed. The *matzebah* therefore does not only serve as an identification of her burial site but also as a reminder of the cause of her premature death.

multiple occasions. The text describes Jacob as crying when meeting Rachel (29:11), when meeting Esau (33:4), and possibly when meeting Joseph (46:29). Similarly, Jacob is recorded as crying and mourning over Joseph's presumed death (37:34–35). Why would the text mention the *matzebah* while omitting any reference to crying or weeping over Rachel? Were Jacob's eyes truly dry? Furthermore, as Jacob's true love, why doesn't Jacob attempt to bury her in the Cave of the Machpelah field?[450]

Why Didn't Jacob Bury Rachel in the Cave of Machpelah?

By answering this question, one will also be able to understand why Jacob presumably restrains his tears and eulogy over Rachel's death as well. Jacob may not have buried Rachel in the Cave of the Machpelah field for a number of reasons.

Primary Matron

Firstly, Abraham, who also had more than one wife, only buried Sarah in the Cave because she was the primary matron from whom the divine chain continued. Sarah was also Abraham's true love, as evinced by his mourning and crying over her death. In addition, Abraham is recorded as feeling bad only about his son Ishmael (and not about Hagar) when Hagar and Ishmael are kicked out of his home at God's and Sarah's command. Not burying Hagar in the Cave thus symbolizes divine rejection and a lack of love.

Isaac and Rebekah were buried in the Cave, with Isaac's love for Rebekah being attested to by the text itself (24:67). Rebekah is also the matron from whom the continuation of the divine chain issues. It is only befitting, therefore, that she be buried in the Cave.

In keeping with tradition, Jacob is aware that he can bury only one of his wives in the Cave of the Machpelah field. He realizes that were he to bury Rachel in the Cave, at this point, it would mean excising the rest of the wives from being his true love. It would also indicate Jacob's belief that Rachel has borne the continuance of the divine chain. This would grant Rachel the status of primary matron and thus deprive Leah of what she so desperately holds on to. Leah knows that she does not have Jacob's heart,

---

450 While Alter uses "kh" for the Hebrew letter "chaf" he spells Machpelah with a "ch." For consistency, I have adhered to this spelling.

but is convinced that because she married Jacob first, she should be granted the primary matron status. She may believe that being the first to marry was also the determinative factor regarding Sarah's primacy over Hagar.

Bilhah and Zilpah are also candidates for burial in the Cave. They are both referred to as Jacob's wives or as the maids of Rachel and Leah respectively.[451] In any case, Bilhah and Zilpah derive their status vicariously from their respective matrons and are thus seen as having the different and inferior status as ancillary wives in comparison to Leah and Rachel. As such, their expectations of being buried in the Cave as the true loves or as the chosen mothers are less likely than Leah's.

However, while the mothers and Jacob understand this, the children of Bilhah and Zilpah believe they are on a par with the rest of Leah's children. They are not aware of any disparate status between their mothers.[452] These brothers would realize that they have been rejected by Jacob and God, resulting in even greater jealousy and hatred than is later evinced against Joseph. Jacob, at this juncture, is conscious of avoiding such actions.

Reliving Shechem

Also, fresh in Jacob's mind is the image of the uncontrolled wrath and vengeance that was meted out to the inhabitants of the city of Shechem. At the close of that narrative, the children pit their zealous brotherhood against Jacob's silent fatherhood. Were Jacob to now bury Rachel in the Cave, the children would attribute Jacob's silence at the rape of Dinah to his callousness towards the daughter of Leah, rather than a calculated silence designed

---

451   Only once is Bilhah referred to as Jacob's concubine and that is when Reuben, not Jacob, lies with her.

452   See 37:2 where the text points out Joseph's companionship with the sons of Bilhah and Zilpah, his father's *wives*.

to protect his daughter, family, and wealth. They would now cast blame on Jacob for the course of events at the city of Shechem.[453] The same wrath exhibited there would be rekindled and the new need to avenge their mother's honor and status would raise the stakes to dangerous proportions. Jacob had already witnessed first-hand that his sons can and will act rashly without his permission or consultation, even at the risk of physically endangering the entire camp. In fear of such a conflagration, whose far-reaching and tragic consequences could result in familial bloodshed, risk-averse Jacob opts to bury Rachel on the road.

However, there is yet another factor which greatly impacts Jacob's decision not to bury Rachel in the Cave—namely, Esau.

Esau

Jacob understood that it is not only the matron issuing forth the continuation of the divine chain who is buried in the Cave, but it is also only the "chosen" male child carrying the divine name who is buried there. It is Abraham who is buried there and it would be Isaac and not Ishmael who would be buried in the Cave.

Jacob has recently been successful in reuniting with his brother Esau after many years of separation against a backdrop of parental favoritism, hate, and deceit. As Esau approached, Jacob was concerned that his brother would annihilate him and his camp. The prospect of consciously repeating a scenario that would engender such hate is surely a risk worth avoiding for Jacob. Would Jacob attempt to bury Rachel in the Cave, Esau may challenge Jacob's rights to the Cave, and this would force the relationship to regress.[454] After

---

453   Add to all the above the possibility that Leah and the children never knew that Leah was not the originally intended bride of Jacob, and the burial of Rachel would raise even more eyebrows. Jacob is not ready to risk an upheaval of all existing norms of the family structure. This is especially true after Rachel's death since Jacob will never be able to tell her the truth of how he felt and of what really happened. As in Jacob's many other life experiences, he must weigh emotional honesty against pragmatic stability.

454   After Jacob's own death, the Targum Pseudo Jonathan (50:13) relates that this very dispute takes place between Jacob's children and Esau and his children and that this led to the slaying of Esau by Hushim son of Dan, or by Judah (Me'am Loez).

making amends with Esau, Jacob found peace and became whole "*shalem*" (33:18). It is this type of serenity that he seeks all his life and rarely manages to enjoy. He is not prepared to reintroduce that strife back into his life.[455]

In addition, as analyzed above, it is later recorded that Esau obliged Jacob and moved his own camp to accommodate the flocks of both parties. Perhaps at this juncture Jacob understands that such cooperation would be vital if he plans to remain in Canaan. Burying Rachel in the Cave may cause renewed strife with Esau and so, Jacob decides not to bury her there.

Yet, aside from his wives, children, and brother, another direct force influenced Jacob's decision—his father, Isaac.

Isaac

Following Rachel's burial, the text records that Jacob reunites with Isaac after spending many years apart. If he did not bury Rachel on the road, would he meet his elderly father and introduce him to his new grandchildren and to the corpse of his son's second wife? Social morays and concern for his father's health would surely preclude such an option.

Also, if Jacob chooses to bury Rachel in the Cave, his first encounter with his father after so many years may pit Isaac as arbiter to choose between him and Esau over who is entitled to the burial rights. The last thing Jacob would desire is to force Isaac to actively choose between him and Esau. To Jacob, such a decision would have far-reaching emotional ramifications beyond the actual decision itself. Throughout the years, Jacob manages to convince himself that Isaac's silence in the aftermath of the usurping of the

---

455 It is unclear, however, how conflict was further avoided at the burial of Leah. The approach of A. Korman (*HaAvot VeHashevatim* pgs. 125–140) explained immediately below would allow for Leah to be buried in the cave peacefully and, indeed, the Midrashim do not mention Esau objecting over her burial there. Korman posits, based on midrashic texts, that Jacob purchased a plot in the cave from Esau at or above market value at the time of the sale of the stew. However, as the Midrash relates that Leah was destined to marry Esau, Leah had already acquired independent rights to a plot in the Cave even though she never marries Esau. When Leah is buried there, Esau believes that Jacob is utilizing the plot he purchased. Jacob believes that he is utilizing Leah's independent plot. Hence, no dispute arises. When it is time to bury Jacob, the dispute arises as to which plot the agreement between Jacob and Esau referred to and whether that plot is still vacant for Jacob or had already been utilized for Leah.

blessings, coupled with Isaac's subsequent blessings prior to departing for Paddan-Aram, signify his approval of Jacob's act. At least it allowed Jacob to believe that Isaac truly loves him no less than Esau and that the favoritism displayed towards Esau in his youth had dissipated or had even been reversed. To chance having Isaac favor Esau over him at this later point in his life would deliver a powerful blow to the basic foundation of Jacob's existence. Jacob, in line with his aversion to risk, naturally shuns any such possibility.

On a more pragmatic level, Jacob fears that he may also lose the right to be buried in the Cave if Isaac decides against him.

Another factor against burying Rachel in the Cave is that since Isaac is still alive, it may be inappropriate to bury anyone of Jacob's generation before Isaac. Such an act could be seen as a sign or a message that Isaac's time has passed. Alternatively, the rights to the Cave may have been part of the rights of inheritance and so long as Isaac is alive no rights are vested to Jacob or to Esau.

Burial on the Road—Ignorance Is Bliss

Jacob also risked little to nothing by burying Rachel on the road. No one would be slighted—Benjamin was just born and Joseph was still a young boy or at most a teenager who, as will be seen from his later behavior surrounding the dreams, has yet to learn the subtleties of social graces. Thus, Rachel's non-burial in the Cave may not be read as an insult to Rachel or her children, especially in light of Jacob's already existing predisposition to favor them.

In addition, it is very possible that none of the children even know about the Cave. It is only after Jacob returns to Isaac's home, and Isaac passes many years later, that Jacob and Esau bury Isaac there. At Isaac's burial, the Cave is not mentioned, although from later references (49:31) we know that Isaac is buried in the Cave. From the textual testimony, the children of Jacob and Esau are not involved. They perhaps tended to their families and did not attend the burial. As further proof that the children were not present, years later, when Jacob makes the children swear to bury him in the Cave, he describes the cave's location and history in detail as if they never heard of it previously. Jacob does not reference their personal experience of Isaac's or Leah's burial in an attempt to jar their memory. All this further supports the idea of their ignorance. He also does not mention that they took part of Leah's burial. On the contrary, Jacob states: "There 'they' buried Abraham and Sarah his wife. There 'they' buried Isaac and Rebekah his wife. And there 'I' buried Leah" (49:31). Jacob details the history surrounding the Cave's purchase at the time of his own death because until then no one had known anything about the Cave's existence. These were details that Jacob himself may have learned from Isaac on his deathbed only years after the sale of Joseph.

Thus, in all likelihood, Joseph did not know of the Cave's existence at the time of his mother's death and it would therefore not insult him to know that she is buried along the road.

Another interesting possibility is that the episode recorded of Jacob's death (49:29–33) allows one to postulate that Jacob himself did not know of the Cave's existence until after he buried Isaac there. Indeed, this is a real possibility that, on its own, neatly resolves the entire issue of why Jacob did not bury Rachel there. He didn't attempt to bury her there because he did not know of the Cave's existence or its significance.

The difficulty with this understanding is that Jacob does not claim ignorance when relaying the details of Rachel's burial to Joseph, and which is meant to provide Joseph with a justification about why Rachel is not buried in the Cave. Instead of claiming ignorance, Jacob mentions the fact of his traveling on the road (48:7).

Given all the above reasons, Jacob does not bury Rachel in the Cave of the Machpelah field and also does not publicly display his full emotional grief.

Regardless of Jacob or the children's knowledge of the existence of the Cave, Rachel is buried, without incident, on the road. Following the burial, the text records that "Israel traveled" (35:21). Netziv[456] explains that in Jacob's attempt to overcome his sorrow over the death of Rachel, only Jacob travels onwards beyond Migdal-Eder to have time by himself. In recording Jacob travelling onwards, the text relates that he pitched "*aholoh*"—his tent—beyond Migdal-Eder.[457] The word *aholoh* is spelled with an ending *heh* instead of a *vav*. In accordance with the principle "*yesh em lamasoret*"

---

456 Commenting on 35:21.

457 As opposed to his concern of showing a public display of mourning and grief, Jacob feels that his travelling alone will allow him the time he needs without arousing animosity.

(literally, there is a mother to tradition, in other words, a reason behind the way things are spelled), the word *aholah* denotes "her tent." Jacob did not pitch his own tent but Rachel's—*aholah*. Jacob finds himself unable to break away from his true love, and therefore clings on to whatever he can, taking Rachel's tent and living in it alone. Jacob is acting out how he wished he lived his life, alone with Rachel.

It is while Jacob is away in his mourning that Reuben lays with Bilhah, whom the text describes here as his father's concubine.[458] What would move Reuben to carry out such an act?

What Is Reuben Thinking?

From later references in the Prophets,[459] the taking of a leader's concubine or that of a former ruler carries with it the defiance and aspiration to be the next leader. Reuben's act, therefore, can be seen as one of defiance and rebellion.[460] According to this understanding, Reuben seeks to replace Jacob. Yet, why would he feel that he needed to do that?

Netziv's understanding, that it was only Jacob who traveled onwards beyond Migdal-Eder in order to be alone, makes the circumstances surrounding Reuben's actions clearer. Rachel dies and Jacob travels on alone leaving the rest of the family behind. Reuben feels a sense of abandonment and neglect. With Jacob's parental authority already shaken by the events at the city of Shechem, Reuben reasons: Is not my mother good enough for my father that Rachel's death should move him so? Are not all his wives equal in his eyes? Does he no longer have children? He still has all of us. How could he just leave?

Were Jacob to have gone for a short time, Reuben may have understood but the text relates that: "It was when Israel *dwelled* in that land" (35:22). It is Israel—alone—who dwelled, settled, in "that" land. Jacob is unable to snap out of his depression. He remains forlorn and despondent, searching for a new raison d'être. The camp he leaves behind is directionless and Reuben

---

458   The text only mentions Bilhah as a concubine on this occasion and its singular usage implies that this was only Reuben's understanding of her status, at least after Rachel's death.

459   See II Samuel 16:20–23; I Kings 12:21–22.

460   For a fuller discussion of this point, see Sarna, *JPS*, pg. 244, note on "Reuben's Wanton Challenge."

reasons that Jacob will not imminently return. As eldest, he must therefore assume the leadership position. By laying with Bilhah, he will force the situation. Jacob will either remain aloof and dejected and Reuben will assume the leadership or Jacob will return to regain control of the family. Reuben also tips the scales in favor of Jacob's return for should he not return, Bilhah will have been reduced to the status of concubine[461] or that of perpetual living widowhood[462] which would reflect on his late wife Rachel.[463] Thus, the text describes his action as "*and Reuben went* and slept with Bilhah." The text could have sufficed by stating: "and it was when Israel dwelled in that land that Reuben slept with Bilhah." The extra verb of "*vayelekh Reuven*—and Reuben went" implies that in order to break the holding pattern that developed, Reuben got up and did something—he slept with Bilhah.

The commentators are split as to whether Reuben actually slept with Bilhah[464] or whether he was attempting to have Jacob adjust his sleeping patterns to favor Leah over the other remaining wives after Rachel's death.[465] According to the latter opinion, this is the second time that Reuben has been the cause of manipulating Jacob's sexual behavior. The first episode is by the incident with the *dudaim*.[466] There, Jacob is navigated toward Leah by virtue of Reuben's *dudaim*. Jacob does not verbalize his resentment at that time towards Reuben and/or Leah. By repositioning the beds with Bilhah in order to have Jacob favor Leah, Reuben is repeating the same dynamic. Reuben forces Jacob to sleep with Leah—the woman he prefers less.

As was analyzed earlier, Jacob's resentment focuses in on Leah as the cause of the conjugal switch and Jacob's inability to shower Rachel with all his love. Leah's children constantly remind him of this simply by

---

461 As that is how Reuben last treated her and saw her, her status under Reuben's rule would be seen as a concubine.

462 Cf. II Samuel 20:3.

463 As Jacob marrying Bilhah was at Rachel's urging as a belittlement of her relationship with him, Bilhah's demotion to concubine would reflect a further cheapening of Jacob's relationship with Rachel. Bilhah's demotion would also detract from Rachel's matron status as Bilhah and Rachel are seen as a single unit with Bilhah's children being deemed Rachel's.

464 Rav Joseph Bekhor Shor commenting on 35:22–26.

465 Rashi commenting on 35:22.

466 30: 14–16. See also Sarna, *JPS*, pg. 244, note on "Reuben's Wanton Challenge," who similarly links the two events.

virtue of their being Leah's children. Reuben's additional acts trigger the same feelings of coercion and resentment which Jacob felt when he awoke next to Leah. The recent event now provokes Jacob to redirect and amplify those negative feelings towards Reuben.

Clearly, this was not Reuben's intention. Reuben selects his tactic very carefully. He is sensitive, perhaps more than the others, to the dynamic that existed between Rachel and Leah. He was the only one who witnessed the exchange between the sisters regarding the *dudaim* years earlier in Paddan-Aram. He heard the tenor of that dialogue and their agreement. As a son of Leah, he understands the misgivings of Simeon and Levi as they challenge Jacob's loyalties at the city of Shechem. Reuben chooses the act that, in his view, will not only resolve the immediate crisis of Jacob's absence, but will also resolve the underlying conflict between Jacob and the sons of Leah. Jacob's absence has heightened the disparity between Rachel and Leah. Reuben sleeps with Bilhah who, as Rachel's maid, is the closest substitute for Rachel at this point or the woman most closely associated with her. Upon Jacob's return, Jacob will have grounds to sever the family asunder forever. He could oust Reuben for his rebellious act and clearly indicate Rachel's primary matron status. As Netziv and Abravanel point out, Jacob actively decides not to ostracize Reuben for this matter, although he could have. Faced with choosing between emotional honesty and pragmatic stability, Jacob once again remains silent for the sake of family unity.

Had Jacob ousted Reuben, Simeon and Levi would retort that when Dinah, Leah's daughter, was brutally raped by an uncircumcised foreigner, Jacob was silent and had even entertained allowing them into the family, but when one of Leah's sons sleeps (consensually?[467]) with Bilhah, he ousts him from the family?![468] All eyes are turned on Jacob for a clear resolution. Jacob's action or inaction upon his return will impact the integrity of the

---

467   Bilhah's motivation to consent to Reuben would seem to imply that Reuben had convinced her that her status, at least after Rachel died, was that of concubine and/or that by being with Reuben she could secure her position as matron in the new family order that Reuben was plotting.

468   Had Reuben's sleeping with Bilhah been by force it would further be an attempt at replicating the events of the rape of Dinah to gauge his father's response. However, the word choice employed is that Reuben slept "*et*" Bilhah, meaning "with" Bilhah, and sounds very different from the objectified language "slept her" "*otah*" used to describe Dinah's and Tamar's rapes.

family structure. The acknowledgement or denouncement of Reuben's act will bring any underlying disparity between the sons of Leah and Rachel into high relief. Reuben undertakes his action thinking and hoping that this issue will be flushed out once and for all.[469]

However, as pointed out above, Reuben's plan for family unity and equality backfires. By coercing the sexual patterns of Jacob and his wives, he only reinforces the original resentment that caused the disunity and fragmentation in the first place.[470] However, despite aggravating Jacob's resentment, Jacob's fury is quashed as he opts for family unity and pragmatic silence. Reuben is not reprimanded for his act and Jacob returns to the family encampment. Reuben erroneously believes that he not only succeeded in bringing about family unity, but also succeeded to demonstrate that there is no favoritism for the sons of Rachel over the sons of Leah.[471] Just as Jacob was silent at the rape of Dinah, he is silent once more at the laying of Bilhah. Reuben infers that the equally deafening silence in the two episodes demonstrates to all that each of the family members is on equal footing in Jacob's eyes. Reuben wishes to show that Jacob's passivity and silence is a result of Jacob's character, rather than a byproduct determined by the identity of the victim.

Echoing Silence

The text closes the sequence of events surrounding Reuben's act with: "And Israel heard" (35:22) which echoes back to: "'And Jacob heard' that [Shechem] defiled Dinah his daughter.... And Jacob was silent" (34:5). Malbim[472] interprets Jacob's "hearing" of Reuben's act to mean: "And Israel heard and understood." Which aspect of the act Jacob understood is not clear. Perhaps Jacob understood the vision of family unity and equality that Reuben was trying to accomplish. When Jacob hears and understands, he decides to remain silent and preserve family unity while harboring any

---

469 This line of reasoning will also explain Reuben's later attempt to save Joseph and clarifies Reuben's puzzling actions there, as will be explained in a later volume of this work.

470 The compounding of this resentment provides a more comprehensive backdrop for the upcoming chapters dealing with Joseph.

471 This disparate viewpoint will play itself out in Reuben's failed attempt to save Joseph from the brothers.

472 Commenting on 35:22.

issues of hurt pride resulting from the matter. He knows that Reuben means well, and keeps Reuben and the rest of the children as part of his family, accepting them with their maternal lineage and their faults. Hence, the text immediately[473] records that: "And the children of Jacob were twelve: The sons of Leah, the first born of Jacob—Reuben"(35:22–23).

Based on Malbim's understanding, the entire section can also read as "And Israel understood that the sons of Jacob were twelve…" that is to say, he understood that he has twelve sons while acknowledging that Reuben is his firstborn but that his favorites are, "The sons of Rachel: Joseph and Benjamin" (35:24).

The text does not record who reported the incident of Reuben and Bilhah to Jacob. As Joseph would naturally be the one to be upset by Reuben's laying, as it offended his late mother's matron status, it is not unlikely that it was Joseph who went to report the incident to Jacob. Perhaps this could be the textual incident referred to later when describing Joseph as bearing ill tidings against his brothers (37:2). This explanation fits in nicely with the textual order of events. In light of the explanations set out above, Reuben would be the only one *not* to be upset by Joseph's tattling about this incident, as Reuben *wanted* Jacob to hear about what he did. Thus, Reuben remains the brother who later still has an inclination to save Joseph. He is the only one to view this tattling as a positive development.

As there is no recorded consequence to Reuben for his act at this point, or any negative reaction upon Jacob's return, the text goes on to record Reuben as still maintaining the status of firstborn (35:23). Indeed, it can be argued that Jacob never discusses or mentions the matter to Reuben, preferring to pick up his paternal role where he left off.[474] As mentioned above, Reuben's attempt to bring about a defining moment to the underlying conflict fails. He is unaware of the depth of Jacob's emotional preference for Rachel and her children and the conscious decisions Jacob made and maintained over the years in order to conceal the truth. Jacob paid a high personal emotional price and will not allow Reuben's brazen act to deter his long-term decision of silence. Thus, it is only on Jacob's deathbed that he

---

473 The cantillations do not even record a formal end sentence pause between paragraphs.

474 As pointed out, this mode of silence on a major familial issue is not unusual for Jacob.

reveals to Reuben that he knew what happened with Bilhah all along (49:4). There, he depicts Reuben as rash. Jacob implies that Reuben's decision to force the situation was impetuous because Jacob would have pulled out of his depression on his own and, in time, would have resumed his parental role without any intervention.[475]

Shattered Expectations

After Rachel dies, Jacob takes in the lessons of losing someone he loves before being able to share his true feelings with them. He internalizes the lesson that life is too short and recognizes that he should not leave things unsaid and miss out on the opportunity to see his father before he dies. It is only now that Jacob feels the impetus to return home to see his father.

> And Jacob came to Isaac his father in Mamre, at Kiriath-Arba, that is, Hebron, where Abraham, and Isaac, had sojourned. And Isaac's days were a hundred and eighty years. And Isaac breathed his last, and died, and was gathered to his kin, old and sated with years, and Esau and Jacob his sons buried him.[476] (35:27–29)

For four chapters, the text has led us on Jacob's odyssey to Canaan. Much occurs along the way and many emotional issues come to the fore for Jacob. His emotionally loaded reunion with Esau occupied the reader and the text for over forty verses. As Jacob almost completely fulfills his youthful vow at Bethel, we, as readers, await the fulfillment of Jacob returning in peace to his father's home. At this juncture, Rachel's dying and Reuben's sleeping with Bilhah bring Jacob back to the camp and allows for the long overdue final leg of the journey to be made to Isaac's home. The heightened sense of expectation of the reunion between father and son after over twenty

---

475 As the chapters of Joseph will painfully illustrate, Reuben's attempts to adjust the father-children dynamic in the hopes of acquiring Jacob's love will never succeed. Unfortunately, perhaps encouraged by his misinterpretation of the dynamics wrought by his laying with Bilhah, Reuben specifically espouses this model of conflict resolution throughout. It is only Judah's later approach of accepting Jacob for who he is, of accepting the disparity between the children of Rachel and Leah and of focusing on reconciliation between the brothers themselves that will ultimately allow for some emotional reunification for the family.

476 Alter's translation.

years of separation fills the air. However, the reader is sorely disappointed as any such expectation is utterly shattered by the absolute silence that the text affords the meeting—*not one word* is granted the patient reader who has looked forward to this moment. What could possibly be the reason that the text would disappoint its readership surrounding such a momentous event?

I believe one may suggest that the text's omission of a heartwarming or heartbreaking reunion maintains a heightened tension around Jacob's stressful existence. As the Midrash comments: "Jacob desired to live in tranquility, the wrath of Joseph leaped upon him,"[477] thus indicating that Jacob's character remains in an eternal state of tension. Jacob, as a risk-averse individual, is constantly seeking to avoid harm and danger. Even at rest, he is concerned about the future and does not focus on the peaceful present. Had the text afforded the reader with a satisfying reunion scene, one may have been lulled into believing that Jacob has finally reached a resting point. The Joseph saga will reveal that to be far from the truth. In a similar vein, even Jacob's teary-eyed reunion with Joseph years later receives little textual attention (46:29–30), as I discuss in a later volume of this work. The heightened tension keeps the reader wanting more as he continues to seek a respite for Jacob that is not forthcoming until many chapters and years later—if at all.

Aside from the literary value mentioned above, the textual silence screams out to the reader that this reunion is not as important or central to the story as we would like to believe. The reader anticipates a watershed event at the reunion. Yet, none is forthcoming. The text's message is that there is nothing to tell. Instead of relaying a disappointing ending, the text prefers to omit the description of Jacob's return home.

Nevertheless, the sparse text leaves us with two hints as to the final state of affairs within the Isaac-Jacob-Esau dynamic. The text relates that Jacob returned to "his" father in Mamre (35:27). Thus, Jacob's perspective viewing Isaac as "his" father remained the case as he returned home. This point is further reinforced as the text also relates that "Esau and Jacob, 'his sons'" buried Isaac (35:29). As opposed to the pre-blessing episode where Jacob was "her" (Rebekah's) son and Esau "his" (Isaac's) son, Jacob and Esau are now both "his" sons. In addition, the harmony between the brothers is no less significant than the textual order and epithets. Esau is listed before

---

477   Rashi commenting on 37:2, paraphrasing Genesis Rabbah 84:3.

Jacob, indicating that Esau retained his "first"born status. Jacob's purchasing of the birthright, the deception by the blessings, the long and tumultuous years at Laban, and the atonement for the deception followed by the reconciliation between the brothers, brings the brothers back to where they began before introducing the quest for venison—Esau is still the firstborn and they are both Isaac's sons. It is this delicate nuance that the text feels important to stress before embarking on the Joseph saga. It is a point that will play itself out again by the brothers who, after the entire Joseph saga, will finally reunite only to find themselves at the same point where they began before the pit: They will accept that Joseph is Rachel's son and that that alone affords him a special bond with Jacob. At the same time, they are all "his" (Jacob's) sons as the text near the close of Genesis records: "And *his sons* conveyed him [Jacob] to the land of Canaan and buried him in the cave of the Machpelah field" (50:13).[478] They are all, therefore, "his" sons, despite the preference for Joseph.

The generational brotherhoods of Jacob and Esau, of Jacob and Laban, and of the dynamics of the brothers of Dinah and their father, now shift to the next generation. Jacob's brotherhood and paternal role take on secondary importance to the dynamics between the sons of Jacob amongst themselves. As the reader begins the Joseph saga, the sons jettison their hereditary paternal link as the "sons of Jacob"[479] and transform into "*his* [Joseph's] brothers."[480] The shift proves fateful.

---

478   Alter's translation.
479   See 34:13, 25, 27; 35:5, 22, 26.
480   See 37: 2, 4, 5, 8, 9, 10, 11, 12, 17, 19, 23.

Afterword

My early years of study in elementary school nurtured me with traditional commentaries and midrashim, and the philosophy that "it's all in there" (Pirkei Avot, end chapter 5). As I grew older and experienced "real life," I looked to the Book of Books for guidance in how to deal with my emotions and experiences.

Unfortunately, perhaps because of my own shortcomings, I could not identify with the life events as depicted there. Unlike Midrashic Abraham, I had not survived being thrown into flames, from which I could draw my unwavering faith. I could no longer shift the sphere of Biblical learning to the national arena where the characters symbolized Jews in a non-Jewish world and imparted a religious message of survival and adherence to the faith, as is the case in vast amounts of Jacob-Esau literature. While these ideas are sorely-needed and the messages are highly relevant, I needed the timeless Bible to deal with the human condition and address my personal life.

With a determination and belief that the Bible will never let me down, I was inspired and motivated to take a fresh look, as evinced in this book, and, once again, I can confidently say "it's all in there."

Some of the ideas developed in this book germinated over twenty years ago, in my teen years, when I wrote for, and served as editor of, the *Young Shaarei Zion*[481] parasha sheet. Throughout the years, as my studies grew

---

481 My synagogue's youth group.

more complex and sophisticated, I discovered that the truths presented in this work contained even greater levels of depth, and their message became ever more significant and necessary. For example, the complete soul-filling euphoria and utter soul-shattering agony of Jacob's eternal and unrequited love for Rachel may as well be copied into my autobiography. The danger of being caught in the grips of materialism in Haran or heeding the call to return to one's homeland echoes discussions that arose surrounding my Aliyah. With a cautious eye I ask myself: "What are my children doing in order to garner my parental love and attention? Do I make them feel that, like Jacob, they need to be someone other than themselves to get my attention?" I repeatedly question whether our adult quest for fairness require that we treat all of our children the "same" as did Laban (and as most estate-planning presumes), or should I learn from Jacob's experience that disparate treatment or divestments based on need is tolerable, maybe even fair, so long as it doesn't express itself as explicit *emotional* favoritism to the exclusion of others? What is expected of me as a parent when faced with a situation of sexual abuse? What is the healthy balance between impulsive, emotional purging and reasoned, practical containment?

Now *this* is the timeless Bible that addresses the issues that God sent my way. It is a Bible that, while not always providing a clear answer or *any* answer, comforts me in identifying my journey as part of the great ancestral path of human existence already trodden. It provides particular results from spectacular experiments dealing with "real life," and they are there for me to draw on and extrapolate upon. It is a Book that I cannot afford to ever put down.

As I admittedly find parallels between the analyses provided in this book and my own life experiences, I am well aware that I will be giving credence to critics who will deny the objectivity of the readings I present here. My initial reaction is to cut down such rhetoric by citing objective evidence, verse after verse, in defense of my ideas, yet, on second thought, I lay down my boxing gloves and, instead, confess to finding Biblical relevance in my life.

After all, isn't that what it's all about?

VERSE INDEX

ABOUT THE AUTHOR

Since his beginnings in the Syrian Jewish community in Brooklyn, New York, Gad Dishi has studied and publicly read from the Bible for over twenty-five years. The technically precise reading demanded of him kept him focused on textual detail from a young age and led him to obtain the title of *Hatan HaTanakh LaTefutzot* (*"Tanakh* master" of Diaspora Jewry – an annual competition televised in Israel).

In this work, Gad Dishi combines his experience as an educator and Orthodox rabbi with his years of education at the New York University School of Law and his legal experience at the Israeli Ministry of Justice and the Israeli Supreme Court. Together with his private practice, these provide him with the knowledge of classical and modern Biblical commentaries while conveying a sensitivity to word choice and close readings that will be cherished by readers of the Bible around the world.